≈

SLAVES INTO WORKERS

≈

Modern Middle East Series, No. 18
Sponsored by the Center for Middle Eastern Studies
The University of Texas at Austin

SLAVES INTO WORKERS:

Emancipation and Labor in Colonial Sudan

Ahmad Alawad Sikainga

UNIVERSITY OF TEXAS PRESS

AUSTIN

∽

To
My parents,
Nagat,
and
Isis.

∽

Requests for permission to reproduce material from this work should be
sent to Permissions, University of Texas Press, P.O. Box 7819, Austin,
TX 78713-7819.

∞ The paper used in this publication meets the minimum requirements
of American National Standard for Information Sciences—Permanence
of Paper for Printed Library Materials, ANSI Z39.48-1984.

Library of Congress Cataloging-in-Publication Data

Sikainga, Ahmad Alawad.
    Slaves into workers : emancipation and labor in Colonial Sudan /
Ahmad Alawad Sikainga
        p.   cm. — (Modern Middle Eastern series)
    Includes bibliographical references and index.
    ISBN 0-292-77694-2 (cloth : alk. paper)
        1. Labor—Sudan—History.   2. Working class—Sudan—History.
3. Slaves—Sudan—Emancipation.   4. Great Britain—Colonies—Africa.
I. Title.   II. Series: Modern Middle East series (Austin, Tex.)
HD8787.S53 1996
331'.09624—dc20   95-37530

CONTENTS

LIST OF TABLES AND MAPS

TABLES

MAPS

A NOTE ON
TRANSLITERATION

In transliterating Arabic words, I have adopted a flexible approach and stressed consistency rather than adhering to a particular system. For Arabic proper names, I have utilized the system used by the *International Journal of Middle East Studies*, without the diacritical marks except for ' to indicate the letter *'ain*. For the place-names of provinces and larger towns, I have used conventional forms, e.g., Khartoum and Kordofan instead of al-Khartoum and Kurdufan. Exceptions, however, are Bahr al-Ghazal, Kassala, al-Ubbayyid and al-Fashir. Titles such as shaykh and qadi were transliterated. For Arabic plurals, I have added *s* to the transliterated word. Finally, in direct quotes and in documentary citations in the endnotes, I have retained the original spelling.

ABBREVIATIONS

CAIRINT	NRO classification for the Cairo Intelligence
Civsec.	Archive of the civil secretary department, Khartoum
CLB	Central Labour Bureau
DRST	Department for the Repression of the Slave Trade
FO	Foreign Office files at the PRO
IJAHS	*International Journal of African Historical Studies*
Intel.	Archive of the intelligence department
JAH	*Journal of African History*
Kh.P.	Archives of Khartoum Province at the NRO
L.E.	Egyptian Pound [LE is used throughout text]
NRO	National Records Office, Khartoum
PRO	Public Record Office, London
Pt.	Piastre
SAD	Sudan Archive, Durham
Sudan Reports	Report on the Finances, Administration, and Conditions of (Egypt and) the Sudan
SWTUF	Sudanese Workers' Trade Unions' Federation
WAA	Workers' Affairs Association

꒰

ACKNOWLEDGMENTS

꒰

This book owes a great deal to many individuals and institutions. Research in the Sudan and Britain was facilitated by generous grants from the Social Science Research Council, the American Philosophical Society, and the Research Foundation of the City University of New York. Numerous librarians and archivists assisted me in my research and I am grateful to them all. In particular, I would like to thank Muhammad Ibrahim Abu Salim, Ali Salih Karrar and the staff of the National Records Office, Khartoum, and Mrs. Jane Hogan of the Sudan Archives of Durham University, England. I owe my greatest debt to the old residents of the Khartoum Daims, Mawrada, and ʿAbbasiyya, from whom I have learned a great deal about the social and cultural history of Khartoum. Their names are listed in the bibliography. I am grateful to Sayyid Hamid Hurreiz, director of the Institute of African and Asian Studies, University of Khartoum for providing me with an affiliation to the institute during the course of my research. Mr. A. J. V. Arthur, former deputy governor and district commissioner in Khartoum in the late 1940s, had graciously shared his experience with me, for which I am indebted. I am grateful to the editors of the *International Journal of African Historical Studies* for allowing me to reproduce material from my article, "Shariʿa Courts and the manumission of female slaves in the Sudan, 1898–1939" which was published in 1995.

Very special thanks are due to Richard Hunt and the Andrew Mellon Fellowship Committee at Harvard University for giving me an opportunity to spend the academic year 1991-1992 at Harvard, and to Thomas Bisson and Leroy Vail who welcomed me to the history department and made its facilities available to me. I am also grateful to the history department at Ohio State University for giving me the time to concentrate on my research.

In writing this book, I have benefited from the perceptive criticism and advice of Jay Spaulding, Martin Daly, Bill Freund, Jay O'Brien, and Claire Robertson who read early drafts of the manuscript. They, of course, are in no way responsible for the views expressed in it.

INTRODUCTION

In the broadest sense this book examines slave emancipation and the development of wage labor in the Sudan under British colonial rule. At the specific level, the study focuses on the fate of ex-slaves and other dislocated people in Khartoum, the Sudanese capital, and on the attempt of the colonial state to transform them into wage laborers. In the Sudanese colonial economy—which emphasized cash crop production—the Three Towns of Khartoum, Khartoum North, and Omdurman became a labor reservoir from which people were sent to different parts of the country to perform agricultural tasks. Hence, the interaction between the city and the countryside and the role of urban workers in the colonial economy form an important part of this inquiry.

It is well known that the Sudan was one of the most active slave-raiding zones in Africa in the second half of the nineteenth century. Moreover, the current ethnic and regional conflicts stemmed, in part, from the country's servile past. There also have been several allegations during the past few years about a revival of slavery in the context of the current civil war.[1] Despite all of this, one cannot find a single book that deals exclusively with slavery.[2] However, the subject has figured prominently in regional and general studies of Sudanese history. The development of slavery in the precolonial Sudanese kingdoms of Sinnar and Dar Fur has been examined by Jay Spaulding and R. S. O'Fahey.[3] Regional studies include those of Lidwien Kapteijns on Dar Masalit and Janet Ewald on the Tegali Kingdom,[4] while the history of the slave-raiding frontiers has been examined by O'Fahey in Dar Fur and by Wendy James in the Upper Blue Nile.[5] The expansion of the slave-raiding frontier into the southern Sudan during the Turkiyya has been dealt with by Richard Gray, and in the eastern

Ubangi-Chari by Dennis Cordell.[6] The conditions that generated the demand for slaves in the northern Sudan and impelled northern Sudanese to migrate to the south have been discussed by Jay Spaulding and Anders Bjorkelo.[7] Certain aspects of the institution of slavery such as military slavery have been examined by Douglas Johnson.[8] These studies have shed light on the slave trade and revealed a great deal about the institution of slavery itself. They demonstrate that slaves had important political, military, and economic roles in precolonial Sudanese kingdoms. They also show that before the nineteenth century slave ownership was a privilege of the ruling elites and that the widespread use of slaves occurred toward the end of the eighteenth century as a result of major socioeconomic changes. These changes included increased commercial contacts with the outside world, the monetization of the economy, and the rise of a local merchant class. Hence, these scholars have challenged the widespread assumption among many Sudanese scholars that slavery was one of the evils brought by the Turks in the nineteenth century. Indeed, Turkish policies expanded the slave-raiding frontier and led to large-scale enslavement. Yet these developments should be seen as a continuation of earlier ones and a culmination of a long-term trend.

However, most of these studies deal with certain regions and focus on the nineteenth century. Moreover, with the exception of two studies, little attention has been given to the subject of emancipation. The suppression of the nineteenth-century Nilotic slave trade was examined by the late 'Abbas Ibrahim, while Taj Hargey's unpublished thesis deals with the abolition of slavery under the Anglo-Egyptian regime in the twentieth century.[9] These works focus exclusively on official policies and actions. The social aspects of emancipation, the fate of ex-slaves and their descendants, and their integration into the labor force, have not been examined.

Similarly, the literature on the Sudanese labor history has focused mainly on the development of trade unions, labor migration, and the formation of the agricultural labor force in government and private schemes.[10] Moreover, most of these studies are either outdated or have focused exclusively on the postindependence period. The manner in which the labor force was created, its major characteristics, and workers' experiences inside and outside the work place remained neglected.

By linking emancipation, ideology, ethnicity, and labor, this study contributes to the debate on the nature of slavery and race relations in Muslim societies, particularly in those areas where enslavement was justified on religious and ethnic bases. During the last two centuries, the Arabic-speaking northern Sudanese have developed genealogies upon which they claim Arab descent, and created ideologies that defined who is free and who is enslaveable. Accordingly, Arab ancestry became the main criteria for freedom while animism and darker skin were associated with servility and hard menial labor. These perceptions were adopted by British officials, who brought their own conceptions, framed by the Western European intellectual tradition and the experience of slavery in the New World. From the beginning, British officials in the Sudan conceived of labor in ethnic terms, with certain perceptions about the working capacity of each ethnic group.[11] Central to these perceptions was the notion that slavery made the Arabic-speaking slave owners lazy and averse to manual work while it made slaves unwilling to work unless they were forced.

However, the attitude of the Sudanese population to wage employment cannot be explained in terms of innate qualities, but by the nature of the colonial economy, working conditions, and the circumstances under which rural producers become wage earners. During the early decades of this century the colonial economy in the Sudan did not create the necessary conditions to impel people to seek wage employment. The majority of the Sudanese engaged in farming and pastoral activities and did not need to become wage laborers until much later. As a result, runaway and liberated slaves became the prime target of colonial labor recruitment. However, this goal remained an uphill battle as ex-slaves sought alternatives or worked on an occasional basis. The opening of the Gezira Scheme and the expansion of cash crop production in the mid-1920s created an unprecedented demand for wage labor that could not be met locally. The solution to this problem was provided by West African residents and immigrants as well as other immigrants from Chad and the western parts of the Sudan. From the 1930s, these people dominated the agricultural labor force in the country. Thus colonial labor recruitment policies resulted in an ethnically segmented labor force. However, with the integration of rural areas into the cash nexus, various Sudanese groups entered the wage labor market. Nonetheless, the labor force remained segmented along ethnic, occupational, and gender lines.

This study is grounded in the growing literature on slave emancipation and labor in Africa that has appeared during the past two decades.[12] There is now a general consensus that European colonial powers in Africa tolerated the institution of slavery for at least three decades after the conquest. However, sharp divisions remain on important questions. Scholars disagree over what manumission really meant and over what happened to ex-slaves after the establishment of legalized freedom. For instance, Frederick Cooper has argued that in East Africa emancipation was a time of struggle for slaves, slave owners, and the colonial state. The vast majority of ex-slaves squatted on the plantations of their former owners or worked for them under different terms.[13] This assumption has been challenged by Fred Morton's assertion that most slaves escaped after the colonial conquest and established their own communities or took refuge in European mission stations on the coast.[14] However, the numerous regional studies in Miers and Roberts' volume attest to the fact that the impact of emancipation and the response of freed slaves varied from one part of Africa to another.[15] Emancipation did not follow a single pattern but differed considerably, depending on local social, economic, and political conditions. Even within the Sudan it is possible to discern important regional variations.

Although the number of studies on slave emancipation in Africa continues to grow, many important themes remain unexplored. Of particular importance is the legacy of slavery and the status of ex-slaves and their descendants in African societies. Moreover, most studies have justifiably focused on rural areas. Little attention has been given to the cities, despite the fact that migration to urban centers appeared to be one of the most attractive alternatives for liberated slaves.

The study of ex-slaves in urban centers will help us understand the various ways in which ex-slaves responded to emancipation and will shed light on the social history of contemporary African cities. Ex-slaves were one of many subaltern groups (workers, migrants, women, prostitutes, domestic servants, etc.) that have, until recently, been left out of conventional historical studies. The study of ex-slaves and other marginalized groups tells us more about the societies that marginalized them, their organization, and cultural values.

The history of urban workers has figured prominently in the works of Frederick Cooper, Paul Lubeck, Peter Gutkind, and Bill Freund.[16] These authors have shifted the focus from trade unionism and institutional labor history to the study of the working class, the workplace, the relations between urban structure and social processes, and the colonial city. On the other hand, Charles Van Onselen, Jacklyn Cock, Claire Robertson, and Luise White have studied the evolution of specific occupational groups such as prostitutes, traders, and domestic servants,[17] while the position of women as migrants and producers in the urban economy has been explored by Claire Robertson, Margaret Strobel, and others.[18] These works deal with the emergence of social classes in the city in the context of the growing impact of capitalism and the socioeconomic transformation that is associated with it. Most important, however, is their concept of the city as a center for the reproduction of labor.[19]

During the colonial period, the Sudanese capital functioned as a population warehouse from which ex-slaves and other dislocated groups were dispatched as laborers to rural areas. Thus, while the city gave many ex-slaves an opportunity to establish their independence and build their own communities, it also became a place where they faced increased repression and coercion. In Khartoum colonial vagrancy laws, a registration system, and other measures to force ex-slaves to work were applied rigorously.

The city was also a place in which different groups competed in an attempt to establish a niche in the urban economy. Ethnicity played a major role in this struggle.[20] In Khartoum ex-slaves established neighborhoods along ethnic lines and constructed new ethnic identities to overcome their servile past and to reintegrate themselves into their former communities.

This book is an attempt to fill a gap in the literature regarding the origin, the evolution, and the character of the labor force in the Sudan. It intends to demonstrate the historical continuity and to show how precolonial forms of labor organizations and ideologies shaped the character of the labor force that emerged under British colonial rule. Indeed this was a result of the pattern of capitalist development in the Sudan under colonial rule and the interaction between Sudanese reality and British concepts. Indeed, there was a close link between the development of the wage labor force and the manner in which slavery was abolished. Ex-slaves became the prime target of colonial recruitment policies and formed the backbone of the labor force during the early decades of this century. They were followed by West African immigrants and other western Sudanese groups. The result was an ethnically and regionally segmented labor force.

The history of ex-slaves and workers in colonial Khartoum will be examined in the context of the socioeconomic transformation of Sudanese society under colonial rule. The nature of the colonial economy determined the fate of ex-slaves, the degree to which different Sudanese groups participated in the wage labor market, and why and how people moved to the city. The discussion of the ethnic segmentation of the labor force is informed by the new literature which perceives ethnic identities as ideological constructs that emerge at certain times and under particular historical circumstances.[21] The central questions around which the inquiry revolves are: what did the establishment of colonial rule and city life mean to slaves, ex-slaves, and other dislocated peoples? And what, on the other hand, did the city and its people mean for colonial officials?

This book follows a thematic as well as a chronological order. Although the main focus is on Khartoum, the bulk of this study is devoted to the evolution of slavery in precolonial Sudan and to the process of emancipation and labor in the rural areas during the colonial period. It is assumed that Khartoum did not stand alone, but was affected by what occurred in the countryside. Hence, each chapter on Khartoum is preceded by a discussion of what went on in the rural areas. For practical reasons this discussion focuses on northern Sudan. Although various forms of servitude existed in southern Sudan, the practice was not as widespread as in the north. Chapter 1 traces the evolution of slavery and labor in precolonial Sudan from the eighteenth to the late nineteenth century. For this chapter I have relied on the accounts of European travelers and on the growing historical literature on the Sudan that has appeared during the last two decades. Chapter 2 discusses slavery and labor during the first twenty years of colonial rule, including the responses of slaves, ex-slaves, and the slave owners to colonial rule. Chapter 3 parallels chapter 2 and focuses on the fate of slaves and ex-slaves in Khartoum, the attempt of the colonial government to convert them into wage laborers, and the role of the Three Towns in the colonial labor system. Chapter 4 covers the period from 1920 through 1956 and examines the major economic and political changes that prompted the colonial government to take active measures to abolish slavery. It also discusses the process of emancipation and the status of former slaves in Sudanese society. Chapter 5 parallels chapter 4 and focuses on the development of the wage labor force, its main characteristics, and the emergence of labor activism. The final chapter covers the same period (1920–1956) but focuses on Khartoum. It examines the social and economic conditions of ex-slaves and workers in the city, the nature of the working-class neighborhoods and popular culture, postwar migration, labor unrest, the struggle of urban ex-slaves for equality, and the response of the colonial government to these developments.

SOURCES

This work is based on heterogeneous unpublished archival and oral material gathered from the Sudan and Great Britain in 1989–1993. In the Sudan, the National Records Office (NRO), Khartoum, is a rich source of information on all aspects of Sudanese history, including the records of the Anglo-Egyptian Government. The principal sources used in this study are the records of the civil secretary department of the Anglo-Egyptian Government, the Egyptian Army intelligence department, the intelligence department of the Anglo-Egyptian Government, provincial reports, and miscellaneous reports. Archival materials in Britain include Foreign Office files at the Public Record Office in London, which include correspondence between British officials in the Sudan and Egypt and the metropolitan government. Other important sources in Britain are the Sudan Archive of Durham University, which contains the private papers of British officials who served in the Sudan and a variety of other documents.

Oral material for this study was collected through a series of interviews with residents of the Khartoum Daims and those of Mawrada and 'Abbasiyya in Omdurman, as well as with former British administrators in Khartoum Province. Collection of oral material on a sensitive subject like slavery is extremely difficult. Because of the stigma attached to slavery, the subject remains taboo in the Sudan. Moreover, slavery has become an explosive political issue in recent years due to its revival in the course of the current civil war. These constraints have limited the scope of this inquiry. Nonetheless, it is hoped that this work will stimulate others to pursue the various aspects of Sudanese labor history that have not been explored in this study.

MAP I

The Sudan

(Left) Sudanese soldiers of the Egyptian Army, c 1904. Sudanese units formed one-third of the invading Anglo-Egyptian force in 1898. R. von Slatin. SAD A38/12.

(Below) Sudanese soldiers on the march, pre-1914. The use of slave soldiers was common in Muslim societies for many centuries. Postcard. SAD 16/6/48.

All photographs are reproduced courtesy of Durham University Library, Palace Green Section.

Slave woman on return to Yambio after thirty years in exile, c 1937.
Many slave women were prevented from leaving their masters, even after
slavery had been officially abolished. A. B. H. Riley. SAD 760/3/60.

A consignment of slaves leaving for Singa with their armed guard, c 1928.
By the late 1920s the Sudanese Government began to take active measures to
suppress rampant slave trading. A. W. M. Disney. SAD 717/1/91.

Freed slave children waiting for milk ration, Kosti, c 1930s. Circular Memorandum No. 60-A-I, issued on 6 May 1925, stated that no person born after 1898 was other than free. M. E. and G. W. Wolff. SAD 743/1/93 and 743/1/94.

Kababish slave women, c 1910. While the majority of male slaves had gained manumission by the time of World War II, many female slaves remained in bondage as late as the 1950s, especially in rural areas. H. A. MacMichael. SAD 587/2/212.

10th Sudanese Battalion Band, pre-1914. The first Sudanese military band was created in 1897. Many former soldier–musicians congregated in the Radif settlements and pioneered the performance of indigenous music using Western instruments. Postcard. SAD 16/6/51.

An ex-slave woman street sweeper, c early 1930s. Official abolition did little to improve the social status of many former slaves. SAD 679/2/37.

Slave at Meroe, 1923. As late as the 1970s ex-slaves continued to
maintain social obligations toward their former masters. SAD 2/15/11.

Bucket removal, c early 1930s. In the absence of modern sewage facilities in the early years of this century, waste was gathered in buckets that were removed by conservancy workers at night. Such jobs were often filled by ex-slaves. SAD 679/2/25.

A camel-drawn bucket lorry on its way to a sewage collection station outside of town, c early 1930s. SAD 679/2/27.

A native mud house, known locally as a *jaloo*, c 1920s. It is typical of the houses built in the Daims. Between ten and fifteen of these structures would sit on an acre of land. F. Addison. SAD 649/1/28.

A native official's residence in Khartoum, c early 1930s. Three or four such red brick houses would be built per acre in the "first-class" areas occupied by European expatriates and senior Sudanese civil servants. SAD 684/5/45.

∽

ONE

SLAVERY AND LABOR IN PRECOLONIAL SUDAN

∽

The whole social system of the northern Sudan grew to depend on the possession of slaves without whom no property could be developed or family maintained.

C. A. WILLIS[1]

Willis, a British administrator who served as assistant director of intelligence in the Sudan between 1915 and 1926, held a view shared by many of his colleagues in the Anglo-Egyptian administration. The notion that all economic activities in the Sudan depended on slaves played a key role in shaping colonial policies towards slavery and labor during the early decades of this century. In order to understand these policies it is essential that we examine not only the ideas that British officials brought with them, but what these officials had actually found in the Sudan at the beginning of this century. Indeed, the conditions that prevailed in the Sudan at the time of the Anglo-Egyptian conquest had deep historical roots and were a culmination of developments several centuries ago. These developments form the central theme of this chapter. The discussion focuses on the evolution of the precolonial labor system and the role of slaves in Sudanese society. Unfortunately, limited space and the nature of the available evidence do not allow comprehensive analysis of these themes. While slavery has received substantial attention,[2] the literature on precolonial labor is scarce. Hence, the following discussion is based on the few historical and anthropological studies that have appeared during the last two decades.

THE PRECOLONIAL LABOR SYSTEM

Between the sixteenth and the nineteenth centuries the northern two-thirds of the Sudan were ruled by the Funj and the Fur kingdoms. The Funj kingdom of Sinnar emerged at the beginning of the sixteenth century and included the Gezira (between the Blue and the White Niles), the northeastern parts of the Sudan, and the riverain region north of Khartoum, until the Turkish conquest in 1821. The Keira sultanate, on the other hand, dominated the western parts of the Sudan from the seventeenth century until 1874 when it was destroyed by Al-Zubair Rahma Mansur, the northern Sudanese slave trader. After a brief revival between 1898 and 1916 the kingdom was incorporated into the Anglo-Egyptian domain.

Funj society was broadly divided into two hereditary classes of nobility and subjects and a category of slaves.[3] Relations between the nobility and their subjects were based on dependence and subordination. While the former controlled the political institutions and economic resources, the latter provided labor and paid tribute. This division was maintained by customary law and was reflected in property ownership, legal rights, and marriage patterns.[4]

Most wealth in Sinnar derived from land, which was distributed by the sultan to members of the ruling elites and to religious leaders. Economic activities varied from one region to another, ranging from rainland cultivation and pastoralism in the central and southern regions, to river-based agriculture along the Nile. In the latter region, agriculture was based on the *saqiya* system. The term saqiya refers to both the waterwheel and the land irrigated by it. A saqiya holding was the common property of those who held a share in the fruits of its cultivation. Cultivation on the saqiya lands was based upon the assumption that cultivators had a right to a share in the fruits of the land but not to the land itself.[5] Under this system agricultural production required the participation of several individuals: the *samad*, or the overseer of production; the *arwati*, who drove the animals that propelled the saqiya; the *turbal*, or laborer who tended the crop; and the *basir*, or craftsman who repaired the waterwheel.[6]

The agricultural work on the saqiya land included cleaning the *kodaig* (a ditch in the riverbank beneath the waterwheel from which the water is drawn), cleaning the *jadwal* (water conduit), and bird scaring. The saqiya had to be worked day and night. The work was divided into two shifts: the *fijrawi* (morning shift) and the *'ishawi* (evening shift). Some agricultural tasks were beyond the capacity of the shareholders of a single saqiya and demanded a different form of organization. These included the construction of the primary distribution canal and the preparation of a new site for saqiya cultivation. These tasks were performed by village work parties called *nafir*, whose service would be reciprocated on other occasions. The nafir was usually supplied with food and drinks such as *marisa* or local drink.

Each community maintained its own system of distribution of the crop to those who contributed to the production process. These arrangements were called *teddan* and were usually agreed upon at the beginning of the cultivation season. The products were normally divided into six major shares, but varied from one village to another.[7] Among the minor claims to be satisfied were those of the *rayyis*, or the sailor of the village's boat; the basir; the *'arabi*, who provided the camels for carrying the crop; and the *haddad*, or blacksmith who repaired the hoes and other tools.

Among the nomads in central and western Sudan, cattle herding was the primary occupation while cultivation was practiced during the slack season. These two activities required a particular form of labor organization which varied from one community to another. However, cattle herding and farming were conducted on a communal basis, and there was a clear division of labor along gender and age lines. The case of the Rufa'a al-Hoi nomads in the southern Blue Nile illustrates this pattern.

The primary form of social organization among the Rufa'a al-Hoi was the tent cluster, which consisted of several independent households.[8] Each household owned its own herds and maintained cooperative relations with the rest of the cluster members. The animals of each cluster were herded by young men who spent several months in the grazing areas until they were replaced by others. Women and old men remained in the settlements all the time. While the former did all domestic work, the latter spent most of their time entertaining guests and helping young boys in making ropes and saddles. Young boys and girls were responsible for bringing water to the camp.[9]

A similar form of labor organization existed among the Baqqara cattle herders in southern Kordofan. The primary unit of social organization among the Baqqara was the camp, which consisted of several households and was associated with a lineage known as *surra*.[10] Cattle herding and cultivation were conducted communally by the camp members. Each cattle owner or a group of cattle owners provided a young man who herded for five days and then was replaced. Adult males herded only if the terrain was difficult and if the grazing was scarce or distant.[11] While grazing land was owned by the whole community, cultivable land was scarce and was privately owned. Yet cultivation was done by extended family members, who normally established their farms close to each other.

In brief, the vast majority of rural producers in precolonial Sudan organized their labor on a communal basis. It is evident that slave labor did not play a significant role in economic production until the nineteenth century. Most important, however, is the fact that the sedentary and pastoral communities in various parts of the country worked at their own pace and developed a work pattern that shaped their attitude toward wage labor in the twentieth century.

THE ROLE OF SLAVES IN PRECOLONIAL SUDANESE SOCIETY

It is important at the outset that we examine what slavery meant in the Sudanese context. Since the appearance of Miers and Kopytoff's book in 1977 there has been a growing debate among Africanists on the nature of slavery in Africa and whether or not it could be equated with slavery in the New World. Miers and Kopytoff have rejected the application of Western concepts of slavery and freedom to other cultural and historical contexts such as Africa.[12] They have argued that African slavery should be viewed in the context of the "rights in persons," which were an integral part of African systems of kinship and marriage. They have further stressed the openness of African societies, in which slaves and outsiders were easily absorbed, above all into the kinship groups of their owners. This position was challenged by Frederick Cooper, Paul Lovejoy, Claude Meillassoux, and others who argued that slavery is the antithesis of kinship, and focused on the use of slaves by particular social groups in their struggle for wealth and power.[13] On the basis of their research in the western Sudan, Lovejoy and Meillassoux have asserted that slavery was the dominant mode of production in this part of Africa. It was a peculiar mode of production that was sustained by violence and by the commercialization of people as commodities. The concept of "slave mode of production" was also applied by A. Sheriff on the East African coast.[14] However, in the precolonial states of the eastern Sudan, slave labor did not play an important role in economic production until the late eighteenth and early nineteenth centuries. Therefore it is important to consider these regional variations when dealing with slavery in Africa. The constituent element of slavery was never static and cannot be understood without reference to time, place, and changing socioeconomic conditions. Even within a single society one finds variations in forms of servitude.

The slave among the Arabic-speaking northern Sudanese is an absolute legal property of the owner. The Arabic terms 'abd (for the male slave) and *khadim* (for the female slave) are clearly defined in Muslim law. According to the Shari'a rules, the only legal method for enslaving a person was that he or she was a non-Muslim who was captured in the course of the *jihad* (holy war).[15] A freeborn Muslim cannot be enslaved. Slaves had both legal rights and disabilities which varied from one school of jurisprudence to another. Technically the owner owned both the slave and what the slave possessed; but if a contract of manumission had been entered into, a male slave was allowed to earn money to purchase his freedom and similarly to pay bridewealth. He could marry, but only with the consent of his owner. While the Hanafi and the Shafi'i schools of jurisprudence allowed the slave to marry two wives, the Maliki permitted him four, thereby making no distinction between the slaves and the freeborn. Theoretically a male slave could marry a free woman, but this was discouraged in practice.[16] If a male slave married a slave woman, the children belonged to the woman's master. A slave woman could marry a freeborn man, including her master, but she should have been freed first.[17] The slave's testimony was not admitted in courts. A slave's penalty for an offense was half that of a free person. If he or she incurred a fine, the owner was held responsible. In civil matters, a slave had no rights or legal power. He could not enter into a contract, or hold or inherit property.

Islam, in general, encouraged manumission (Arabic *'itq*) and provided several procedures to facilitate it. The first method was *mukataba* or a contract of manumission between the owner and the slave whereby the latter would pay the former a fixed sum of money. The second was *tadbir*, by which the master would declare that his slave would be free after his death. A third method was a verbal proclamation by the master that his slave was free. Fourth, a slave could be freed as a *kafara* or penance for accidental homicide, breaking an oath, or some other offense.[18]

There is no reason to assume that such strictures are any more effective among Muslims than among other people. The status of slaves in many parts of the Muslim world and their day-to-day existence were determined by social reality more than religious norms. For instance, the vast majority of slaves in northern Sudan were obtained through raiding and purchasing. Captives included many Muslim groups such as West Africans and Western Sudanese. Moreover, before the Anglo-Egyptian conquest, manumission was rare.

Institutionalized servitude, which became a pervasive feature of Sudanese society during the Turco-Egyptian period (1821–1884), predated the coming of the Turks. The use of slaves was common in both the Funj and the Fur kingdoms. Yet slave ownership in Sinnar was a prerogative of the sultan and the ruling elites.[19] Slaves were obtained through organized raids from the non-Muslim population in the southern hinterland of the kingdom and from the Nuba Mountains. The bulk of the captives were drafted into the army and settled around Sinnar, the capital, and a few were appointed as court officials. Surplus slaves were exported and provided a major source of wealth for the sultan.[20]

Like the Funj, Fur society was marked by rigid social divisions. The Fur kingdom emerged around the middle of the seventeenth century in Jabal Marra and was ruled by a hereditary royal lineage known as the Keira. The ethnic core of the sultanate were the Fur, an indigenous African group who adopted Islam.[21]

The use of slaves was a conspicuous feature of the kingdom. As in Sinnar, slave ownership was a privilege of the ruling elite. Slaves were used as soldiers, laborers, eunuchs, bureaucrats, and concubines. Slave ownership among the Fur nobility was also a symbol of prestige and social distinction.[22] Slaves were obtained through barter and organized raids from the southern hinterlands of the state which included Dar Fertit and parts of the present-day Central African Republic.[23] The use of slaves also affected the balance of political power within the kingdom. Royal slaves were stationed at al-Fashir, the capital, and were used by the sultan as a counterweight to the hereditary Fur nobility.[24] Eunuchs occupied the highest rank in the servile caste. One of the most powerful posts they held was that of *aba shaykh dali*, the governor of the eastern half of the sultanate and controller of the palace. Some holders of this post became kingmakers and threatened the hereditary rights of the Fur nobility. Other royal slaves were advisers, inspectors-general, personal emissaries, spies, and confidants who controlled access to the sultan.[25] Concubines also played a powerful role, particularly after the establishment of the capital at al-Fashir. Offspring of favorite concubines reached higher positions and sometimes succeeded the sultans. Slave ownership was a major source of wealth for the sultan. Slaves were deployed as agricultural laborers on his estates outside the capital. Moreover, the sultan had an exclusive monopoly over the export of slaves.[26]

The eighteenth century was a watershed in the history of both kingdoms. Funj society underwent major political and social changes that led to a large-scale use of slaves. These changes included increased commercial contacts with Egypt and the Middle East, the arrival of a large number of Muslim merchants and holy men, increased use of currency, and the emergence of an indigenous merchant class.[27] Members of the new middle class dominated external trade and adopted an Arab identity by constructing genealogies tracing their origin to an Arab ancestor. A central feature of the lifestyle of this class was the possession of slaves.[28] Slave ownership became a vehicle for social mobility and transformed the balance of power within Funj society. Since most new merchants were originally farmers or nomads, slave ownership relieved them from farming and pastoral activities and allowed them to devote their energies to trade. The same applied to religious leaders and provincial nobles. Gradually, these powerful groups challenged the authority of the Funj king. By the end of the eighteenth century the Funj kingdom disintegrated and was finally destroyed by the invading armies of Muhammad 'Ali in 1821.

Growing commercial exchange and the monetization of the economy in Dar Fur increased social differentiation and the centralization of authority and affected communal forms of land ownership. A new system known as *hakura* was introduced toward the end of the eighteenth century, according to which the sultan gave land grants to merchants, holy men, members of the royal family, and other influential figures.[29] The extent to which slaves were used on these estates is not clear, but undoubtedly the hakura owners belonged to the ruling elite and used slaves extensively.

Both the Funj and Fur kingdoms obtained slaves from non-Muslim groups south of their borders. With the increased demand for slaves in the late eighteenth century, the southern peripheries of these states were transformed into slave-raiding frontiers with a complex pattern of interaction between Muslim and non-Muslim groups. An elaborate system of ideological and ethnic notions emerged along these frontiers. A brief examination of these notions will help us understand the ideology of slavery and the creation of ethnic identities in the Sudan.

SLAVE-RAIDING FRONTIERS AND THE IDEOLOGY OF SLAVERY

Most slaveholding societies in Africa and elsewhere created ideologies that justified enslavement.[30] These ideologies legitimized enslavement of non-members of the society. Determining the legitimate target of enslavement has been an important part of Muslim ideology. Medieval Arabs created a number of ethnic labels and stereotypes about African peoples. Such ethnic labels included Zanj, for the inhabitants of the east African coast, Dar al-Nuba for the people of southern Egypt and northern Sudan, and Habash for Ethiopians.[31]

Following the Muslim conquest of Egypt in the seventh century, the Christian kingdom of Nubia became a major source of slaves for Muslim

Egypt.[32] The conclusion of the *baqt* treaty between Nubia and the Muslims opened the former to "muslim traders (particularly slave-traders) who gradually carried the frontier of Islamic influences deep into the country."[33] The treaty required the Nubian king to send an annual tribute of 360 slaves to Egypt. After the rise of the Funj and Fur kingdoms and the spread of Islam and Arabic in the northern Sudan, the slave-raiding frontier moved farther south. Adoption of an Arab identity by northern Sudanese had become a major criteria for distinguishing them from the non-Muslim people of the south. However, the adoption of a particular identity entails the development of certain perceptions about others. Northern Sudanese Muslims created derogatory ethnic labels to refer to non-Muslim groups in the south. These generic names included Fertit below Dar Fur, Janakhara below Wadai, and Shankalla below Sinnar. Hence, the slave-raiding frontier was defined in ideological, ethnic, and geographical terms. The inhabitants of Dar Fertit, the Nuba Mountains, and the Upper Blue Nile became prey for northern Muslims.[34] The term Fertit was used by the people of Dar Fur to describe the non-Muslim and stateless societies south of the Bahr al-Arab. As a label associated with inferiority and enslavement, Dar Fertit was a "state of mind."[35] As the slave raiders moved southward, Dar Fertit was pushed farther south. Several versions of Fur oral traditions describe the origin of the Fertit. According to one account, the Fur and Fertit have a common origin; they were descendants of twin brothers known as "Fir" and "Firat." The children of Firat scattered and became Fertit. Another version indicates that the Fertit were the original inhabitants of Jabal Marra, the heart of the Fur sultanate, and after the Islamization of the sultanate were forced to move south and split into several sections such as the Binga, Kara, Shaiu, Indiri, and Yulu.[36] Patron-client relations developed between Dar Fur and Dar Fertit as successive rulers of the former asserted their hegemony over the latter. They selected suitable rulers capable of collecting tribute, established trading facilities, and bestowed upon them traditional Fur titles such as *maqdum* and sultan. The most eminent vassals of Dar Fur in Dar Fertit were the ruling families of the Feroge, Nyagulgule, Binga, Kara, and of some sections of the Kreish.[37]

The Funj kingdom also had a dynamic southern frontier. This was inhabited by several non-Muslim groups such as Berta, Uduk, Burun, Jum Jum, Meba, etc. For several centuries these communities were easy prey for the Christian kingdom of Ethiopia and the Muslim kingdom of Sinnar. Both Muslims and Christians used generic names to refer to these animist groups. To the Ethiopians, they were known as Shankalla, a term that implied low social status.[38] To the Funj, they were known as Hamaj or riff-raff.[39] The incorporation of this area into the Funj kingdom took place in the sixteenth century; the rulers converted to Islam, intermarried with the Funj royal family, and identified themselves as Funj.[40] Ironically, a century later in 1762, the Hamaj, in alliance with the new merchant class and other discontented groups, overthrew the Funj ruling family and established a regency.[41]

Another major source of slaves for Sinnar and Dar Fur was the Nuba Mountains in southern Kordofan. The eastern part of the Nuba hills was ruled by the kingdom of Tegali which emerged in the sixteenth century. Its rulers adopted Islam, established close links with the Funj, and supplied them with slaves in exchange for luxury goods.[42]

The ideological and ethnic distinctions should not be taken too far. Displaced persons, whether Muslim or non-Muslim, could be enslaved, particularly at times of war and famine.[43] For instance, following the overthrow of the Fur sultanate in 1874, many members of the royal family fled to Dar Masalit where they were enslaved.[44]

In the eighteenth century, Dar Fur became Egypt's major trading partner and slave supplier. Dar Fur's slave export to Egypt was estimated at 3,000 to 4,000 annually.[45] Slaves were carried off by the *jallaba* (traveling merchants) from the Bahr al-Arab region, across the desert, and through the market towns of al-Fashir, Kobbei, al-Ubayyid, Shendi, Berber, and Dongola. They were sent to Egypt through the desert routes and to the Middle East through the Red Sea.

For instance, the Swiss traveler John Lewis Burckhardt estimated that about five thousand slaves were sold annually at Shendi in the early nineteenth century.[46] In these towns male slaves were classified by age into the following categories: *khumasi* (under 10 years of age), *sudasi* (above 11 years), and *baligh* (15 years or older). The slave's age determined the price. A male sudasi was sold for fifteen Spanish dollars, a khumasi for twelve dollars, and a baligh for eight dollars. However, female slaves, particularly Ethiopians, commanded higher prices. They were desired as concubines and domestic servants.[47] Young girls sold for twenty to twenty-five dollars. It was estimated that more than half of the slaves exported to Egypt were females.[48]

However, the bulk of the captives were sold in the Sudan. As pointed out earlier, by the early nineteenth century, slave ownership in the Sudan had become a major feature of the lifestyle of the new middle class. Burckhardt reported that in the major towns: "there is scarcely a house which does not possess one or two slaves, and five or six were frequently seen in the same family."[49]

Slaves in the northern riverain areas were used as laborers in the fields, looked after cattle, and did most of the domestic work. Once obtained, young boys were circumcised and given Muslim names. However, slaves were given peculiar names such as Sabah al-Khayr (good morning), Jurab (leather bag), 'Ata Minnu (God's gift) and the like. Burckhardt described Sudanese slavery as benign. According to him slaves were "seldom flogged, are well fed, are not over-worked, and are spoken to in a kind manner."[50] The slave was taught to call his master *abuy* (my father). However, the status of the slave cannot be determined by treatment. The slave was still considered an object and the absolute property of the owner. The slave could be punished, transferred, or sold at the owner's will. When counted, the slave was referred to as *ras* (head), a term used for cattle. The status of slaves can be illustrated by the following northern Sudanese expression: "never trust a black slave; whip him well, and feed him well, and the work will be done."[51] As we shall see later, the position of slaves in the northern Sudan continued to deteriorate, particularly in the mid-nineteenth century.

The Fur and the Funj were large-scale kingdoms with centralized systems of authority. To understand how slavery affected and was affected by the balance of power in the society, we may consider the case of Dar Masalit in the Sudan-Chad border region. Until 1874, Dar Masalit was under the sultanates of Wadai and Dar Fur. However, after the collapse of Dar Fur in 1874 and the outbreak of the Mahdist revolution, a local millenarian leader established a sultanate in 1883.[52] Before the rise of the sultanate, slaves were acquired as domestic and agricultural laborers and to expand the owner's kinship.[53] Slaves did much of the same work as the freeborn laborers but performed heavier tasks. Slave labor "was not used to maximize production for the market" but "to make life easier and more comfortable for the slave owners."[54] However, the emergence of the kingdom affected the institution of slavery and the role of slaves in Masalit society. The new ruling elites employed slaves as soldiers and eunuchs, a practice that did not exist before. In this way slaves helped consolidate the political power of the ruling elites.[55]

Until the beginning of the nineteenth century, slave ownership in the Sudan was still a privilege of the nobility and the new merchant class. Large-scale use of slaves by other social groups occurred a few decades later as a consequence of the transformation of Sudanese society under Turco-Egyptian rule.

SLAVE TRADE AND SLAVERY DURING
THE TURKIYYA, 1821–1884

It is commonplace that Muhammad 'Ali's desires to acquire Sudanese slaves for his new army and to exploit the country's natural resources were the main motives behind his conquest in 1821.[56]

Following the conquest, the new regime moved swiftly to realize these objectives. During the first twenty years, the government organized slave raids that were directed toward the old slave-raiding regions of the Nuba Mountains, the Upper Blue Nile, and Dar Fur.

In the Upper Blue Nile, the government tried to incorporate the southern hinterland of the former Funj kingdom by administering the area directly, or by creating local clients who were capable of supplying captives.[57]

Raids were conducted annually during the dry season by government regular and irregular troops. Early raids south of Sinnar brought about 1,000 captives. Expeditions to the Nuba Mountains resulted in 2,000 captives, of whom 800 were sent to Egypt. Between January and May 1824 a total of 4,000 captives were gathered in Dongola, from which they were sent to Egypt.[58] These figures did not satisfy Muhammad 'Ali, who urged his officials in the Sudan to intensify their efforts. Several raids were conducted in Dinka and Shilluk lands in the White Nile area, but they did not bring in sufficient numbers. The greatest effort was directed toward the Nuba hills from which thousands of people were captured during the first two decades of Turkish rule.[59] Captives included a large number of women and children who were sold in Egypt and the Sudan. The number of men suitable for military service remained far below the Pasha's expectation. Despite Muhammad 'Ali's efforts to ensure the safety of captives, the difficult desert journey, illness, and exposure to new climates took a heavy toll.[60]

Sudanese slaves fulfilled several functions for Muhammad 'Ali. Although priority was given to military recruitment, slaves were deployed in agriculture and military workshops in Egypt and were sold to individuals to generate revenue for the government. The prices of slaves in Egypt in 1837 are shown in Table 1.[61]

It is clear that the most desired categories were young boys and young Ethiopian females. The former were drafted into the army; the latter were used as concubines. Slaves were also given to government soldiers in lieu of salaries. This practice was discouraged in the late 1830s as a result of European pressure on Muhammad 'Ali to stop the slave trade.

TABLE I
Price of Slaves in the Nineteenth Century

Males	
young boys (12–15 years)	400–500 piastres
Dinka grown male	70–100
Ethiopian boy	600–1,000

Females	
young girls	200–400
Dinka grown woman	100–200
Ethiopian girls	600–1,000

By the late 1830s, it became clear to Muhammad 'Ali that the use of Sudanese slaves in the Egyptian Army was a failure. Muhammad 'Ali attended to other resources such as gold, gum arabic, livestock, and ostrich feathers. The slave trade was left to private merchants, particularly after the White Nile opened for navigation in the late 1830s.

ADVENT OF PRIVATE MERCHANTS, 1840–1881

The opening of the White Nile and the introduction of new navigation and military technology was a turning point in the history of the Nile Valley. These developments paved the way for the integration of the Upper Nile and adjacent territories into the northern trading network, with far-reaching consequences. Successive waves of European, Middle Eastern, and northern Sudanese traders (known collectively as Khartoumers) rushed to the south. Eager to appropriate the natural resources of these regions, the merchants established fortified settlements known as *zaribas*, from which they conducted their trade in ivory, ostrich feathers, and livestock. As they depleted these resources, the Khartoumers turned to the slave trade.[62]

At another level, Turkish rule in the northern riverain regions brought profound socioeconomic changes that generated a great demand for slaves and created massive social dislocation. These included government intervention in the economy and the alteration of the land tenure system, imposition of heavy taxes on saqiyas (waterwheels), and the levying of tribute in slaves. For instance, the application of the Shari'a laws of inheritance led to massive fragmentation of land. Moreover, traditional rights of land became transferable, a situation that did not exist before. This led to the emergence of a new class of landlords who began to rely on slave labor, and created a large group of landless peasants who had no alternative but to join the ranks of the slave traders in the south. Although outward migration from this region was not new, it increased dramatically by the mid-nineteenth century. Most emigrants were Danaqala, Ja'aliyyin and Shaiqiyya.[63]

These impoverished peasants sought refuge and fortune in remote parts of the country. In the Upper Blue Nile, they were called "watawit" and faced a hostile local population. However, by the mid-nineteenth century, the watawit established themselves in the Sudan-Ethiopia border region. They settled down gradually, married local women, and established trading networks in the Sudan and across the border in Ethiopia. They employed local people to produce gold which was exchanged for firearms from Ethiopia. With these firearms, the watawit plundered the local communities such as the Berta, Gumus, Uduk, and others. A number of slave-based chiefdoms emerged and thrived well into the twentieth century.[64]

Another area which attracted northern immigrants was the Upper Nile and the Bahr al-Ghazal. These immigrants were employed as soldiers and sailors by the big merchants, while some became prominent slave traders. The latter were best exemplified by Al-Zubair Rahma Mansur, a Ja'ali from al-Jayli, who arrived in the Bahr al-Ghazal in the mid 1850s and became the dominant slave trader in the region. With the help of his *bazingir* (slave army), Al-Zubair carved out a large empire in the Bahr al-Ghazal and adjacent territories from which he dispatched thousands of slaves to local and external markets.

By the mid-nineteenth century, government duties and taxes had forced European merchants to leave. Their position was taken over by northern Sudanese. These adventurers raised private armies from local communities and extended slave raids over a vast area stretching from the White Nile to the Chari and Uele Basins. Thousands of people were captured and exported to northern Sudanese and external markets. It has been estimated that Al-Zubair alone exported about 1,800 captives annually.[65] In this way, the Khartoumers undermined the position of the Fur sultanate in the southern hinterlands. The old sultanate itself was finally conquered by Al-Zubair in 1874.

The Khartoumers continued to reign supreme until the late 1870s. However, by that time the Turco-Egyptian regime came under great pressure from European governments and humanitarian groups to stop the rampant slave trade. Efforts during the previous two decades had failed, owing to the lack of resources and personnel. However, a series of measures were taken under Khedive Isma'il (1863–1879). He employed European officers such as Samuel Baker and Charles Gordon and entrusted them with the task of incorporating southern provinces into the Turco-Egyptian domain. These early efforts focused on the suppression of the slave trade rather than on the institution of slavery itself.[66] European officials shared the assumption that slavery had always been an integral part of Sudanese society and could only be eradicated gradually.[67] Moreover, these officials undermined their own efforts by employing slave traders and acquiring slaves themselves. Despite the annexation of equatorial provinces and the establishment of military posts on the White Nile, the overland slave trade continued to persist. However, following the conclusion of the Anglo-Egyptian Anti-Slavery Convention in 1877, General Gordon, with the help of Romolo Gessi, launched massive assaults against the Khartoumers in the Bahr al-Ghazal. These campaigns destroyed many zaribas and led to the execution of Sulayman, son of Al-Zubair, in 1879.[68] Moreover, with Gordon's encouragement, the Baqqara of southern Kordofan attacked the merchants' caravans that passed through their land. But although government measures dealt a serious blow to the jallaba and the small traders, they did not affect the big merchants. Some, such as Ilyas Umm Birayr, enjoyed government protection and held official posts.[69] In 1875 Ilyas was appointed governor of Shaqq and, for a short time, governor of Kordofan.[70] Despite the destruction of the zaribas, the process initiated by the Khartoumers persisted for several decades.

The power vacuum created by the destruction of the zaribas was filled by new adventurers—local leaders, ex-slaves, and ex-soldiers—who replicated the methods of their former patrons and expanded the slave-raiding frontier farther west. The most notable was Rabih Fadlalla, an ex-slave who had become one of Al-Zubair's leading generals. After Sulayman's death, Rabih reassembled the remaining bazingir and raided the inhabitants of Dar Fertit. Threatened by the government, he moved farther west to the Chari region. From there Rabih's conquests engulfed the Lake Chad area and brought him to the eastern marches of Hausaland and the Borno kingdom, which he eventually destroyed.[71] Before leaving the Chari Basin, Rabih installed Muhammad al-Sanusi as sultan of Dar al-Kuti in the upper Ubangi-Chari. The latter established a kingdom from which he raided the local communities. He supplied the trans-Saharan trading network with large numbers of captives until his kingdom was destroyed by the French in 1911.[72]

Besides Rabih and Al-Sanusi, the warlords included Al Nur 'Anqara, one of Al-Zubair's lieutenants; Surur and Rafai of the Zande; and Bandas Hakim of the Kreish.[73] They were helped by the firearms which flowed into the region in ever-increasing numbers. Hence the process initiated by the Khartoumers haunted the region for years. Perhaps the most important legacy of the Turco-Egyptian abolition was that it became a model that was followed by the Anglo-Egyptian regime in the twentieth century. Rather than abolishing slavery, both regimes tried to curtail the slave trade.

MILITARY SLAVERY

Despite the growing number of studies on slavery in Africa, little attention has been given to the system of military slavery. The study of military slavery provides a better understanding of the complex nature of the institution of slavery. The use of slave soldiers was common in Muslim societies for many centuries.[74] The merits of military slavery are obvious: it helps the ruler create unquestioning loyalty and obedience—a quality less likely to be found among freeborn recruits. Moreover, as outsiders, slave soldiers were not likely to have a base of support among the local population. Such soldiers, it was assumed, would have no loyalty but to the ruler who bought and employed them.

Military slavery has had a long history in the Sudan. As we have seen, slave soldiers formed an important part of the military establishment of the precolonial Sudanese kingdoms of Sinnar and Dar Fur. Moreover, Muhammad 'Ali gave military slavery a new life, even as it disappeared from the Islamic heartland with the massacre of the Mamluks in Egypt in 1811 and the Janissaries in Turkey in 1826.[75] The most significant aspect of Sudanese military slavery was its persistence throughout the nineteenth and early twentieth centuries and its social impact in the Sudan and neighboring countries.

After the conquest of Sinnar in 1821, Muhammad 'Ali established a large camp at Aswan in southern Egypt to receive Sudanese captives. However, the Pasha's initial optimism faded owing to the failure of his local officials in the Sudan to obtain sufficient numbers and to the high mortality among captives on the road to Egypt. Many who arrived at the training camp died of fever and other diseases. Yet Muhammad 'Ali urged his generals to intensify their slave raids and to send as many captives as they could.[76]

Upon their arrival in Egypt, recruits were vaccinated and clothed. Those found unfit for military service were enlisted as water carriers, cooks, messengers, etc. Since most captives came from the non-Muslim groups in the southern and western Sudan, they were converted to Islam by religious shaykhs appointed by the Khedive.[77] They were then given education and training.

The new army was modeled after the French Army, but it retained Turkish titles. Training was entrusted to French, Spanish, and Italian instructors.[78] In 1823 there were six regiments of four thousand men each.[79] Sudanese units were placed under a *diwan al-jihadiyya*, established in 1821.[80]

Due to the high rate of death and desertion among Turkish and Egyptian troops in the Sudan, Sudanese jihadiyya were stationed in different parts of the country. They were responsible for defense and internal security. Besides the jihadiyya, there were irregular troops known as *bashbuzuq*, recruited from the Arabic-speaking groups in the northern Sudan such as the Shaiqiyya. They collected taxes and raided for slaves.

Besides garrisoning the Sudan, the jihadiyya were used on several occasions by Muhammad 'Ali and his successors in their foreign ventures. They were among the six battalions that the Pasha sent to Greece in 1823 to help quell a revolt there. They also participated in the Khedive's effort to consolidate his rule in the Hijaz against numerous Wahabi revolts. However, disease and the climatic conditions in Arabia led to a heavy death toll among these soldiers. Consequently, Muhammad 'Ali turned to the Egyptian *fallahin* (peasants) for his military needs, although recruitment of Sudanese slaves continued on an ad hoc basis.

In later years the government used various methods to obtain slaves, such as inducing tribal leaders to supply slaves in lieu of taxes. In Egypt itself, wealthy families avoided military conscription by presenting slaves instead of their sons.[81] On certain occasions tribal leaders and local rulers in the southern Sudan were required to provide the government with a certain number of recruits, who sometimes included their own sons. For example, during his visit to the Sudan in the late 1850s, Khedive Sa'id Pasha requested Sultan Ibrahim of Dar Fur, Ibrahim Sabun, the Dinka chief of al-Kawa, and 'Adlan Badi of Jabal Bulli to send their sons to Egypt to be drafted into the army. 'Adlan's son, 'Abdullahi, enlisted in the army, rose to a high rank, and participated in major campaigns.[82]

Perhaps the most notable feat of the Sudanese jihadiyya was their participation in the international force sent by Napoleon III to suppress the Mexican revolt in 1862. Upon the emperor's request for black troops, the

Khedive Sa'id dispatched 447 Sudanese soldiers. In Mexico they proved fierce fighters, but they soon grew tired and homesick. As a result of this, as well as of the objection of the U.S. Government to the presence of foreign troops in the Americas, the soldiers returned to Egypt in 1867, where they were honored and decorated.[83]

There are no accurate figures on the total number of Sudanese troops. In the 1860s they were estimated at 10,644.[84] Their pay, food, and clothing were poor. Sometimes soldiers were not paid for months. As a result, those stationed in the provinces often pillaged local communities for food and tribute. The government entrusted them with tax collection, which meant that soldiers spent much of their time away from headquarters. This led to a decline in military discipline and low morale. On top of that, the jihadiyya were abused by their Egyptian and Turkish officers. It is not surprising, therefore, that desertion and revolts were common. One of these revolts occurred in 1844 in Wad Medani where the jihadiyya killed some of their Turkish officers and fled to Sinnar. It was only after a great deal of difficulty that the revolt was suppressed.[85] The most serious revolt took place in 1865 in Kassala. Soldiers of the Fourth Regiment killed several officers and besieged the town for twenty-six days. The revolt was finally suppressed with deception and diplomacy. The survivors were executed or given long prison sentences. Following the revolt, Sudanese units were transferred to Egypt, where a large number of soldiers were discharged and the rest were attached to other army units.[86]

The antislavery measures of the 1870s greatly reduced the supply of new slaves and had a disastrous effect on army recruitment, to the extent that the governor-general of the Sudan seriously considered drafting 1,500 prisoners from Egypt. But the conquest of Dar Fur in 1874 created a new source of recruits. To prevent desertion, all recruits from Dar Fur, from sergeants downward, were branded with the Arabic letter *jim*, for jihadi, or regular soldiers.[87]

During the course of the Mahdist revolution (1881–1884) the jihadiyya remained loyal to their patron and fought against the Mahdist rebels. However, following the collapse of the Turco-Egyptian regime many were absorbed into the Mahdist Army. After the collapse of the Turkish regime some Sudanese jihadiyya were trapped with Emin Pasha's in Equatoria. These soldiers scattered in East Africa, where their descendants formed what came to be known today as the Nubi communities in Kenya and Uganda.[88]

Turco-Egyptian rule helped military slavery grow in yet another way. The slave traders in the south raised their own armies. The rise of these private armies was associated with the zariba system. Each zariba was surrounded by a large number of local people who produced food and worked as porters. These camps resembled small towns with a heterogeneous population and a highly stratified social structure. At the top were the zariba owners. Below them were the *wakils* (agents) who had proven organizational or military abilities and had gained the confidence of the Khartoumers. Another category was the jallaba who conducted trade and bartered goods in the camps. The largest group in the camps, however, was the merchant armies. This group may be divided into two categories: the *'asakir*, who were drawn from the Danqala and the Ja'aliyyin and other northern Sudanese groups, most of whom were peasants, recruited in Khartoum. They were given six months' salary in advance from which they purchased necessities. However, the 'asakir were constantly in debt to the agents who overcharged them for goods. The most profitable undertaking for them was slave raiding from which they received a small portion of the booty.[89] They were provided with firearms and served as guards, escorting the caravans, and conducting the raids.[90] The second category of soldiers was known as the *furukh* or bazingir, who were recruited from the local population and formed the backbone of the merchants' armies. They were most useful for their knowledge of the countryside.[91]

During the government campaign against the slave traders, many bazingir remained loyal to their owners, while others defected to the government. After the collapse of the Turkish regime, most of the bazingir were absorbed into the Mahdist Army, where they formed the backbone of the jihadiyya. The career of Hamdan Abu 'Anja amply illustrates this process. Abu 'Anja was from the Mandala group. He served under Al-Zubair and later joined the Mahdist forces. He became a prominent general after the fall of al-Ubayyid to the Mahdists in 1883. In 1887, Abu 'Anja led the Mahdist expedition against Ethiopia, but died of cholera or typhoid in Gondar.[92]

SLAVES IN THE AGRICULTURAL AND DOMESTIC SECTORS

In examining the role of slaves in the Sudan, it is important to emphasize regional variations. The use of slaves depended on the degree of socioeconomic transformation, particularly on the commoditization of agriculture and land. By the mid-nineteenth century, commoditization prevailed in the riverain areas north of Khartoum, particularly in the Dongola and Berber provinces.

Before the nineteenth century, most agricultural work, especially in the riverain areas, was done by free peasants. By the middle of the century slaves had begun to play a dominant role in agricultural production. This was one of the major changes that resulted from the alteration of the system of land tenure and the promotion of cash crop production. Following the conquest, Muhammad 'Ali urged his officials to "modernize" agriculture and to introduce new techniques. Special attention was given to saqiya irrigation in the Dongola and Berber provinces. Hundreds of Egyptian artisans were sent to the Sudan to build saqiyas and dig canals. In addition, new cash crops such as sugarcane and rice were introduced.[93] To facilitate the export of these crops to Egypt, efforts were made to improve river and land transportation. Coupled with this was the regime's policy of taxing the saqiyas at a fixed rate, which required intensive labor within each unit. Moreover, traditional land rights became transferable, a situation that did not exist before.[94] Many individuals began to expand their land holdings at the expense of others. This led to the emergence of a new class of landlords who began to rely on slave labor.

By mid-century the new landlords began to exploit free peasants by using a precolonial system known as *shayl* (credit) to extend their influence over a community of indebted cultivators, maximizing their income in the form of grain and labor services. At the same time they altered the teddan system to their advantage. Before the mid-nineteenth century the distribution of crops produced by the waterwheel was negotiated at the beginning of the cultivation season. The new landlords changed the terms by increasing the size of their share and crippling the bargaining position of the tenants.[95] The latter responded by migrating to remote regions of Kordofan and Dar Fur or the southern provinces where they joined the slave traders.

The terrain and the system of land tenure in northern riverain areas did not allow the growth of a plantation system. Slave labor (of both sexes) served as an adjunct to family labor, performing the same work as free peasants. In addition to clearing the land of trees, sowing, weeding, harvesting, and storing the grain, male slaves dug the canals and looked after livestock.

In the central rainland of Kordofan, slave labor expanded cultivation, particularly in the southern parts of the province, inhabited by the Baqqara. Their proximity to the slave-raiding areas in the Nuba Mountains and south of the Bahr al-Arab allowed them to obtain a large number of slaves. During the heyday of the slave trade, the Baqqara became the principal allies of the jallaba whose caravans passed through their territories.[96] The Baqqara employed slaves in agriculture while they pastured the cattle.

Moreover, many immigrants from the northern riverain regions had settled in Kordofan and combined commerce with agriculture. During the early days of the Turco-Egyptian conquest, these merchants acted as brokers between the government and the Baqqara who were required to pay taxes. The Baqqara supplied the jallaba with slaves in exchange for the latter's assumption of their taxes.[97]

The major slave owners in Kordofan were the big merchants who migrated from the northern riverain areas to this region. These merchants lived in towns such as al-Ubayyid and owned fertile land in areas known as al-Khayran north of al-Ubayyid and in southern Kordofan, where they grew wheat, sorghum, and cash crops such as tobacco, using many slaves to work on these plots.[98] The wealthiest merchants in Kordofan were Ilyas Umm Birayr and Ahmad Dafaʿ Allah, who migrated from the Shendi region.[99] They also employed slaves as domestic servants. Slaves were obtained through purchase from the jallaba and through organized raids. For example, Ahmad Dafaʿ Allah and his brother ʿAbdalla frequently raided the Nuba Mountains and obtained a large number of captives. They retained some and gave others to the government to be drafted in the army.[100] Wealthy merchants owned between fifty and one hundred slaves. In addition to agricultural labor, slaves were also used as soldiers. The use of slaves, therefore, helped merchants to become power centers and to consolidate their economic and political position in the region.

With the increased slave supply and government restrictions on slave export in the mid-nineteenth century, the local people also began to rely on agriculture. It was reported that in the 1860s most households in Kordofan possessed at least one slave. The extensive use of slaves allowed local farmers to expand their landholding by opening new fields for cultivation.[101]

The socioeconomic changes in the nineteenth century had a great impact on the status of slaves in the northern Sudan. The increased supply meant that slaves could be obtained cheaply, and this affected their position in the society. Slaves in the northern Sudan were marked by cultural, physical, and social attributes and relegated to the bottom of the social hierarchy. Slave owners in nineteenth-century northern Sudan sold slaves born in their households and used them as collateral for loans and tribute.[102] Slaves were distinguished from the freeborn by their peculiar names such as "Sea of Lust" and "Patience" for women, and "Good Morning" and "Friday" for men. Although the majority of slaves assimilated into the culture of their owners, spoke Arabic, and became Muslims, they were still regarded as inferior. They were not fully integrated into the owners' communities, particularly in marriage.

In East Africa and the New World, the plantation system concentrated slaves in one locality. Slaves in the northern Sudan were scattered among various households. Resistance was more of an individual action which often took the form of desertion and escape. Flogging or heavy work frequently led to escape. Subtle forms of resistance included slaves' attempts to create their own communities and to build a life of their own within the society that enslaved them.

FEMALE SLAVERY

The preponderance of female slaves in Africa—and their double jeopardy as slaves and as females—has been stressed in numerous studies.[103] Robertson and Klein emphasize the fact that the majority of slaves in Africa were females and address the question of why women were more desirable than men by looking at the roles they played in economic production in particular.[104] While some scholars have argued that female slaves were valued for reproduction and the expansion of the owner's lineage, others have stressed the importance of their productive role.[105] The latter group have argued that reproduction was not limited to childbearing and child rearing, but included various domestic functions.[106] To a large extent, the Sudan conforms to the pattern that prevailed elsewhere in Africa in that female slaves outnumbered their male counterparts. Although there are no accurate figures to support this assumption, it is evident from colonial records that females formed the bulk of the slave population. Shortly after the Anglo-Egyptian conquest of the Sudan in 1898 the new government conducted a survey and established a register in which the names of slaves were recorded. Although the reliability of this survey is questionable, it does provide some clues as to the number of female slaves in the country. In Dongola Province, for instance, the number of slaves was estimated at 15,468 at the beginning of this century; of those, 9,908 were women and 5,560 were men.[107]

A central issue in the debate on female slavery is the position of slave women in Muslim societies.[108] The recognition of concubinage in Islam overshadowed the productive function of female slaves in these societies, distorted colonial antislavery policies, and delayed their manumission.[109] Concubinage is recognized by the Shari'a, which contains elaborate rules regulating it. In his study of slavery in Islam, Mahmoud 'Abd al-Wahab

Fayid rationalizes concubinage, arguing that it satisfied the sexual desires of the female slaves and thereby prevented the spread of immorality in the Muslim community.[110] Concubinage implies a monogamous relation between the slave woman and her master. In reality, however, female slaves in many Muslim societies were prey for members of their owners' households, their neighbors, and their guests.

A slave concubine who bore children to her master would be elevated to the status of *um al-walad* (mother of his child), and their offspring were considered equal to the master's freeborn children. Such a woman could not be sold and was to be freed upon her master's death. If a man claimed a female slave as a concubine before a Shari'a court she could establish a claim at his death, which would entitle her to a share in his estate. However, in the Sudan the addition of an inheritor to the share of the estate was often resented by freeborn members of the family. Freeborn wives preferred their husbands to keep female slaves as concubines rather than marry them, because as concubines they would still be their servants. If the concubine was manumitted, she could not have legal status as a wife; she would be living with her master as his mistress and her children would be regarded as bastards. If a slave woman deserted her master, she lost the custody of her children. If the slave woman had children from a man who did not belong to her owner's family, the children would be considered as the property of the owner. The same applied if she had children from another slave.

It would be misleading to determine the conditions of female slaves by simply looking at these rules. It is essential that we look beyond Quranic injunctions for the treatment of slaves and examine how they actually lived and how the law was used in specific historical situations.

In the Sudan, from the beginning, women formed the bulk of the slave population and played major productive and reproductive roles. Young girls, particularly Ethiopians, commanded higher prices as they were desired as concubines and domestic servants.[111] For instance, in one case a young male slave was sold for fifteen Spanish dollars, but his female counterpart was sold for twenty to twenty-five dollars.[112] Throughout the nineteenth century, young girls commanded higher prices.[113]

Female slaves had a significant social and political role in precolonial Sudanese society. In the Fur kingdom, for instance, concubines had considerable political influence. Offspring of favorite concubines reached high positions and sometimes succeeded the sultan.[114] In Dar Masalit, concubines expanded the kinship groups of the rulers.[115] Ownership of female slaves affected the role of women in Sudanese society. In the riverain regions, before the nineteenth century, freeborn women performed domestic tasks and worked in the fields. By the mid-nineteenth century, middle- and upper-class women refrained from physical labor and adopted a new style of dress which reflected their new roles as secluded women. Unmarried girls also demanded female slaves as part of the bride-wealth so that they could be relieved from menial labor.[116]

Although young girls were used as concubines, they also played a major role in economic production. They were assigned to light tasks such as cattle grazing and minor domestic chores. As soon as they reached adolescence they became easy prey for the males of the owner's household and their guests. In old age female slaves were relegated to the field or hired out as servants.[117] In addition to their labor, female slaves were valued because of their potential for biological reproduction.[118] Owners often hired out their female slaves as prostitutes and lived on their earnings. Children of prostitutes were considered slaves since they had no legitimate father to recognize paternity.[119] This practice persisted in the twentieth century and was noted by a colonial administrator who wrote:

> The most paying thing from the point of view of the master is to get his slaves to have children without laying any claim to paternity, and the children are merged into the household as the labor of the next generation.[120]

In urban centers female slaves were used mainly for domestic service, often including the provision of sexual services. In nineteenth-century Khartoum, for instance, slave women were taken as concubines by many European residents. Some women found shelter with Christian missions and were converted to Christianity.[121]

Before the nineteenth century, slave ownership was a privilege of the nobility and the ruling elites. As a result of the increased supply of slaves during the Turkiyya, other groups such as peasants and nomads began to own slaves. Although the majority of the slaveholders were males, freeborn women also owned slaves. In Dar Masalit, for example, royal women owned the female slaves working under their supervision.[122] It is not clear whether or not common women owned slaves. But since the Shari'a allowed them to inherit property, it is possible to assume that they could inherit slaves or a share in a slave. One of the most important examples of women slave owners was Sitt Amna who lived in the upper Blue Nile area in the early years of this century. During the first two decades of colonial rule, she received a continuous influx of slaves from her husband, Khojali al-Hasan, who lived on the Ethiopian side of the border. Their clandestine activities undermined colonial antislavery policies, until Amna was finally convicted of slave dealing in the early 1920s.[123]

Slave women, in particular, were viewed by the Arabic-speaking northern Sudanese as promiscuous and were so degraded that society's moral values did not apply to them. They were given to slave men as wives and to freeborn men as concubines. In Dar Fur for instance, slave women were pressured to offer sexual services to owners' relatives and guests.[124]

URBAN SLAVERY: KHARTOUM DURING THE TURKIYYA

While the overwhelming majority of slaves in the Sudan were deployed in agriculture in the rural areas, from almost the beginning slavery was also urban. Many Sudanese towns such as Shendi, Berber, and al-Ubayyid had a large complement of slaves and they were as much a part of the system as those who toiled in the fields. These towns owed their success to their location on the trade routes which linked the Sudan with the outside world. It was through these towns that the country's produce—including slaves—was exported to the outside world, and imports were distributed to the countryside. During the Turkiyya these towns functioned as principal markets and military garrisons. They formed enclaves of cosmopolitan life in an agricultural and nomadic country.

The largest of the Sudanese towns was Khartoum, the capital of the Turkish Government and the headquarters of business firms. In Khartoum, slave traders such as Ghattas, Kuchuk 'Ali, Muhammad Khayr, and Idris Wad Daftar established the headquarters from where they sent expeditions to the south. It was not a coincidence that the slave traders in the south were known as Khartoumers.

By the mid-nineteenth century, Khartoum developed from a small fishing village to a city. In 1843 its population was estimated at 13,000.[125] By mid-century Khartoum had grown into a cosmopolitan city with a population that included Europeans, Egyptians, Middle Easterners, and northern Sudanese, most of whom owned slaves. According to Licurgo Santoni, the director of posts in Upper Egypt and the northern Sudan, "no matter how poor a Nubian is he possesses two to four slaves of both sexes. The comparatively well-off have any amount of them."[126] In 1883 the slave population in Khartoum was estimated at 27,000, or two-thirds of the total population.[127] However, these figures were based on sheer guess, and it is not clear whether all of these people were slaves. It is possible that many of them were ex-slaves, discharged soldiers, or other immigrants.

The majority of slaves in Khartoum were used in the domestic sector or as porters, while others were recruited into the army. A few attained high ranks. Adham al-'Arifi from Tegali reached the rank of *qai'm maqam* and for a few months in 1872 became acting governor-general. Another slave from Tegali, Faraj Muhammad al-Zayni, was Gordon's chief of staff, charged with the defense of Khartoum during the siege of the Mahdists.[128] Some discharged soldiers were employed as private troops or boatmen on Nile expeditions. In the 1870s and 1880s a dockyard existed at the Muqran, which employed a large number of slaves and wage laborers.

Discontented slaves of both sexes often took their cases to government officials. Fearing that, if liberated, slaves would turn to prostitution or thieving, government officials would usually try to convince the slaves to remain with their owners. If all failed, male slaves would be sent to the army while their female counterparts would be deployed to the military depots and married off to the soldiers from their home areas. Other female slaves were employed as launderers, water carriers, and domestic servants.[129]

In Khartoum each community lived in a particular quarter. Ex-slaves, discharged soldiers, and workers congregated in Salamat al-Pasha, Hay al-Nuba, Hay Kara, and Haboub Darabani.[130] These slums were located in the southern part of the city.[131] Another overcrowded quarter was al-Munjara, which housed dockyard workers and their families.[132]

These communities had a rich cultural life, full of festivities and ceremonies. The Italian missionary, Pellegrino Matteucci, described at some length an archetypical carnival of Sudanese slaves and ex-slaves in Turkish Khartoum. One day each year the slaves boycotted work and gathered at the Muqran to party. People wore attire from their home areas or other colorful costumes, played music, and danced. They elected a "king of the slaves" and staged satires on the behavior of their masters.[133] Matteucci wrote:

> Everyone was laughing, for the slaves had laid aside their chains—though tomorrow they will be enchained anew. Almost every tribe of Central Africa was represented on the great plaza—from Wadai to the equator, from the Mongbetu to the Galla, not a single tribe was missing.[134]

Matteucci thought he could distinguish forty-two tribes, but named only the Shilluk, Nuer, Bongo, "those from Darfur," and the "Rajjaf" (Bari, perhaps). It is not clear how many of these people were actually slaves, as many European visitors tended to associate all black Sudanese with slavery.

KHARTOUM SLAVES AND CHRISTIAN MISSIONS

Liberated slaves in Khartoum became a major source of converts for European Christian missionaries who arrived in the Sudan in the early 1840s. In 1842 Luigi Montuori, a priest of the Vincentian order, arrived in Khartoum with the Belgian consul-general to Egypt. With the latter's help he obtained permission from the Turkish governor to open a church and school.[135] However, as a result of shortage of funds and apathy of European residents, the mission was abandoned in 1845. This short-lived attempt was soon followed by a far-reaching one. In 1846 the pope created the Apostolic Vicariate of Central Africa, and the mission in the Sudan was entrusted first to the Jesuits and later to the Franciscans. In February 1848 Father Ryllo and his party arrived in Khartoum. Through the help of Shariif Hasan, a Turkish merchant residing in Khartoum, they obtained a mission site at the west end of the town.[136]

From the beginning, the missionaries considered asylum for liberated slaves an essential part of their duties.[137] They opened their first church on the Feast of Pentecost, and soon founded a school for slave children whom they bought in the slave market. Besides the catechism, Arabic, Italian, arithmetic, singing, and drawing were taught. Most children enrolled in the school were orphans.[138]

The missionaries also targeted ex-slaves who had been freed by British and other European agents in the Red Sea and White Nile regions. According to Comboni's baptism register, 684 people were baptized in the Sudan between 1842 and 1898, the vast majority of whom were slaves.[139] The main ethnic groups from which the slaves came were the Dinka, Nuba, Bari, and Oromo from Ethiopia.

In general, converts adopted biblical or Italian first names but kept their African or Arabic names (examples: Antonio 'Abdallah, Vittorio 'Abdallah, Caro 'Abdalkhair, Carolina Adam, and so forth). The register gives little information about the religious background of the converts. However, judging by their last names, it can be assumed that some were Muslims, though adoption of Arabic names without conversion to Islam was and is common in the southern Sudan and the Nuba Mountains.

The regulation of asylum and the conversion of freed slaves to Christianity became a thorny issue between the missionaries and the Turkish administration in the Sudan. While the government permitted the missionaries to offer asylum and baptize slaves they had freed, the missionaries went further and sheltered runaway slaves. As a result, the mission stations were subjected to frequent police raids.[140]

One of the most controversial aspects of the mission's activities was the practice of "concubinage." Many bought young female slaves from the local market and lived with them without legal marriages.[141] Legal marriages were rare in Khartoum, particularly before the establishment of the Christian mission. Licurgo Santoni related that of the forty or forty-two European residents in Khartoum in the 1870s, only three or four were legally married.[142] This situation produced a large number of illegitimate children. Following the establishment of the mission, these children were christened and some concubines were canonically married.[143]

A few examples illustrate this pattern. Marie Peney was an Oromo woman from western Abyssinia. Her husband, Alfred Peney, chief medical officer of the Sudan, took her as a concubine soon after his appointment in 1850 and married her in 1855. Peney died in 1861 not far from Gondokoro while preparing to attempt the discovery of the White Nile's sources. Adolfo Antognoli was with him when he died and accompanied the widow back to Khartoum. In 1864 he married her. On Antognoli's death Marie married his business partner, Flaminio Finzi Magrini, a Ferrarese Jew, and left the Catholic church to which she later returned. She died in Cairo in 1891.[144] Eugene de Prussenarere de la Wostyne from Ypres, a doctor who spent the years from 1856 to 1864 in the Sudan, married an Oromo slave woman. She was given to him by an Arab shaykh from al-Massalamiyya. She was christened as Amina Mariam. After his death she married Martin Ludwig Hansal, the Austrian vice-consul.[145] Caterina Zaynab was born near Holy Cross, a mission station on the Upper Nile between Bor and Shambe. In 1861 she was sent for education to Verona and in 1867 returned to Egypt where she became a teacher in Bishop Comboni's school in Cairo. In 1874 she married an Italian carpenter, Ceasare Ongano, in the mission church in Khartoum. A child, Maria Vincenza, was born and christened in Khartoum but died in infancy. Caterina, now a widow, next married Ernst Marno Bey, an Austrian in the Egyptian Government service. They had a son, Jakob Ernst, born in 1880, who died in Khartoum in 1955.[146]

Fearing the social stigma at home, many Europeans abandoned their African wives and children in Khartoum and returned alone. Santoni depicted the situation:

At this moment there are Abyssinian women with children begotten by their dead European masters and who live in the greatest poverty. Some become the mistresses of newly arrived Europeans and the children of former unions are cast out into the streets and merge with the native population. Some Europeans have deserted their own wives and children in their own lands and have formed new and illegitimate families here.[147]

While a few orphans and illegitimate children found shelter with the missions where they received basic education, the great part fell into misery and lived by begging in the streets. Still, some mulattos established themselves as physicians, engineers, and teachers in Egypt and the Sudan. Examples include Musa Peney of the Suez Canal Company, Yusuf Peney of the Egyptian State Railways, and Adolf Haggenmacher, an engineer on the construction of the Blue Nile Bridge in Khartoum.[148]

Young boys and girls were sent to Europe to receive training in theology, reading, arithmetic, and other technical skills such as weaving, blacksmithing, and shoemaking. The missionaries hoped that these evangelized Africans would return to Africa and spread Christianity in their communities. At the beginning, Sudanese students were trained at the Mazza Institute in Verona. In 1867 a missionary training center was established in Cairo, followed by the Nigrizia Institute in Italy.[149] It is appropriate here to examine the careers of a few. Giuseppe Habashi was an Ethiopian slave who was baptized in Khartoum in 1851 and then taken by the Franciscans to Verona to be trained in theology at the Instituto Mazza. Habashi was ordained as a priest. He returned to Khartoum and later went to Egypt and Palestine.[150] Female slaves also found a niche among the missionaries. For instance, Bakhita, a slave from Dar Fur, was baptized in Khartoum and sent to Italy in 1890 where she became a nun. She died at Schio Vicenza and was regarded as a saintly woman.[151] Some like Don Luca were taken to Europe and settled there permanently. He was a Dinka slave freed in Egypt in 1854 and taken by the missionaries to Lubiana where he remained for the rest of his life.[152]

Conversion of ex-slaves to Christianity led to the emergence of a Christianized African community in a predominantly Muslim society. These evangelized Africans played a significant role in the spread of Christianity in their own communities in the southern Sudan and the Nuba Mountains, particularly after the Anglo-Egyptian conquest in 1898. For instance, Margherita Cassina, a Golo slave baptized in Khartoum, remained there throughout the Mahdiyya. After the reconquest, she accompanied the

Catholic missionaries to the Bahr al-Ghazal and helped them establish a mission among her people in Wau. Margherita lived in Wau until her death in 1935.[153]

The outbreak of the Mahdiyya in 1881 and its subsequent victories dealt a serious blow to the missionary activities. By 1883, they left the Sudan and were not able to return until the establishment of Anglo-Egyptian rule in 1898.

SLAVERY AND THE SLAVE TRADE DURING THE MAHDIYYA

The Mahdist revolution of 1881 emanated from a conjunction of religious, political, and economic factors. The Anglo-Egyptian officials assumed that the outbreak of the Mahdiyya was a response to the antislavery measures in the late 1870s. In her study of the Tegali kingdom, Janet Ewald has pointed to tensions between the wealthy traders supported by the government and the jallaba, against whom government actions were directed.[154] It was small traders, poor farmers, and herders who joined the Mahdist movement. Personal interests and rivalries between the big merchants played a major role in their attitude towards the Mahdiyya. For instance, Ahmad Dafa' Allah remained loyal to the government, while Ilyas Umm Birayr supported the Mahdi. Before the Mahdiyya, Ilyas was a strong supporter of the government and became the governor of Kordofan until 1879 when he was removed. He resented this decision and later joined the Mahdi.[155]

The initial military success of the Mahdiyya may be attributed to its ability to integrate the merchants' private armies. At another level the Mahdi appealed to slaves, promising them freedom and salvation.[156] In other words, the outbreak of the Mahdiyya gave many disaffected groups an opportunity to rise against the Turco-Egyptian regime.

SLAVE TRADE DURING THE MAHDIYYA

Under the Mahdist state (1885–1898) the slave trade resumed but not on its previous scale. There were several reasons. First, the Mahdist state was largely cut off from the external world and hence could not export slaves on a large scale, especially since the British attempted to enforce antislave trade measures in Egypt and on the Red Sea. Second, local demand increased because the Mahdist state needed a large number of slaves for its armies as well as for agricultural production. Finally, continuous warfare between the khalifa and his neighbors made the slave trade a hazardous business. Hence, slave raids were conducted to meet the local demand. In his attempt to incorporate southern provinces, Khalifa 'Abdullahi, the Mahdi's successor, sent several expeditions to Equatoria, the Nuba Mountains, and the Bahr al-Ghazal, but these did not bring in sufficient numbers.[157]

The khalifa devised several methods to recruit slaves. For instance, slaves who deserted their masters and went to Omdurman were not permitted to return; if capable of bearing arms, they were drafted into the army.[158] Rudolf Slatin reported a daily sale of slaves in Omdurman. However, the purchase of male slaves was forbidden, as they were considered a monopoly of the Khalifa. Any person wishing to dispose of a male slave had to send him to the Bayt al-Mal (the treasury), where a nominal price was paid. If it was found that he would make a good soldier, he was recruited for the army. If found unsuitable, he would be sent to work as a laborer in his master's fields.[159] On the other hand, the sale of women and girls was allowed, provided that a paper was signed by two witnesses, one of whom should be a *qadi* (judge), certifying the sale. According to Slatin, this system was introduced because slaves frequently ran away from their masters and were often caught and resold by others.

The khalifa also tried to use religious rationales to justify his slavery policies. He called for the opinions of the qadis on such issues as manumission and runaways.[160] In one instance, the khalifa asked the qadi for an opinion as to whether or not such runaways could become property of the *mulazimin* (guard corps) if they were not claimed by their rightful owners within twenty days. But as no persons living outside the mulazimin quarter were permitted to enter the enclosure, it was not possible for the masters to look for their runaway slaves there. On these grounds, the qadi suggested that runaway slaves should be exposed in the marketplace for a short time. If no one claimed them, they should become the property of the Bayt al-Mal. As the khalifa had previously given instructions to his mulazimin to retain all slaves belonging to the Nile Valley groups and to return only those who belonged to his kinsmen from the west, the qadi's opinion did not please him. He disregarded it.[161]

Another method through which slaves were obtained was the Mahdist campaigns against rebellious groups in the Nuba Mountains, upper Blue Nile, and the Bahr al-Ghazal. Through these punitive expeditions many people were captured and sent to Omdurman. These captives were taken as *ghanimas* (war booty). Provincial administrators, particularly in

Kordofan, Dar Fur, and Bahr al-Ghazal, sent large numbers of captives regularly to Omdurman. Suitable males were absorbed into the jihadiyya; the rest were given to prominent emirs.[162] The jihadiyya also kept many female slaves as wives and concubines.

Because of the limited supply, theft of slaves became common in Omdurman. Slaves were enticed into other people's homes or induced to leave the fields, then thrown into chains and carried to distant parts of the country, where they were sold.[163]

Under the Mahdiyya, the basic tenets of slavery remained. Slaves fulfilled agrarian and domestic functions. After the establishment of his rule, the khalifa paid great attention to agriculture. To ensure the security of his regime, the khalifa encouraged his Baqqara kinsmen to migrate from Kordofan and Dar Fur to Omdurman and the central parts of the country. Many Baqqara settled in the fertile regions of Gedarif and the Gezira where they were given the best land, which led to great friction between them and the riverain population.[164] At the same time farmers were required to pay an annual tribute from their produce to the Bayt al-Mal. The concentration of a large number of people in Omdurman created a great demand for grain and became a heavy burden on farmers. This was evident in the large quantities of sorghum sent from the Gezira and Gedarif.[165] At the same time the Baqqara pillaged villages along the Nile and confiscated crops as well as slaves. As a result many people fled from the riverain areas.[166] The problem was exacerbated by lengthy military campaigns against Ethiopia and Egypt. In brief, agricultural production declined sharply during the Mahdiyya.

The major beneficiaries of slavery during the Mahdiyya were the Mahdist state, members of the Mahdi's and the khalifa's families, and leading emirs.[167] Most individuals resided in Omdurman but owned large agricultural estates in the distant provinces. For instance, it was reported that emir Ahmad Muhammad Shariif employed ninety-eight slaves on his agricultural estates in Halfaya, Aba Island, and elsewhere. Mahmoud wad Ahmad claimed that he owned thirty-three female slaves in Omdurman and fifty-nine in Kordofan.[168] Besides their slaves, members of the Mahdi's and the khalifa's families obtained labor from their followers through other methods. The *ansar* (loyal followers of the Mahdi) provided their daughters to work in the Mahdi's and the khalifa's households. This voluntary labor was an expression of loyalty and earned *baraka* (blessing or grace). Although these women were not slaves, they received no remuneration for their service.[169]

MILITARY SLAVERY DURING
THE MAHDIYYA

The Mahdist state, like its predecessors, relied heavily on slave soldiers. As mentioned above, most Mahdist soldiers had served in the Turco-Egyptian Army and in the merchants' bazingir. Some occupied prominent positions in the Mahdist Army and played a major role in its campaigns. Al Nur Muhammad 'Anqara was a Dongolawi who had enlisted in the Turco-Egyptian cavalry. After his discharge he joined Al-Zubair and became the khalifa's chief of staff in Dar Fur. He later defected to the government side with 2,000 bazingir, and was promoted by Gordon to *qaim maqam* and appointed governor of Lado. In 1882 'Anqara commanded the government forces besieged in Bara by the Mahdists. He surrendered the town in 1883, joined the Mahdi and became an emir. During the last years of the Mahdiyya he was stationed in Gedarif, where he surrendered to Anglo-Egyptian forces.[170]

Another major source of recruits were the Mandala, the servile dependents of the Baqqara. Two of the most prominent Mahdist generals were Mandala: Hamdan Abu 'Anja and Zaki Tamal, who led the Mahdist armies against Ethiopia in 1887.

Slave soldiers were organized into separate units called jihadiyya. The jihadiyya were armed with rifles and bandoliers and later displaced the volatile ansar.[171] The overall command of the jihadiyya was placed in the hands of Hamdan Abu 'Anja. Apart from their military tasks, the jihadiyya performed administrative and police functions. They collected taxes and maintained law and order in the outlying districts. The jihadiyya were not paid regularly at first, although they later received the equivalent of a quarter of a dollar per month. They were, however, entitled to rations of grain. To supplement their income, the jihadiyya engaged in theft, robbery, and other illegal activities.

However, the incorporation of former Turco-Egyptian soldiers into the Mahdist forces was a major source of problems. Many of these soldiers remained loyal to their old patrons. There were continuous tensions between them and the ansar. Their discontent was manifested in 1885 when a unit stationed in al-Ubayyid revolted, killing the deputy governor and a large number of the ansar, and took refuge in the Nuba Mountains. After suppression of the uprising, 'Atron, the leader of the revolt, was captured and beheaded.[172] Because of their continuous defiance, the jihadiyya were supplanted by the mulazimin, into which the khalifa incorporated his own kinsmen—the Baqqara—as well as a significant number of servile recruits. The mulazimin were considered more trustworthy and hence were allowed to keep their arms and ammunition.[173]

URBAN SLAVERY DURING THE MAHDIYYA

Urban slavery was also conspicuous during the Mahdiyya. Following the overthrow of the Turco-Egyptian regime and the fall of Khartoum to the Mahdists in 1885, the capital was moved to Omdurman. A year later, the khalifa ordered the destruction of Khartoum, and the city's population was transferred to Omdurman. Although Khartoum was abandoned in favor of Omdurman, some of its residents (including many slaves) remained in the old quarters of al-Munjara, Salmat al-Pasha, and Burri. These neighborhoods formed the nucleus of what came to be known as the Khartoum Daims.

In addition to slaves from Khartoum, Baqqara immigrants brought slaves with them. Moreover, Omdurman became the headquarters of the government in which servile troops were stationed and the largest slave market in the country existed near the Bayt al-Mal or the treasury. Joseph Ohrwalder and Slatin (both Mahdist prisoners whose accounts should be treated with great caution) reported a slave market called Suq al-Raqiq near the Bayt al-Mal. This was a house built of mud bricks in which fifty or sixty women of various ages were sold on a daily basis.[174] Slaves were arranged in lines under the open sky; their bodies were bathed in oil to preserve the gloss of their skin. Purchasers made minute examinations and asked all sorts of questions to ascertain the physical and mental qualities and the reliability of the slaves. The salesmen were required to produce certificates showing the slave's tribal origin and their legal title of ownership.[175] Young females were usually kept apart from the rest, as they were generally selected as concubines. They were subjected to serious scrutiny. Ethiopian males were thought of as ill-fitted for hard work and were usually employed in the domestic sphere. Prices paid for slaves ranged as follows: for an old working male slave, fifty to eighty dollars; for a middle-aged woman, eighty to one hundred twenty dollars; and for a young girl, one hundred ten to one hundred sixty, depending on her looks.[176] These rates varied according to market value or special demand for a particular ethnic background. In addition, as a way of expressing their loyalty, many Mahdist Baqqara raided neighboring communities and offered their captives to the khalifa, who would then distribute them to his emirs.[177] The number of slaves in each household was usually small, but the practice was widespread.

Tasks performed by urban slaves varied. Male slaves were enlisted in the army or deployed in the agricultural estates of their owners outside the capital. Their female counterparts were used as domestic servants.[178]

Although reliable figures are not available, oral informants assert that females constituted the bulk of slaves in the city.[179] These women performed a wide range of tasks. In addition to domestic work such as carrying water and grinding grain, female slaves were given as presents at weddings and circumcisions. Large-scale warfare and the high rate of death among men created a large number of unattached women in the capital. This became evident after the fall of Khartoum in 1885. Female slaves became property of the Bayt al-Mal. Many were distributed to the Mahdi's followers.[180]

Female slaves lived in the households of their owners but were subjected to constant abuse and harsh punishment.[181] Freeborn women in the masters' households were reportedly even harsher toward female slaves, especially if jealousy was the cause of anger. This led to resentment among slaves, who seized any opportunity for revenge.

Continuous Mahdist military campaigns meant that most men were dispatched from the capital to frontier provinces. A large number of women, particularly slaves, engaged in prostitution and in selling local drink.[182] Despite Mahdist edicts against drinking, brewing local drink continued clandestinely in Omdurman.[183] In 1888 the Khalifa ordered all unmarried women in the capital to marry within one month or be handed over to the Baqqara as concubines.[184] The order targeted female slaves. As a result many were forcibly married, but these marriages did not last.

Both Ohrwalder and Slatin give a grim picture of the life of slaves in Omdurman. According to the latter, slaves were "huddled together in wretched quarters, and eventually found homes amongst the poorest quarters of the population."[185] A male slave's dress consisted merely of a rag tied around his loins.[186] They were overworked and mistreated. Whatever money they earned belonged to the master. Although manumission was recognized, it was rare.

The prevalence of slavery in Omdurman and the khalifa's policy of settling western and southern groups in the city in specific quarters have shaped the ethnic composition of the city. Omdurman was roughly divided into three residential zones. The northern and northwestern zones were inhabited by riverain northern Sudanese, Blue Nile Arabs, and Egyptians and other foreigners. White Nile Arabs settled north and northeast of the mosque. The southern zone was inhabited mainly by immigrants from Kordofan and Dar Fur, West Africa, and southern Sudanese groups such as the Binga, Kara, and others. This zone was subdivided into smaller *fariqs*, each inhabited by a particular group of people. The jihadiyya were garrisoned in this part of the city, in the quarter known as al-Kara. One of the most striking features of southern Omdurman was the prevalence of people from the old slave-raiding frontiers of Dar Fertit in the southwestern Sudan and in the eastern part of what is today the Central African Republic. Most of these people were probably brought by Mahmoud wad Ahmad during his campaign in that region. The Feroge established their own quarter under their sultan, Musa Hamid. The Tama settled in Fariq Tama, while the Fur settled in Fariq Abu Kadok. The Dinka were settled in Hay al-Surujiyya. The Kreish, the Banda, the Binga, and other Fertit groups established themselves in Fariq Fungur.[187] To this day the southern part of Omdurman, which includes present-day al-Mawrada and 'Abbasiyya, is inhabited by people from western and southern Sudan. Following the Anglo-Egyptian conquest, many discharged soldiers from the Egyptian Army joined their kinsmen in these neighborhoods. From these quarters, the first urban workers were drawn at the beginning of this century.

CONCLUSION

Although slavery was a major feature of precolonial Sudanese society, economic production was maintained by free laborers and was conducted on a communal basis. Moreover, slave ownership was a privilege of the nobility and the ruling elite. Only at the end of the eighteenth century, as a result of the socioeconomic transformation of Sudanese society, did slave ownership become widespread. The main beneficiaries of slavery in the northern Sudan were merchants, tribal heads, and religious leaders. The Turco-Egyptian conquest of the Funj kingdom in 1821 consolidated trends that were already under way. It also initiated new ones. The regime's policies with regard to taxation, commerce, military recruitment, and land tenure generated great demand for slaves and created massive social dislocation. At the same time, new military and naval technology led to the incorporation of the slave-supplying regions and expanded the slave-raiding frontier. However, the widespread use of slaves did not lead to the emergence of a plantation system or to the development of the so-called "slave mode of production." Slaves had important political, economic, and domestic roles not only in the rural areas, but also in the urban centers.

✍

TWO

SLAVERY AND LABOR IN
THE SUDAN, 1898–1919

✍

Between many of the Sudanese slaves and their Arab masters there had developed in the course of years an affectionate attachment like that which often prevailed between the Negroes in the southern states of the U.S.A. and their owner, and in such cases slaves were unwilling to break away. They regarded their owners as their father, who had cared for them all their lives; indeed many Arabs treated their slaves as members of their own family.[1]

H. C. JACKSON

There is no status of slavery in the Sudan. There is however a considerable number of Sudanese who for one reason or another are living in a state of domestic servitude.[2]

C. A. WILLIS

These statements encapsulate the views of the first generation of British officials in the Sudan toward the institution of slavery and explain the Anglo-Egyptian Government's slavery and labor policies. The application of these policies, their impact on the slaves and the slave owners, and the efforts of the colonial government to transform ex-slaves into wage laborers are the main themes of this chapter. The discussion revolves around the questions of how the situation at the end of the nineteenth and early twentieth centuries affected government policies toward slavery and labor, and what the establishment of the Anglo-Egyptian regime meant to Sudanese slaves and slave owners. The colonial period was a time of struggle for slaves, slave owners, and colonial officials, each with their own interests and constraints. The nature of this struggle and its outcome form a central part of this inquiry.

BRITISH VIEWS OF SUDANESE SLAVERY

Despite the fact that the Sudan was one of the most active slave-raiding zones in Africa in the late nineteenth century, and despite British rhetoric, slavery and the slave trade continued to persist for several decades after the Anglo-Egyptian conquest.

One of the major factors contributing to the continuation of slavery was some senior British officials' perception of Sudanese slavery, which was framed by Western intellectual and historical experience. They feared that a sudden abolition would lead to vagrancy and prostitution. In this respect, colonial officials were guided by the post-emancipation experience in the New World. This cautious strategy had been developed in Asia and was later applied in Africa.[3] Also, officials' perceptions of Sudanese slavery derived, in part, from the slave owners themselves with whom administrators were closely associated. According to C. A. Willis:

> The reactionary official takes his cue from the Arab, with whom he, as was pointed out above, is in closer touch than the slave. He likes order and discipline, and he wants to see production increase and habits of thrift and industry encouraged, and all these seem to be available under the system of domestic slavery.[4]

In other words, colonial officials shared the slaveholders' view that without discipline the slave would be idle, mischievous, and even dangerous.

Another factor was the assumption that slavery had always been an integral part of Sudanese society and that most economic activities were performed by slaves. British officials were convinced that a sudden abolition would lead to economic collapse. They also believed that slavery in the Sudan had corrupted both owners and slaves, making the former indolent and the latter unwilling to work unless forced. Therefore, they made serious efforts to keep slaves with their owners and targeted runaway and liberated slaves for labor recruitment.

One of the most instrumental figures in shaping government policy toward slavery was Rudolf Slatin. In view of his long experience in the Sudan during the Mahdiyya, he was considered an authority on local customs and traditions. Slatin himself had owned domestic slaves during his captivity in Omdurman.[5] Throughout his term (1900–1914) as inspector-general of the Sudan, Slatin discouraged the emancipation of slaves, arguing that this would adversely affect the economic well-being of the country. Another senior official, H. C. Jackson, spoke for many when he wrote:

> Liberation would have resulted in the abandonment of most of the cultivation along the river-banks, the loss of many of the flocks and herds of the nomad Arabs and the consequent death of thousands of innocent individuals who, through no fault of their own, had been brought up under a social system that was repugnant to Western ideas, but accepted as an indispensable condition of their everyday lives. More than this, to have freed all the slaves would have meant letting loose upon society thousands of men and women with no sense of social responsibility, who would have been a menace to public security and morals. And, finally, the whole Arab population might have risen against what they regarded as a gross injustice; for, after all, they had bought their slaves and paid for them.[6]

They would be destitute, immoral, and irresponsible, British officials argued; ex-slaves would have no idea of what freedom entailed and would find it difficult to survive without the paternal guidance of owners.

It is not surprising, therefore, that government officials turned a blind eye, denied the existence of slavery, and deliberately avoided using the term, resorting instead to such euphemisms as "domestic servants." The implicit assumption in this term is that slaves in the Sudan were born in the family and became members of the owner's household, and that domestic slavery was basically benign.[7]

However, the most important factor that shaped the government policy toward slavery was the colonial economy itself.

THE COLONIAL ECONOMY, 1900–1919

From the beginning, the Anglo-Egyptian regime considered agriculture as the best hope for the Sudan's economy. This view was confirmed by the availability of vast tracts of arable land and the abundant water supply. However, for political and economic reasons the new regime adopted a cautious strategy during the early years. Large-scale capitalist enterprise, with its attendant social and political consequences, was deliberately avoided. The Anglo-Egyptian officials believed that the Sudanese economy had been severely disrupted during the Mahdiyya. From their perspective, the immediate task was the revival of agricultural production.

One of the most critical issues the new regime faced was the question of land tenure. The large-scale dislocation, abandonment of land, and forceful appropriation of property during the Mahdiyya led to endless disputes immediately after the conquest. Settlement of these disputes was considered essential for the revival of the economy and thus became the first priority of the government. Between 1899 and 1905 a series of ordinances were enacted, surveys were conducted, and a commission to settle claims was established. The government claimed for itself all land not privately owned and established the right to acquire land through eminent domain. Individual titles could be established on the basis of possession, receipts of rent, or profit from the land.[8]

However, regional variations in the land tenure system were sources of innumerable problems. In the northern riverain areas, for instance, there were conflicting claims over the *jarf* (the land between the water's edge and the bank proper) and the saqiya land (the land above the bank irrigated by the saqiya). In the Gezira major disputes arose over the boundaries between irrigated land and rainland. Farther away from the Nile, conflicts involved tribal leaders who claimed all tribal lands and members of their tribes who cultivated the land but did not own it. In short, land tenure continued to preoccupy the government for many years.[9]

From the perspective of this study, the colonial economy guaranteed the continuation of slavery. In the riverain areas in the far north, serious efforts were made to revive and expand saqiya irrigation. Loans of money and grain were provided to farmers for saqiya erection and cattle purchase. In Dongola Province a loan of LE 500 was given, and in 1903 the government announced a year's exemption from taxes on land irrigated by newly erected saqiyas.[10] The number of saqiyas increased from 8,902 in 1904 to 10,075 in 1913. The amount of cultivated land rose from 1,100,000 feddans in 1904 to 2,100,000 feddans in 1913 (1 feddan=.038 acres). The main crops cultivated were sorghum and date palms.

As we have seen in chapter 1, saqiya cultivation was labor intensive and required the mobilization of diverse resources. Since the nineteenth century slave labor had played a vital role in agricultural production in this area. However, the continuous fractionalization of land by the Islamic rules of inheritance and the amount of effort needed for production had created a pattern of outward migration from this area to other parts of the country.

This pattern continued after the conquest and involved both free peasants and slaves. Halfa Province, for instance, had witnessed a massive exodus of people—including slaves—to Egypt during the last days of the Mahdiyya. In its attempt to revive agriculture, the Anglo-Egyptian administration tried to repatriate these refugees. By 1900 about 1,500 had returned.[11] However, economic conditions in the province were not attractive and slaves continued to drift to Egypt and other parts of the Sudan. At the beginning of this century the slave population in the province was estimated at between 6,000 and 7,000.[12] Within a few years their numbers decreased to fewer than a thousand.[13]

In Dongola Province, about 20,517 slaves were registered in 1900, constituting 15 percent of the total province's population.[14] As in Halfa, cultivable land in this province was limited to a narrow strip along the river bank and economic opportunities were few. The inhabitants had often fallen prey to famine, particularly at times of low Nile. As a result there was a strong tendency among the population of this province to migrate to other parts of the Sudan. Slaves were particularly vulnerable during bad years. For instance, during the famine of 1913 many slaves were abandoned by their owners.[15] As a result, outward migration was common for both free peasants and slaves. Hence, despite an increase in the number of saqiyas erected, agricultural production was marked by fluctuations.

Further south in Berber Province, a different situation prevailed. This was one of the largest slaveholding regions in the Sudan. During the first decade of colonial rule this area witnessed the introduction of European estate cultivation by concessionaires, which was based on the Egyptian model.[16] Availability of arable land and the extension of the railway line between this province and Port Sudan offered great prospects for cash crop production. Concessions were offered to individuals and private companies of European, Egyptian, and Middle Eastern origin. These estates were established at Zeidab, Berber, Damir, Kabushiyya, Kelli, and Shendi. The average size of an estate was 1,000 feddans. Crops grown included cotton, sorghum, and wheat. The Zeidab estate was owned by Leigh Hunt, an American businessman, who organized the Sudan Experimental Plantations Syndicate in 1904. He was granted a concession of 10,000 feddans, and by 1906 he was growing cotton on an experimental basis.[17]

From the beginning the operations of these estates depended on wage labor. The companies had great difficulty in obtaining a steady supply. The great majority of the rural population was engaged in farming or pastoralism and was not willing to become totally dependent on wage employment. Labor shortage led to higher wages, thereby increasing the cost for the estate owners.[18]

Labor shortage continued to plague the estate farms, and by 1907 most of them began to switch to the tenancy system. According to this system, the company would supply tenants with water and cash advances to meet cultivation expenses, in exchange for specified sums of rent. In this way the problem of labor was transferred to the tenants. The first estate that switched to this system was the Zeidab farm. After two years of experimentation, the company rented all its cultivable land to tenants in 1908. A total of 1,776 feddans of cotton and 800 feddans of wheat were cultivated by tenants, most of whom were local Ja'aliyyin.[19] The Fadlab estate followed suit in 1909.

As pointed out earlier, Berber Province was one of the largest slaveholding regions in the Sudan. In the eighteenth and nineteenth centuries, market towns such as Shendi, Berber, and Damir were meeting points for slave caravans, and the inhabitants received a constant supply of slaves. Moreover, many of the slave traders in the nineteenth century came from this area. Examples are Al-Zubair Rahma and Ilyas Umm Birayr. The total number of slaves registered in the province in 1900 was estimated at 19,615.[20] However, as in Halfa and Dongola provinces, cultivable land in the northern part of Berber was limited and irrigation was based on the saqiya. As a result many slaves left for the fertile land in the southern part of the province where agriculture was based on pump irrigation. The concentration of these estates in Berber Province offered opportunities to many slaves in the province. For instance, in 1908 the Zeidab estate employed from 3,500 to 4,000 laborers.[21]

By 1910, the tenancy system was the dominant form of state sponsored, irrigated cultivation, particularly in the Blue Nile and Kassala provinces. In the latter, cotton had been cultivated in the Tokar and Gash Deltas since the Turkiyya. Under the Anglo-Egyptian regime the cultivated area increased from 7,000 feddans in 1907 to about 18,000 in 1908, and to 39,000 feddans in 1910.[22] Tenancies were given to local tribal shaykhs and immigrants from the riverain areas such as the Ja'aliyyin, Shaiqiyya, and Danaqla. However, it was Blue Nile Province, with its fertile Gezira, that offered the greatest prospects for cotton production. Experimentation with cotton cultivation began in 1911 at Tayba station and was managed by the Sudan Plantations Syndicate. The main impetus for cotton growing was the decline of Egyptian and American cotton production and the growing needs of the Lancashire textile industry. In 1910 the Gezira yield was 8,700 tons, which realized LE 235,000. Production increased to 11,800 tons in

1917, realizing LE 610,000.[23] This success became a major incentive for post–World War I expansion and the predominance of cotton as the Sudan's main cash crop.

In addition to irrigation, the government also encouraged rain-based agriculture, especially in the White Nile, Gedarif, and Kordofan provinces. Cash crop production was considered the only means for generating revenue and ending the Sudan's financial dependence on Egypt. Sorghum and sesame were exported in large quantities after 1910, which led to food shortages and precipitated famine on several occasions.[24] However, the most important export item besides cotton was gum arabic which was grown in Kordofan. Gum arabic accounted for 20 percent of the Sudan's revenue during the early years of this century.

In brief, the main beneficiaries of the colonial economy were tribal shaykhs, religious leaders, and merchants. The last were particularly conspicuous in the growing export trade, in which they had gained preeminence during the Turkiyya. In other words, colonial economic policies strengthened the position of the slaveholding classes throughout the northern Sudan. It should be no surprise that slavery and the slave trade persisted and were tolerated during the first three decades of colonial rule.

PERSISTENCE OF SLAVERY AND THE SLAVE TRADE

During the tumultuous period of the Anglo-Egyptian conquest, slave owners were able to acquire new slaves through various methods. Immediately after the conquest, the government supplied some tribal leaders with arms to pursue Mahdist remnants and to reestablish their authority. Many of them used these arms to conduct raids and acquire new slaves. Numerous examples may be given. In Berber Province, for instance, the *ansar* (Mahdist followers) raided the Ja'aliyyin and took many slaves.[25] Consequently, during the Anglo-Egyptian campaign, the Ja'aliyyin supplied the Anglo-Egyptian Army with intelligence on the Mahdist forces. As a reward, they were given rifles with which they seized slaves from the ansar.[26] Similarly, Munhil Khayr Allah, head of the Shanabla, was given arms after his surrender in Omdurman in 1898 and was instructed to return home. On his way, he captured many slaves. 'Abd al-Rahim Abu Dagal, the Hamar leader, used the arms he obtained from the government to capture about 1,000 slaves from the Nuba Mountains.[27] Nomadic

TABLE 2

Number of Slaves in the Gezira, 1905–1912

	1905	*1912*
Rufaʻa	4,900	5,311
Hasaheisa	5,969	7,065
Kamlin	?	4,383
Wad Medani	?	5,867

groups such as the Kababish, Bishariyyin, and Hawawir began to steal slaves from the sedentary population along the Nile.[28]

Along the White Nile and in the Gezira the introduction of cash crops and the existence of market towns such as Kosti, Sinnar, Kurmuk, and Jabalayn generated a great demand for labor.[29] Groups such as the Lahawiyyin raided the Berta and Gumus on the upper Blue Nile. It was reported that the Lahawiyyin had a small number of slaves at the beginning of the century, but within a decade or so their slaves numbered about 10,000.[30] The Sudan-Ethiopia border region was another source of slaves for the central Sudan. Export of slaves from this area was facilitated by the presence of northern Sudanese merchants and a ready supply of firearms from Ethiopia and Djibuti. These merchants established commercial networks across the border and their activities remained unnoticed by the government. For instance, Khojali al-Hasan, a Jaʻali from Shendi, settled among the Gumus in Ethiopia and established a trading network with his wife, Sitt Amna, who lived on the Sudan side of the border.[31]

The expansion of cash crop production in the Gezira led to an increase in the number of slaves in the province. This is evident from the figures in Table 2.[32]

In White Nile Province a mixed economy of herding and rainland cultivation developed. Wealth in livestock contributed to successful farming and, in turn, allowed individuals to build up herds. The combination of these activities created great demand for labor. In addition to mobilization of family labor, local shaykhs employed a large number of slaves.[33]

Toleration of slavery meant the continuation of the slave trade, which was revived along the old slave-raiding frontiers of Dar Fertit, the Nuba Mountains, and the Upper Blue Nile, which were not yet fully pacified. In addition to these sources, Dar al-Kuti and the Sudan-Ethiopian border region supplied a large number of slaves.

In Kordofan Province the Baqqara resumed raids against the Dinka in the south and the Nuba Mountains in the southeast. They supplied Nuba chiefs with rifles in exchange for slaves.[34] Farther west, Dar Fur remained outside the government's control until 1916. With the defeat of the Mahdist state by the Anglo-Egyptian forces in 1898, 'Ali Dinar, grandson of the former Fur sultan Muhammad al-Fadl, returned from exile in Omdurman, seized the capital, al-Fashir, and defeated the Mahdist puppet sultan Abu Kuada. The Anglo-Egyptian Government was unwilling at that time to undertake the additional burden of ruling this distant province. 'Ali Dinar was therefore recognized as the ruler of Dar Fur as long as he was "obedient" to government authority and paid nominal tribute.

One of the immediate concerns of the new sultan was the definition of his borders. Although 'Ali Dinar directed his attention mainly to the northern and western frontiers, he also relentlessly tried to restore Dar Fur's hegemony over the southern peripheries. The sultan invoked residual loyalties among former Fur clients in Dar Fertit to obtain slaves for his new army. 'Ali Dinar acquired slaves from the traditional reservoirs of Dar Fertit, Dar Runga, Dar Sila, and Dar Kara. Slaves were obtained by state-sponsored raids and through the nominally subordinate Baqqara who raided the west African pilgrims and the Dinka across the Bahr al-Arab. In 1903 'Ali Dinar's army was estimated to have 6,000 riflemen and 1,700 cavalry, the bulk of whom were servile recruits.[35] Apart from his servile bodyguard, 'Ali Dinar surrounded himself with eunuchs and concubines. Thus the political and domestic use of slaves, which was common in precolonial Dar Fur, was revived by 'Ali Dinar.

GOVERNMENT POLICY TOWARD SLAVERY

The policy of the Anglo-Egyptian administration toward the institution of slavery did not differ from that of its counterparts elsewhere in Africa. For economic, political, and ideological reasons slavery was tolerated for several decades.

The ambivalence of the Sudan Government toward the institution of slavery can be understood through an examination of its legislation and ordinances and the way in which they were enforced. Six months after the conquest, Kitchener, the new governor-general, issued the much-quoted Confidential Memorandum to Mudirs: "Slavery is not recognized in the Sudan, but as long as service is willingly rendered by servants to masters it is unnecessary to interfere in the conditions existing between them."[36] The essence of government policy, therefore, was to abolish the legal status of slavery, but maintain the system under a different guise. At the same time colonial officials made a distinction between "slavery" and the slave trade and tackled each separately. They assumed that if the influx of new slaves were stopped, slavery itself would gradually die. According to a senior official:

> What we ought to do is to leave the slaves quietly in the possession of their masters until they either disappear through death or are set free by manumission, and to devote our efforts solely to preventing the slave-raiding and slave-hunting, by means of which the market for this article of commerce is stocked, an article for which there will always be buyers for a long time to come.[37]

In chapter 1 we have seen how this strategy was adopted by the Turco-Egyptian administration and how the institution of slavery continued to thrive despite the attack on the slave trade. Nevertheless, concern with the slave trade rather than slavery became the dominant feature of Anglo-Egyptian Government policy during the first twenty years.

According to the Anglo-Egyptian Slave Trade Convention of August 1877, the slave trade in the Sudan was to have stopped by 1880. But implementation of this measure was hindered by the outbreak of the Mahdiyya and the establishment of an independent state thereafter. A new convention for the suppression of the slave trade was signed by Great Britain and Egypt in 1895.[38] Prior to that a Department for the Repression of the Slave Trade (DRST) was founded in Egypt in 1880 and was attached to the Egyptian Ministry of the Interior. The Anglo-Egyptian Convention of 1899 stated that "The importation of slaves into the Sudan, as also their exportation is absolutely prohibited. Provisions shall be made by proclamation for the enforcement of these regulations."[39] Consequently, a branch of the DRST was established in the Sudan under the directorship of Captain A. M. McMurdo.[40] With its headquarters in Cairo and inspecting officers at Khartoum and in the provinces, the department extended its operation to the Sudan and began to tackle the rampant slave smuggling and child abductions in remote parts of the country.[41] The main duty of the department was to stop the slave trade across the Sudanese borders. Ordinances to this effect were published in 1901 and in 1903 and sections 279–290 of the Sudan Penal Code were issued specifically for this purpose.[42] However, the code did not refer to slavery but provided for punishment for offenses such as kidnapping, abduction, and forced labor. But the vast area of the Sudan, the poor communications, and the lack of staff and funds rendered the application of these measures difficult. Moreover, the organization of the department itself was a major handicap. Although its location and center of activities were in the Sudan, the headquarters of the department were in Egypt and the Sudan Government had no jurisdiction over its officials. The department appointed its own inspectors who set up posts throughout the country, assisted by their own mounted police and camel corps. They could make arrests and issue warnings without reference to local authorities.[43] Following its reorganization in 1905 the department divided its force into three branches with headquarters at al-Rusairis in the Blue Nile Province, al-Ubayyid, and Khartoum. Although the department's activities were closely tied with the Sudan Government, its officials were continually at odds with senior officials such as Governor-general Wingate and Inspector-general Slatin, who were reluctant even to admit the existence of slavery. Right from the beginning these senior officials viewed the department as an unwelcome intruder and a representative of the Anti-Slavery Society in Britain. Slatin did not hide his hostility toward Captain McMurdo, who continued to encourage his officers to intercede in disputes between slaves and their owners. Slatin often complained to Wingate that the department's activities were posing a serious danger to government relations with the locals.[44] He then began to press for the transfer of the director and to bring the department under the jurisdiction of the Sudan Government. This was achieved in 1911 when McMurdo was transferred to Cairo and the department was placed under the Sudan police. His successor, Major H. V. Ravenscroft, was more conforming.[45] After that the activities of the department were reduced considerably, and following the resignation of Ravenscroft in 1914 the remaining staff were amalgamated with the provincial administration and were completely controlled by the Sudan Government.

During the decade and a half of its existence the department made considerable progress in curtailing the slave trade along the Sudan's borders. Although large-scale and open sale of slaves within the Sudan was largely suppressed, the smuggling of small numbers of children and women continued along the Sudan-Ethiopian border, the frontier shared with the French possessions to the west, and along the pilgrimage routes to the Hijaz. In this vast territory slave dealers could easily evade government patrols. According to consular reports, hundreds of slaves continued to be smuggled across the Red Sea throughout the first three decades of this century.[46]

In the meantime slavery was tolerated and the slaves were encouraged to remain with their owners. Colonial administrators made every possible effort to check the departure of slaves and persuade runaway slaves to return to their owners. Administrators usually provided the slave with freedom papers but then tried to persuade the owner to take the slave back as a paid servant. If successful in convincing both sides, the official would enter the slave's name in a register, fix the amount of wage, and not interfere further in the situation.

The second official document that dealt with the subject of slavery was Circular Memorandum No. 10 of January 1902. This stated that slaves should remain with their owners as long as they were well treated and adequately fed and clothed.[47] It also called for the return of runaway slaves and prevented their migration to towns. The circular also required registration of slaves in each province. Further, it stipulated that all children born of concubinage would be free when they were old enough to look after themselves.[48]

In 1905 the government introduced the Vagabonds Ordinance, which allowed the prosecution of unemployed runaway slaves in towns. (The application of vagrancy laws will be discussed in chapter 3.) More important, however, was the establishment of the Central Labour Bureau in the Intelligence Department in 1905. Its main task was to register slaves and to discourage them from leaving their owners without "good reasons."[49] G. S. Symes, who was in charge of the bureau, wrote: "our chief concern was to control and check the exodus of slaves from agricultural districts."[50]

Despite the institution of vagrancy laws and the registration system, the exodus of slaves from agricultural districts did not stop, a situation that enraged their owners. While the registration scheme was successful in some provinces such as Dongola and Khartoum, it failed in others. There was no consistency in the vigor with which district officials implemented ordinances. As slaves left, farmers were forced to do their own cultivation or hire expensive labor, which decreased agricultural production.

Faced with an unpredictable government that announced measures against the slave trade but was often lax in enforcing them, slave owners responded in a variety of ways that ranged from open rebellion to economic adjustment to the acquisition of new slaves. For instance, antislavery measures were one of the main reasons behind the Talodi uprising in 1906. The population of this area consisted of ex-slaves originally from the Nuba Mountains. After their settlement in Talodi, they themselves began to acquire slaves. In response to the liberation of 120 slaves by an administrator, the slave owners revolted, killing forty-six people, including the *mamur* (local official). They were joined by others and attacked the government garrison for three days. However, the revolt was suppressed by a combination of government troops and Baqqara men, resulting in the killing of

400 rebels.[51] The same tale of anger was also evident in the Wad Habouba uprising in the Blue Nile Province in 1908. An investigation into the causes of the revolt revealed that slave emancipation was a major factor. One of the major grievances expressed by prisoners interrogated afterwards was that their land remained unproductive and their crops were not harvested because of the loss of slaves. Moreover, many slaves left during the cultivation season.[52]

In response to government policy slave owners tried either to keep their slaves or acquire new ones. As the supply declined the remaining slaves changed hands as owners found it more profitable to hire out their slaves for varying periods. In the riverain areas, landowners developed an elaborate system of crop sharing and introduced limited mechanized agriculture. In the Gezira, farmers who lost their slaves resorted to rainland cultivation instead of the labor intensive irrigation.

In 1907 the government replaced the 1902 circular with Circular No. 22. This addressed three major issues: runaway slaves, the acquisition of female slaves by soldiers, and the registration system. It was stated that slaves had the right to leave their masters if they wished. However, any slave who was found in the city without any means of "honestly" earning a living would be prosecuted under the Vagabonds Ordinance and might be required to provide a surety for "good behavior" for one year, in default of which the slave might be imprisoned until one was produced.[53] Sudanese soldiers of the Egyptian Army were prohibited from taking away female slaves under the pretext that they were relatives. In this regard, provincial administrators and Shari'a judges were given the power to settle disputes which involved complex issues of marriage, concubinage, and so forth. Finally, provincial officials were urged to conduct slave registration with a great deal of care and to seek the help of local administrators.

These measures were taken seriously in provinces where the demand for labor was high. The governor of the Red Sea Province told his inspectors that "in every case in which it is known that a servant has been with his master since the Mahdiyya, a special endeavor must be made to arrange a settlement between master and servant."[54] Since the government was hiring many liberated slaves, the governor urged that owners should be allowed to visit their slaves in order to persuade them to return after they finished their employment with the government. If a slave refused to return, he should be asked to pay the *fidya* (money payable in a lump sum or by installment, but never in monthly payments, to be continued indefinitely, and assessed on the basis of the owner's estimate of the value of the slave).[55] The system of fidya was instituted to compensate the owners.[56] A slave would be freed after the completion of the payments. Failure to make the payments would render the slave liable to arrest.[57]

Similar steps were taken in the Blue Nile Province. W. P. D. Clarke, an inspector in the province, wrote: "I suggest that they [freed slaves] be kept directly under government control and made to understand that they owe a return to government for their freedom."[58] He further recommended that freed slaves should be made to live in definite quarters in the towns and not be allowed to leave these quarters without a permit. The shaykhs of the quarter should supply the government with a list periodically showing how many of its residents were employed. Ex-slaves residing in these quarters should be the first to be called upon for labor.[59] The inspector had already tried these measures in the Malakiyya quarter in Wad Medani and recommended that they should be applied in other towns. "I believe," the inspector wrote,

> that these measures would have a great effect in reducing crime, in improving the supply of labor, and also in removing a great source of emotion to ex-owners of Sudanese, part of whose grievances is to see their former slaves living in a state of uncontrolled indolence.[60]

The governor of the Blue Nile Province supported the scheme and tried to justify it on moral, material, and political grounds. On the moral level, the absence of control would lead slaves to crime and drunkenness. On material grounds, the registration of freed slaves would, in his view, help to solve the serious labor difficulty the government was facing. On political grounds: "nothing would give the Arab population who are seeing their slaves gradually disappearing, more satisfaction than to know that such Sudanese [slaves] are being properly controlled and worked by the government."[61] The governor's proposals received the support of the civil secretary who favored the idea of confining freed slaves to special settlements. However, when it came down to the practical level, the director of intelligence acknowledged the difficulty of implementing these measures owing to the lack of personnel.[62]

Nonetheless, ex-slaves continued to defy these rules and drift to urban centers. In 1911, for instance, the governor of the Red Sea Province reported that many slave owners complained about their slaves leaving for stations on the Nile–Red Sea railway line, particularly between Aradeib and Mismar to take the trains to Atbara, after which they scattered and could not be traced. As a remedy, he suggested that instructions should be given to all stationmasters between Salloum and Mismar not to issue tickets to such persons unless their destination was Port Sudan.[63] The assistant director of intelligence took the matter seriously and wrote to the director of the Railway Department requesting application of these measures. According to him, tickets should not be issued to slaves unless: 1) they were accompanied by a "responsible" individual who could account for them; and 2) they were able to produce their registration book. He further stated that these regulations should apply only to the "Sudanese labouring class" and should not affect merchants or bona fide pilgrims.[64] The traffic manager of the railways proposed the establishment of police posts along the railway line to enforce these measures.[65]

Runaway slaves continued to preoccupy colonial administrators throughout the first twenty years of this century. But as it turned out, their assumption that runaway slaves would become criminals in towns proved to be false. In the mid-1920s, administrators admitted that ex-slaves were responsible for a small percentage of petty crimes in the urban centers.[66]

After World War I colonial officials began to debate and reevaluate government policy toward slavery. This was a result of increasing pressure by humanitarian groups in England, and by the departure of Slatin in 1914 and Wingate in 1916, who had tried hard to maintain the status quo. After a great deal of discussion, a new document was issued at the end of 1918, was ratified in March 1919, and came to be known as Circular Memorandum No. 33.[67]

The new circular formed the basis of government policy toward slavery and replaced all earlier ordinances on the subject. It contained fifteen points among which the most important was the continuous use of the official euphemism "Sudanese servants" instead of slaves. They were defined as "persons who were in a state of slavery or are considered as such by natives."[68] Second, it stated that such persons had the right to leave their owners if they wished, and could not be compelled or persuaded to return against their will. The bulk of the text dealt with the conditions of those slaves who left their owners and went to towns. It empowered provincial officials to use the Vagabonds Ordinance to conduct exhaustive investigations with the ultimate aim of reconciling masters and discontented slaves.[69] The document was intended to appeal to humanitarian groups in England; its provisions were rarely enforced.

RESPONSE OF SLAVES AND EX-SLAVES

The response of slaves and ex-slaves to colonial rule in Africa has been a subject of scholarly debate over the past two decades. Some scholars have reported massive desertion in the wake of colonial conquest, particularly in French Sudan and northern Nigeria.[70] A similar assertion has been made by Fred Morton who maintained that the majority of slaves on the East African coast had escaped and established independent communities.[71] This contrasts with Frederick Cooper's earlier argument that many slaves became squatters on the old plantations.[72] In general, the slaves' responses to colonial conquest did not follow a single pattern. How and why particular slaves chose particular options was determined by factors such as kinship and family ties, the nature of slavery in the particular society, and economic and social prospects after departure. Most significant, however, were gender differences. The main consideration for female slaves was whether or not they had children and if they could get custody. Another distinction lay between old and newly acquired slaves; it is likely that desertion was more common among the latter than the former. In brief, even within a single colony one may find numerous regional and gender variations in the slaves' responses.

In the Sudan, it is not entirely clear who and how many left, but, given the attitude of the colonial administration, it is possible to assume that during the first twenty years, most slaves (particularly females) remained with their owners. Moreover, the majority of those who gained manumission did so outside official channels. Table 3 shows the total number of slaves freed by the government between 1911 and 1922.[73]

TABLE 3

Number of Slaves Freed between 1911 and 1922

Year	Number of slaves freed	
	Male	Female
1911	113	192
1912	115	148
1913	152	212
1914	191	217
1915	128	176
1916	99	149
1917	165	417
1918	149	318
1919	184	317
1920	157	263
1921	178	307
1922	95	212
	1,726	2,928
Grand Total	4,654	

These figures do not give a complete picture and must be taken with caution. First, there is no accurate information about the total number of slaves in the Sudan. After the Anglo-Egyptian conquest, the government tried to register the slave population in the country, but the official registry was far from accurate. In some provinces, registration was not carried out at all, while in others, it was limited to those slaves who lived near district headquarters. The above table shows the number of freedom papers issued by administrators. In many cases slaves were liberated by unrecorded official verbal proclamation.[74]

Given the ambivalence of the colonial government and its tacit alliance with the slaveholders, it may be assumed that the majority of slaves who gained manumission did so through escape and desertion. However, the response of slaves to colonial conquest requires detailed regional studies. Therefore, our assessment is general and speculative.

Desertion occurred during and immediately after the conquest. The chaotic situation at the end of the Mahdiyya and in the early days of colonial rule allowed many slaves to escape.[75] Some returned to their original homes, while others joined ex-slave settlements in different parts of the country. There were several types of ex-slave communities that attracted runaway slaves. They included ex-soldiers, remnants of Mahdist jihadiyya, and communities that were founded by liberated and runaway slaves in the late nineteenth century. However, escape was a risky venture for it often led to misery, insecurity, and disappointment. The need for food and shelter forced many to sell themselves back into slavery or to attach themselves to whomever provided them with the basic necessities.[76]

In Kassala Province in the east, the existence of fertile vacant lands induced many slaves to break away and become farmers. Kassala attracted runaway slaves from other provinces. For instance, slaves moved from Sinnar Province and settled on farms around Gedarif.[77] Since the nineteenth century ex-slaves and refugees had established independent settlements at Qallabat, Gedarif, and Nugarrah. Some of these settlements were founded by remnants of the Turco-Egyptian and Mahdist armies. In their attempt to assert their independence and show their defiance, runaway slaves in this province chose obscene names for their villages, such as *tiz umm al-Sayyid* (lit. the master's mother's behind).[78] These communities became focal points for fugitive and liberated slaves.

In the Blue Nile Province, the expansion of cash crop production created some opportunities for slaves. The majority of manumitted slaves became agricultural laborers on private or state owned farms, while others moved to the urban centers such as Wad Medani, Sinnar, and Khartoum where they became a source of irritation for colonial administrators.

In the White Nile Province, as we pointed out, many tribal leaders established agricultural estates and began to import slaves. This province continued to receive a large number of slaves from the Sudan-Ethiopia border region, the Nuba Mountains, and the Upper Nile Province. However, many slaves drifted to the colonies of discharged soldiers in places like Kosti, Hillat 'Abbas, Malakiyya, and Quz.[79]

In the provinces of Kordofan and Dar Fur, the vast majority of slaves remained in servitude. The nature of the kinship system among the Baqqara (which allowed limited integration of ex-slaves),[80] the remoteness of these provinces, the lack of economic opportunities, and the laxity of colonial officials were major factors. Moreover, the proximity of these regions to the old slave reservoirs meant that new slaves were constantly acquired. At the beginning of the century, the slave population in Kordofan was estimated at 40,000. Twenty years later, there were still 25,000 registered slaves. The total number liberated by the government between 1915 and 1925 was about a thousand.[81] However, the existence of communities of ex-slaves and discharged soldiers became a major incentive for some slaves to break away. For example, a large settlement of some 10,000 slaves was established in the Nuba Mountains.[82] On the other hand, Dar Fur remained outside government jurisdiction until 1916 because its slave trade had been revived by 'Ali Dinar; most slaves in Dar Fur remained in bondage for several decades.

Judging by the attitude of liberated slaves, it is clear that they had their own version of freedom. To them, freedom meant autonomy more than anything else. They moved away and established their own villages, or joined communities of discharged soldiers, or went to settle in urban centers. The best known of these communities was the Malakiyya in the Upper Nile near Renk. It was founded by survivors of the khalifa's army after the battle of Um Duwaykrat in 1899 and numbered about 5,000 people.[83] Other ex-slave settlements emerged in towns such as Daim Zubair, Wau, and Raga in the Bahr al-Ghazal Province. These towns were established originally as military camps by slave traders in the nineteenth century. Their residents included a substantial number of ex-soldiers and former slaves. Since most of these people had originally been enslaved in these regions, they may be considered "returnees." However, many of the returnees were captured at a young age, and had been living in servitude, far away from home, for many decades. They lost their ethnic ties, spoke

Arabic, and became Muslims. The presence of these Muslim elements among non-Muslim groups was a major concern for British officials, especially with the announcement of the Southern Policy in 1929.[84] According to C. A. Willis, "the main objection to the Malikia [sic] settlements is that it introduces a nominally Mohammedan element into a province that is otherwise refreshingly pagan."[85] These settlements also included a large number of children kidnapped during the early years of colonial rule and retrieved by government agencies. Some of them were attached to mission stations where they received education. They became part of an elite group that played an important role in the political and social life of the south.

FEMALE SLAVES AND THE COLONIAL REGIME

While male slaves had to grapple with the antipathy of government officials and the resistance of their owners, slave women faced even greater obstacles to emancipation. As noted in chapter 1, female slaves had important productive and reproductive roles. According to official estimates, they constituted three-fourths of the slave population in the Sudan at the beginning of this century.[86] Moreover, acquisition of female slaves continued during the first twenty years of this century.[87] As male slaves began to leave, the labor of slave women became even more vital and owners made every possible effort to prevent their manumission. The owners were supported by colonial officials who viewed all female slaves in Muslim societies as concubines. In their view, liberating them would break up families and disrupt domestic arrangements.[88] Consequently, all disputes between female slaves and their owners were regarded as family matters and referred to the Shari'a courts. Furthermore, these officials were apprehensive of the social consequences of manumission and felt that, if liberated, slave women would become prostitutes and join the idlers and vagabonds in the cities. According to Willis, "The alternative of declaring all the slaves free on the decease of the master would be to turn a number of women and children upon the world without any means of support."[89] As in the southern United States and the Caribbean, the immorality of slaves remained an integral part of the officials' perception of slaves, particularly of female slaves.

Female slaves had few choices. For the most part the colonial wage labor was open to men only,[90] and therefore flight would mean economic insecurity, and in some cases, loss of children. During the early years after the conquest, slave women faced economic hardships. As a result, many of them attached themselves to Sudanese soldiers in the Egyptian Army as wives or concubines. It was reported that each soldier had at least four or five women. This situation alarmed colonial officials who feared that this would anger the slave owners and lead to the loss of labor.[91] Soldiers continued to acquire female slaves, especially during military campaigns against local revolts. For example, during the Talodi uprising in the Nuba Mountains, soldiers took a large number of Nuba women. A local holy man in al-Ubayyid complained to the authorities that these women were his slaves and demanded their return. Despite intervention from Khartoum, the commander of the expedition refused and declared that he had married the women off to his soldiers.[92]

Other female slaves had no alternatives but to become prostitutes or sell local drinks, even at the cost of economic insecurity and loss of children. Widespread prostitution and venereal diseases, especially among soldiers of the Egyptian Army, caused great anxiety. The government decided to build special quarters for prostitutes in different districts and required them to take regular medical examinations.[93] Unlike male slaves who could earn money to pay the fidya, female slaves did not have that option. If a female slave wanted to marry a freeborn man, he was required to pay the fidya on her behalf before the marriage took place. The fate of slave women was, therefore, determined by their owners and government officials. Their manumission became a legal battle that was fought in the Islamic courts.

The primary sources of law in the Sudan under the Anglo-Egyptian regime were English law, Islamic law, and customary law. The administration of these laws was controlled by a judiciary. The judiciary was organized into two separate and independent divisions, the civil and Shari'a divisions, with a supreme court for each. The civil division administered English law and customary law, in both civil and criminal matters; the Shari'a division administered only Islamic law to Muslims in personal matters. A council comprised of the legal secretary of the Sudan Government, the grand qadi, and the chief justice was created to resolve conflicts between the civil and Shari'a branches.[94]

The Shari'a courts were created by the Sudan Mohammedan Law Courts Ordinance in 1902. According to this ordinance, three courts were created, comprised of a High Court, Mudiriyya Court, and district courts. The district court consisted of a single qadi (judge), the Mudiriyya of a single qadi with a deputy appointed when deemed necessary. The High Court consisted of the grand qadi who acted as president, the *Mufti* (an expert in Islamic law) of the Sudan, and one or more other members.[95] These courts were to decide any question regarding marriage, divorce, guardianship of minors or family relations, *waqf* (trust), and other personal or family matters. The grand qadi was authorized to issue from time to time, with the approval of the governor-general, regulations regarding the decisions, procedure, constitution, jurisdiction, and functioning of the Shari'a courts. A series of judicial circulars was issued by the grand qadi throughout the colonial period. Some of these circulars were of an administrative nature, defining the way in which the courts were to perform some of their duties; other circulars defined the substantive law to be applied. It was the last which constituted the chief medium for reform; they were all based on reforms either already promulgated or at least under consideration in Egypt. In other words, reforms carried out in the Sudan reflected the views of Egyptian theologians, not least because until the 1940s all the grand qadis who served in the Sudan were selected from Egyptian jurists.[96]

Despite the fact that the majority of Sudanese Muslims followed the Maliki school of jurisprudence, the Shari'a courts followed the Hanafi school introduced during the Turco-Egyptian period. However, the predominance of the Hanafi school was by no means absolute, since the Shari'a Supreme Court had the power to authorize the application of rules derived from other schools of jurisprudence.[97]

By assigning the cases of female slaves to the Shari'a courts, colonial authorities created a major barrier for them and made them susceptible to the intrigues of their owners. Moreover, conflicts within government legislation regarding slavery and the Shari'a courts began to emerge from the beginning.

Since Muslim law superseded the secular code in family matters, slave owners astutely tried to take advantage of the legal complications inherent in the Shari'a with regard to the status of female slaves by claiming them as concubines, thereby denying them the possibility of manumission.[98] A child custody case that was settled in the Shari'a court in Dongola Province in 1902 illustrates this situation. The case involved a widow and the female slave of the deceased husband. The dispute occurred over the custody of the thirteen-year-old son of the slave woman. The slave woman claimed that the boy's father was her deceased owner who recognized the paternity of the child many years before his death. However, the owner's widow claimed that her late husband never recognized the paternity of this boy. She contended that the boy's father was a slave to whom the slave woman had been married for many years. She, therefore, argued that the boy should be considered a slave and should belong to her as part of her husband's estate. She then brought two witnesses to support her case. However, the court questioned the credibility of the witnesses and ruled that the boy was free and should remain with his mother.[99] This case typifies the kind of problems female slaves had experienced throughout the colonial era.

Even when childless, female slaves were denied freedom by their owners who produced fake marriage certificates. In 1902 a legal circular was issued by the grand qadi requiring masters who raised such claims to produce documentary evidence showing that a lawful union had been contracted and stating the amount of bridewealth paid. However, if the judge was satisfied that the marriage was legal, he would rule in favor of the owner, giving him the right to retrieve his female slave.[100] The circular also dealt with cases in which masters claimed the children of their female slave. It was ruled that if a man applied for the custody of these children because their mother disobeyed him, the court, after investigating the case, might rule in his favor and grant him the custody of children.[101]

Since Shari'a law is immutable, government officials had no alternative but to limit their jurisdiction and authorize local administrators to settle disputes between masters and female slaves. But there was no consistency or clear policy and decisions were made on an ad hoc basis. The Shari'a courts continued to rule in favor of the slave owners. If, for instance, a female slave was liberated by a district official, the slave owner would take his case to the Muslim judge who often ruled in his favor. In fact, civilian administrators themselves were still apprehensive of slave women with children. The legal secretary argued that emancipation of such women would transform a category of children considered legitimate by the Shari'a court into bastards and deprive them of their rights of inheritance.[102] This position was supported by the grand qadi, Muhammad Amin Qura'a, who emphasized the tangible benefits of the Shari'a for concubines and their children.[103]

The delegation of slavery cases to the Muslim courts provided owners with a strong weapon through which they were able to keep their slave women. Hence, most female slaves remained in bondage well after their male counterparts gained their freedom. In the mid-1920s a senior colonial official admitted that "at present moment, the real problem of slavery in the Sudan concerns only women."[104]

EX-SLAVES IN THE EGYPTIAN ARMY

One of the most important features of Sudanese slavery was the widespread use of slaves as soldiers. As discussed in chapter 1, slave soldiers formed the backbone of the Turco-Egyptian Army. Moreover, the bulk of the Sudanese battalions raised in Egypt in the 1880s consisted of slave and ex-slave soldiers. They included former Turco-Egyptian and Mahdist jihadiyya and runaway slaves. In other words, slave soldiers were inherited by the successive regimes that ruled the Sudan. This meant that these soldiers served under different patrons, which created myriad problems of loyalty and control. In 1882, Sudanese troops fought with their Egyptian counterparts against the British invaders.[105] However, after the occupation, the old Egyptian Army was disbanded and the British began to create a new force. New recruits were drawn from the Egyptian *fellahin* (peasants), Sudanese slaves, and former slaves living in Egypt. Because most Sudanese soldiers were old and lacked discipline, preference was given to those who came directly from the Sudan over those who had been residing in Egypt for a long time.[106]

During the period from 1885 until the conquest of the Sudan in 1898, the British in Egypt relentlessly tried to augment Sudanese units from recent arrivals. With the exception of the Twelfth Sudanese Battalion, the rest of the Sudanese units were recruited from those who came directly from the Sudan.[107]

As observed earlier, one of the most important characteristics of military slavery was the way in which slave soldiers changed their allegiance to different patrons. Sudanese slave soldiers who were part of the Turkish jihadiyya formed the backbone of the new units. Some of these soldiers played a significant role during and after the Anglo-Egyptian conquest of the Mahdist state. The careers of 'Ali Jaifun and 'Abdallah Sa'id Bey amply illustrate this point. The former was a Shilluk from Fashoda. He was captured as a young boy by the Baqqara and handed over to the Turkish Government as part of a tax payment. He enlisted in the army and fought in several government campaigns. He was a member of the Sudanese battalion that was sent to Mexico in 1863. After his return he joined the Sudanese garrison in the eastern frontier. During the Mahdist revolt he fought in the defense of Kassala. After the fall of Amideb to the Mahdists, Jaifun escaped to Masawwa and was taken to Egypt. He was then posted to the Tenth Sudanese Battalion in 1889 and promoted to *Yuzbashi* (captain). He fought the Mahdists at Tokar and during the Nile campaign, after which he was promoted *Sagh qolagashi* (major).[108] 'Abdallah Sa'id was born into a slave family captured in the Nuba Mountains in the nineteenth century. He joined the Turkish jihadiyya and was posted to the eastern frontier. Following the defeat of his battalion by the Mahdists in 1891, he was transferred to Egypt. He then fought in the Nile campaign between 1896 and 1898, and later received several promotions until his retirement in 1918.[109]

Sudanese units were separated from the Egyptian fellahin and were organized into six battalions, with four English officers per battalion of 759 men.[110] The first company was raised on 1 May 1884. Its recruits were largely drawn from the remnants of the Turco-Egyptian troops who had been stationed at Dongola and Berber and who retreated to Egypt after the fall of Khartoum.[111] A Tenth Sudanese Battalion was raised on 2 January 1886 and was dispatched to garrison Suakin. A year later the Eleventh Sudanese Battalion was formed, followed by the Twelfth, in November 1888, and the Thirteenth in June 1889. By that time the whole Egyptian Army numbered 12,633 officers, non-commissioned officers, and men, and comprised fourteen battalions of infantry, five squadrons of cavalry, six battalions of artillery, two camel corps, and support units.[112] Just before the conquest of the Sudan, the Fourteenth Sudanese, Fifteenth Egyptian, and Sixteenth Egyptian battalions were raised.[113]

Sudanese units formed one-third of the invading Anglo-Egyptian force in 1898 and were in the vanguard of the advancing army. They showed an unwavering loyalty to their patrons and fought fiercely against the Mahdists at the battles of Atbara and Karari. Immediately after the battle of Omdurman many Mahdist jihadiyya were absorbed into the Egyptian cavalry, and the Fifteenth Egyptian Battalion became a Sudanese battalion.[114]

RECRUITMENT POLICIES IN EARLY YEARS

Two of the major problems that faced the authorities after the conquest was the replacement of old soldiers and the lack of suitable recruits. Prior to 1903, enlistment in the army was for life or until one was medically unfit for further service.[115] Recruitment policies of the Condominium Government did not differ very much from those of the Turco-Egyptian regime in that they were shaped by ethnic stereotypes. The non-Arab groups in the Nuba Mountains and in the south were singled out for their "superior" military qualities. Even before the Anglo-Egyptian conquest, senior British officers such as Wingate had placed great hopes on enlisting the "cattle owning negroes" of the southern and western Sudan.[116] The inhabitants of the Bahr al-Ghazal were described as the "most warlike in the Sudan" and "capable of making excellent soldiers."[117] Liberated and runaway slaves also became prime targets for the army. On the other hand, recruitment of Arabic-speaking groups was generally avoided. The "Arabs" were considered "as uncertain and difficult to regulate by ordinary methods of discipline as the American Red Indian, and so are only fitted for irregular service."[118] In other words, the British continued the recruitment policies of their predecessors. But the system of military slavery requires a constant supply of slaves, mainly from outside the domain of the state.[119] In this regard, the non-Muslim groups in the Nuba Mountains and in the southern Sudan, which were not fully pacified, seemed to be ideal for the army.

However, the Condominium Government had great difficulty in attracting suitable recruits from these groups. In 1904 a Recruiting Commission was established in the Bahr al-Ghazal to recruit southerners, but failed to produce enough men. As in the case of wage labor, the majority of these people had no compelling need to enlist in the army. Moreover, conditions of service in the army, poor pay, and insecurity after discharge were major disincentives.

Unable to obtain voluntary recruits, the government resorted to coercion. For instance, many Mahdist jihadiyya captured during the Anglo-Egyptian campaign were absorbed into the army against their will.[120] Moreover, in the course of punitive expeditions in the south and in the Nuba Mountains, young people were captured and enlisted by force.

However, runaway and liberated slaves comprised an important pool for recruits. The 1910 Administrative Regulations targeted the following categories of people for military recruitment: runaway slaves who refused to return to their owners; slaves who refused to work or are liable to prosecution as vagabonds or idle persons; slaves or ex-slaves without permanent employment; and young boys without occupation.[121]

Enlistment of slaves into the army, however, led to numerous frictions between military authorities on the one hand and provincial officials and the slave owners who wanted to keep slaves on the land on the other. Discontented owners were mollified by payment of money in small installments (usually fifty piastres per month) from the conscript's wage.[122] Runaway slaves were enlisted after a two-week probation during which their personal histories were investigated to the greatest extent possible. Slave owners often used this period to persuade their slaves to return. At the same time many slaves changed their names and addresses, rendering it difficult for owners to trace them and for the authorities to check their background. Military authorities and civilian administrators continued at odds over this issue. While the former demanded that the probation period should be limited to twenty-four hours, the latter insisted that it should be extended to one month. A compromise was finally reached in 1923 when the army agreed that a voluntary arrangement would be made between slaves and their owners whereby the former would reimburse the latter.[123]

The sons of old soldiers and their descendants were another source of recruits. A number of ex-officers from Sudanese units who were interviewed by the author in 1978 related that their fathers had also served in the Egyptian Army. For example, Muhammad Faraj 'Allam joined the Eleventh Sudanese Battalion as a commissioned officer in 1908. His father was an officer in the Egyptian Army and returned to the Sudan at the time of reconquest.[124] Another prominent officer in the Egyptian Army was Zahir Sirur al-Sadati, who enlisted in the Thirteenth Sudanese Battalion in 1910. His father had been in the Mahdist jihadiyya and was captured at the battle of Atbara and then sent to Wadi Halfa, where he enlisted in one of the Sudanese units.[125]

Colonial recruitment policies led to the concentration of certain ethnic groups in the army. Although the regional and ethnic composition of units cannot be established precisely, a preference for the Nuba, Dinka, Shilluk, and other non-Arab groups is clear.[126] A list of seventy-five officers retrenched in 1931 reveals that forty-six were from the southern Sudan, Dar Fur, and the Nuba Mountains. Of those, eleven identified themselves as Dinka, nine Fur, seven Nuba, four Baqqara, three Shilluk, three Fertit, two unknown, two Zaghawa, two Kanjara, one Borno, one Berti, and one Bergo.[127]

The Sudanese battalions were stationed in different parts of the country and became responsible for the maintenance of internal security. They were usually the nearest to and the first to confront any uprising; reinforcements would come later. They played a significant role in the pacification of the country during the first two decades of colonial rule. These units suppressed all the major revolts that arose against the British in different parts of the country.[128] In addition to fighting, Sudanese troops were relegated to menial jobs. Together with Egyptian troops, they were used in the construction of the railway line which was laid down during the campaign.

Throughout the first two decades of this century, Condominium officials complained about the shortage of suitable recruits for the army. Even when they succeeded in obtaining soldiers, colonial military authorities had to deal with the continuing problems of desertion and rebellion. Many of those forcefully recruited escaped at the first opportunity. Furthermore, poor working conditions and mistreatment by British officers led to numerous mutinies.[129]

Like the Chikunda in Mozambique and the bazingir in nineteenth-century southern Sudan, Sudanese soldiers tried to establish their niche in the colonial economy by acquiring slaves.[130] After the battle of Karari in 1898, these soldiers ransacked Omdurman, entering houses and taking a large number of slaves under the pretext that they were siblings.[131]

One of the most serious mutinies occurred in 1900. In reaction to the rumor that the Egyptian Army would be sent to South Africa, the Eleventh and Fourteenth Sudanese battalions broke into the armories and took several thousand rounds of ammunition. It was only after a great deal of negotiation that the soldiers returned the ammunition. Subsequent investigation revealed that most of their grievances were related to conditions of service and mistreatment by British officers.[132] However, the British held the Egyptian officers responsible for urging on their Sudanese counterparts. They also blamed those Sudanese officers who had received training in the military school in Egypt, as well as the ex-Mahdist jihadiyya.[133] After that the British began to view contacts between Egyptian and Sudanese soldiers as dangerous. It was for this reason that the removal of Sudanese cadets from the Cairo military school occurred, and a military school was established in the Sudan in 1905.[134]

The continuing problem of recruitment and the growing suspicion of the Egyptian Army prompted the Condominium officials to adopt a new strategy. This involved the establishment of the so-called territorial units among non-Muslim populations in the south and in the Nuba Mountains. These units would be recruited locally and stationed in their own areas. From the perspective of British officials this strategy would serve several purposes. First, it would encourage voluntary enlistment. Second, it would pave the way for the removal of the Egyptian Army. Finally, it would create an opportunity for getting rid of the "Moslemizing influence in the shape of Egyptian officers and fanatical Sudanese N.C.O.s and very gradually dropping the Moslem conditions in all Sudanese Battalions of the Egyptian Army."[135] Consequently, an Equatorial Corps was founded in the south in 1914, and during the same year a Nuba Territorial Company was established in the Nuba Mountains.[136] These units were paralleled by the Eastern Arab Corps, the Western Arab Corps, and the Camel Corps that were founded in the northern Sudan. These territorial units formed the nucleus of the Sudan Defence Force which was officially established in 1925.

Each unit drew its recruits from the local population of the area in which it was stationed. Soldiers for these units were recruited from the Arabic-speaking northern Sudanese to counter the "detribalized Negro Sudanese" who lost their identity and became a fertile ground for the spread of Egyptian nationalism.

FROM SOLDIERS TO CIVILIANS

The greatest challenge many of these soldiers faced was after their discharge. In attempting to maintain control over retired soldiers and, at the same time, relieve itself from any fiscal commitment toward them, the government established a series of "Colonization Schemes" in which soldiers were settled.

In line with its policy of discouraging the influx of ex-slaves into towns and its need for agricultural labor, the colonial administration decided to settle retired soldiers in separate agricultural communities in different parts of the country. Another motive behind this policy was to establish a measure of control over these ex-slave soldiers.

Candidates for colonization schemes were selected by their commanding officers prior to the end of their service and were subjected to a great deal of scrutiny. After the selection, each person was allowed to settle with his family at a site of his choice. The majority were directed toward the agricultural districts in the Blue Nile, Sinnar, Kassala, and the White Nile provinces.[137] Each soldier was to be provided with a piece of land as well as farming implements, a seed loan, grain, and food rations until his first crop was harvested. After a trial period of two or three years, he became owner of his plot provided that he had complied with all the rules of the colonies. During this "probation" period colonists were exempted from all taxes, but they were required to commence repayment of the loan immediately after the first harvest. Colonists were not supposed to desert the settlement or mortgage either the land or the crop without the consent of the local district inspector, in which case they were required to reimburse the government for all the assistance they had been given.[138] Discipline in the colonies was maintained through a headman who was appointed by the government, usually from the senior officers or the first settlers. For instance, 'Abdallah Sa'id Bey, who was mentioned earlier, was commander of the reservists in Kassala;[139] 'Abdallah 'Adlan became the head of the Radif settlement in al-Ubayyid; and Emir 'Abd al-Hamid was put in charge of the Radif quarter in Kosti. These headmen were paid nominal salaries and became responsible for the collection of taxes and grain as well as the distribution of food and the settlement of newcomers. The location and population of these colonies are detailed in Table 4.

Despite official rhetoric, ex-soldiers were totally forgotten after their discharge. An inspection tour by Wingate in 1914 revealed that the great majority were living in squalid conditions. In Kosti, for instance,

TABLE 4
Settlements of Discharged Soldiers

Province	Colony	Date established	Number of settlers
Kordofan	al-Ubayyid	1922	134
	Um Rawwaba	1922	19
	Rahad	1922	32
	Abu Zabad	1922	6
Funj	XIV	1902	148
	Tawfiqiya	1902	59
	'Abbud	?	16
	Mukhtara	1905	7
Blue Nile	Ghabbosh	?	116
	Hilimi 'Abbas	?	114
	Keila	?	77
	Hasan	?	11
	Makwar	?	45
Nuba Mountains	Hillat al-Radif	1907	211
Upper Nile	Tawfiqiyya	1920	25
White Nile	Kosti	1905	425
	'Abbasyyia	1901	41
	Khor Agwal	1901	42
	Jabalayin	1914	26
Kassala	Gedarif	?	108
	Daim 'Abbas	?	?
	Gharb al-Gash	?	286
Dar Fur	Salamat al-Pasha	1920	51
Total			1,999

150 ex-soldiers complained that they did not receive the financial assistance they were promised and that they were starving.[140] It is not surprising that some ex-slave soldiers either returned to their owners or engaged in brewing local drinks and criminal activities. However, the establishment of agricultural schemes in the Gezira and Gedarif created employment opportunities.

From the perspective of this study, the significance of these settlements is that they became magnets for freed and runaway slaves and became nuclei of ex-slave communities. By the second decade of their existence, these settlements had become open communities and military authorities had begun to lose control over them. The presence of a large number of ex-slaves in these quarters was viewed by officials as a sign of social decadence that would lead to prostitution and criminal activity. In the early 1920s the whole scheme was reviewed, a subject that will be examined later.

THE DEVELOPMENT OF THE
WAGE LABOR FORCE

Despite the absence of large-scale capitalist enterprise in the Sudan, the establishment of colonial rule created a great demand for labor. The extension of the railway system, swamp clearing in the south, road construction, the building of a new harbor at Port Sudan, etc., all required a great deal of manpower. But as in other parts of Africa, the colonial government in the Sudan had tremendous difficulty creating a steady and reliable supply of labor during the early years. Indeed, the reasons were not unique to the Sudan. The great majority of the population was engaged in farming, pastoralism, and trade, and there was no compelling need for them to sell their labor in exchange for wages.

British approaches to emancipation and wage labor in the Sudan, and in Africa in general, were shaped by the postemancipation experience in the New World, by the industrial revolution and the rise of the working class in Europe, and by the conditions they found in the colonies. In the Sudanese context, the conceptual framework through which the British tried to rule was essentially evolutionist. They classified the Sudanese population into distinct categories, each with its own physical and cultural characteristics.[141] These assumptions were specifically linked to labor. Accordingly, the Sudanese people were classified into three categories: Arabs, Sudanese, and Fallata, with the assumption that each had certain qualities.

The creation of ethnic categories and stereotypes pertaining to labor was common throughout colonial Africa.[142] Everywhere European colonial powers faced similar problems as the vast majority of the population either showed little interest in wage employment or did not work steadily.[143]

The formation of ethnic categories was an interactive process, shaped by both colonial administrators and the people they ruled. For many centuries the Arabic-speaking northern Sudanese had developed genealogies in which they claimed an Arab ancestry. However the term "Arabs" was used by administrators to refer to all the inhabitants of the northern Sudan, some of whom did not even consider themselves Arabs. To British officials these people had "slave-owning mentality" and were lethargic and "averse to heavy manual work."[144]

Similarly the term "Sudanese" was applied to ex-slaves and all non-Arab groups in the south and the Nuba Mountains. The British adopted this term from the Arabic-speaking northern Sudanese themselves. It is commonplace that this term was applied by medieval Arab writers to the inhabitants of the Sahelian belt. In the Sudan, the term was associated with servile status and was not limited to actual enslavement, but embraced all non-Arab groups from whom slaves were captured. British officials believed that the "Sudanese" were energetic but needed discipline and supervision. They were considered "the unskilled [workmen] of the Sudan, and excellent manual laborers [sic] when the whim of the moment or the rare pressure of necessity induce them to labour."[145] Indeed, the notion that slaves were lazy and had no incentive to work was popular among planters in the New World and elsewhere. For instance, during the course of abolition in East Africa, a member of the East Africa Commission wrote:

> It should always be remembered that one of the principal curses of slavery, apart from its immoral character and its economic failures, was the production of the slave mind. A human being accustomed to slavery, when freed, seems to have lost all incentive to work.[146]

Similarly, Fallata was a pejorative term applied by Arabic-speaking northern Sudanese to all immigrants from West Africa and Dar Fur, who had settled in the Sudan for several centuries. The term "Fallata" was not a definitive ethnic category, but was associated with hard, menial, and unskilled agricultural work. According to Mark Duffield, the term did not have derogatory connotations before the twentieth century.[147] In precolonial times West Africans came to the Sudan mainly in transit to or from Mecca, and some settled as cultivators, especially along the Blue Nile. Most of these early immigrants were Fulani religious teachers who were known as Takarir and enjoyed great respect in the Sudan. One of the oldest West African settlements was established in the early nineteenth century at the village of Shaykh Talha on the Blue Nile.[148] However, the greatest exodus from Nigeria to the Sudan occurred after the British conquest of the Sokoto caliphate at the beginning of this century. Members of the Sokoto ruling family led their followers in a *hijra* (emigration) to the east and were joined by many people from the eastern emirates. Eventually, the majority of these people settled in the Sudan. In 1906 Mai Wurno, son of the Khalifa Muhammad Attahiru, settled in Shaykh Talha, which came to be known as Mai Wurno. West African immigration increased over the next few years and by 1912 the population of Mai Wurno was estimated at 4,000. Besides Mai Wurno, several other settlements were established in the southern parts of the Blue Nile. Most of the later immigrants were poor farmers who had no alternative but to become agricultural laborers in the Blue Nile and Kassala provinces. According to one colonial official: "the influx of West African tribes will materially benefit the labor market as these people, unlike most of the Sudanese, are anxious to make money."[149] They were further described as "the most useful population," who "were thrifty hard working people, willing to work for small wages."[150] From the beginning, the colonial officials saw the usefulness of Mai Wurno for labor recruitment. As early as 1911, he was given 3,000 acres of land and was authorized to collect grain and recruit laborers on behalf of the government.[151]

The failure of the colonial government to recruit the Arabic-speaking northern Sudanese cannot be explained by ethnic stereotypes or innate qualities. It had something to do with the nature of the colonial economy itself and with the circumstances under which nonwage producers become wage laborers, the nature of work they were required to perform, and the kind of incentives they were offered. In the early days, the colonial economy in the Sudan did not alienate the rural producers from their means of production, or force them to seek wage labor, or to become totally dependent on it. Unlike in white settler or mineral exporting colonies in other parts of Africa, rural producers in the Sudan did not face displacement during the early phase of colonial rule. Out of fear of renewed political unrest, taxation was kept to a minimum as senior British officials were convinced that the imposition of heavy taxation during the Turco-Egyptian period had been a major factor behind the Mahdist revolution.

The crux of the problem was not that the so-called "Arabs" did not work, but that they did not work steadily. As in other parts of Africa, the rural producers in the Sudan were accustomed to working at their own pace. Their attitude toward wage employment was shaped by certain cultural values and work ethics.[152] Moreover, the kinds of jobs available and wages offered were not attractive. The main demand was for hard, menial, unskilled, and low-paying jobs in public works and in the agricultural sector.

The failure of the government to recruit the so-called "Arabs" convinced its officials that these people would not work and that even if they did, the quality of their labor would be poor. For example, in 1903 when Slatin was dispatched to Suakin to contact the local Beja shaykhs and mobilize their followers, the results were disappointing; the performance of the 300 men recruited was unsatisfactory. Although they worked more steadily than was expected, the quality of their work was considered inferior by colonial officials.[153] Moreover, employment of the nomads, who refused to work for less than five piastres per day and rations, was considered expensive. A year later, the experiment with the Beja was declared a complete failure: "the majority of them, on the first fall of rain in the mountains, gave up their work, being thoroughly tired of it and longing to get back to their homes."[154] The government had to import Egyptian, Yemeni, and Eritrean laborers. Moreover, on several occasions, various departments resorted to prison labor.[155] At the same time technical jobs were held mainly by Egyptian, European, and Middle Eastern immigrants.

Colonial officials concluded that slaves were the only group suitable for hard and unskilled labor. Therefore, runaway and liberated slaves became the main target for labor recruitment by the Central Labour Bureau (CLB) established in 1905 for this purpose. Although the main function of the bureau was to register slaves, it came to embrace the entire labor question by regulating and directing their movement. The clerical work and registration were conducted in the office of the assistant director of intelligence in Khartoum under the supervision of the inspector-general.[156] Heads of government departments were instructed not to recruit workers except through the CLB to which they had to submit all labor requirements at least a month in advance. Provincial governors were allowed to employ local labor from their own provinces without reference to the bureau, but they were required to comply with the bureau's guidelines if they needed labor from outside their provinces. All heads of departments were required to submit a monthly report showing the amount and sources of labor employed during the month. One of the most important tasks of the CLB was to create and enforce a uniform system of wages.

The CLB started operations in January 1906. Two years later it was reported that the supply of skilled laborers for government work as well as for private employers was adequate. But its attempt to transform ex-slaves into wage earners failed, as many slaves refused to subject themselves to colonial work discipline. As one official put it: "the slaves, for the most part consider that the best use they can make of their newly acquired liberty is to labor as little as possible."[157] By 1910 the total number of slaves registered by the Bureau was just over 11,000. The registration was successful in some provinces but failed in others. Indeed, not all registered slaves were actually employed.

Ex-slaves who worked for the government did so at their own pace. They took advantage of high wages—which were caused by a labor shortage—and worked on a part-time basis. In the urban centers in 1908, for example, an unskilled laborer could earn between ninety piastres and one hundred thirty piastres per month and live on ten to fifteen piastres for the same period.[158] A person could work for a few days in a month to make a living. As one official put it: "I think it would be difficult to get any Sudanese from the vicinity of Khartoum."[159] Idleness and disorder were explained in racial terms and the presence of released slaves in towns became a subject of constant lamentation:

> The deplorable migration of Sudanese ex-slaves from agricultural provinces, the Gezira and Berber, to the large towns; where they were forming an ever-increasing population whose natural indolence, untempered by any imperative necessity of working for a livelihood, and the lack of responsibility, caused them to become not only a direct economic loss to the country at large, but even a menace to the more orderly and law-abiding member of the urban community.[160]

It was urged that steps be taken in the near future to exercise adequate control over this "semi-idle population in the best interest of the Sudanese themselves as well as for the benefit of the native Arab cultivators."[161] This meant the adoption of a more aggressive approach to, and a rigorous application of, the registration system.

The first step was to convert the CLB from an essentially statistical agency into an executive organization responsible for all acquisition and allocation of labor.[162] A new system of registration was introduced in June 1909.[163] The new system was specifically designed to control the ex-slave population and keep them on the land, and to prevent those without documents from obtaining employment in towns: "every Sudanese who is not a cultivator and owner of his own land is now obliged to have a registration form (labor book)."[164] It was clearly stated that the purpose of this scheme was to "discourage Sudanese slaves from leaving their masters without good reasons and to distinguish between the genuine laboring class and the parasitical elements."[165] Under the new system, any person who did not have proof of gainful employment was summarily imprisoned as a vagabond. All laborers applying for registration were required to produce evidence of their mode of living during the previous eighteen months. In this way ex-slaves and dislocated persons living in towns were rounded up and sent to various projects all over the country.[166]

The reluctance of the rural population to seek wage employment and the failure of the government to recruit ex-slaves created a major crisis for the regime and led to stiff competition among government departments. This in turn resulted in high wages as each department began to offer different rates to attract laborers. Fears were expressed that any rise in wage scales would reduce the supply of agricultural labor and have a deleterious effect on production in this vital sector of the economy.

In 1910 the CLB was reviewed; inaccuracy and the failure to keep up-to-date records were cited. Although government departments and provinces were required to hire registered slaves, these regulations were often ignored, thus diminishing any value the system may have had. In areas where casual labor was available, the system had little impact and the CLB failed to intervene in a lasting or significant way. But administrative problems alone do not explain the government failure to control the labor of ex-slaves, which was due in equal part to the attitude of ex-slaves themselves toward colonial wage labor and to the choices they made.

However, the period after 1910 seemed to be a turning point. For the first time it was reported that the supply of labor was far in excess of demand. This was indeed a result of changing conditions in the countryside. The low Nile and light rainfall created serious hardships in rural areas, especially in the northern provinces of Dongola, Halfa, and Berber, which were hit by famine and starvation. It was reported that about half of the population of Debba in Dongola Province had died in 1913–1914.[167] The governor of the province gave the following description of the situation:

> On entering a village in the Districts, (Debba, Korti, and Khandak) one is surrounded by hundreds of starving women and children, all practically naked. They have nobody to support them, their male folk having left the province months ago in search for work elsewhere. There are no cattle, no crops . . . The number of deaths from starvation is increasing weekly, principally among children. At Debba bodies have been picked up at dawn, of children who have crawled in during the night.[168]

Drought and famine had forced many people to migrate from the riverain areas to the cities. It is not clear whether all these immigrants were slaves; it is safe to assume that they included many landless free peasants as well as slaves. The latter took advantage of the situation to leave their owners, who had little desire or ability to force them to stay.

Another contributing factor was imposition of a new system of taxation on cultivators. Up to 1912 taxes were kept light for political and economic reasons. The sedentary population paid nominal taxes on land, animals, and crops. Nomads paid an annual tribute based on an approximate assessment of their cattle, and a royalty was imposed on gum, ostrich feathers, and ivory. However, in 1912 the administration decided to withdraw the annual Egyptian subvention on which the finance of the Sudan depended. Consequently, taxes had to be raised.[169] As a result many cultivators began to abandon their land and they flocked to the towns. Extension of the railway system to remote parts of the country and the conquest of Dar Fur in 1916 increased the rate of immigration to the cities. However, this was temporary relief, for once conditions in the countryside improved, farmers returned to their land.

After 1913 the CLB was seldom used, and indeed the registration system was abandoned during the First World War. Although the bureau continued to exist, a new scheme for labor recruitment was devised in 1918. Accordingly, all future recruitment was to be conducted by provincial officials through native administrators.[170] But in view of the acute labor shortage, no provincial governor was willing to allow any laborer to leave his province to work in another. In May 1918 the governors of the Red Sea, Dongola, and Berber provinces asked the government to restrict recruitment in their provinces, a demand that was supported by Khartoum.[171] Finally, in 1921 the CLB was transformed into a Labor Committee which was merely a statistical agency. By that time the colonial economy had entered a new phase, that of the Gezira Scheme and cotton production, both of which had lasting effects on the labor market.

CONCLUSION

For political, ideological, and economic considerations the Condominium Government tried to maintain the status quo and tolerated the institution of slavery during the early decades of this century. Nevertheless, the establishment of the colonial economy generated a great demand for wage labor. Unable to attract enough workers, the colonial regime targeted liberated and runaway slaves for its labor requirements. However, the conversion of ex-slaves into a stable work force proved to be a difficult task, as many of them sought alternatives. They migrated to the cities, established settlements on vacant land, and found sanctuary in the communities of discharged soldiers. In response, the government resorted to various methods of coercion such as the vagrancy laws and the registration system. It was in the cities that these methods were rigorously applied and the greatest effort to force ex-slaves to work was made.

THREE

SLAVERY AND LABOR IN
KHARTOUM, 1898–1919

T his chapter focuses on the experi-
ence of slaves and ex-slaves in Khartoum during the first twenty years of
colonial rule. It attempts to answer the two questions raised in the previous
chapter: What did the establishment of colonial rule and city life mean for
urban slaves and rural ex-slaves who migrated to the capital? And what,
on the other hand, did the city and its people represent for colonial rulers?
For many liberated slaves and displaced people the city was an area of
freedom and opportunity. During the early years of colonial rule, Khartoum
was a place to gather from dislocation, to rejoin kin, or to return home to
after the displacement of the Mahdiyya. However, for colonial officials, the
relative independence enjoyed by ex-slaves and the presence of a "floating"
population in the city became an anathema. It was a violation of their ideal
of an orderly city and a potential source of myriad social problems. Yet the
presence of these elements in the capital was also a blessing: former slaves
represented a potential source of much-needed labor. Thus, from the
beginning, several measures were taken to control and use this floating
population in the emerging colonial economy. The Three Towns of
Khartoum, Khartoum North, and Omdurman became a labor reservoir
and a center for labor circulation. People left the countryside for the city
to escape slavery, famine, and other disasters, and found themselves redeployed to the rural areas as laborers.

ANGLO-EGYPTIAN CONQUEST AND
ITS AFTERMATH

At the time of the Anglo-Egyptian conquest Khartoum was a ruined and largely deserted city. As we have seen in chapter 1, Khartoum was destroyed in 1885 and its inhabitants were transferred to Omdurman, which became the capital of the Mahdist state. During the Mahdiyya the population of Omdurman grew considerably as a result of the mass migration of the Baqqara and other Mahdist supporters. This population movement involved a large number of slaves who accompanied their owners to the capital. Slaves formed the bulk of the jihadiyya units that were stationed in Omdurman. Coupled with this was the continuing slave trade which increased the servile population in the city. In 1895 the population of Omdurman was estimated at 150,000.[1] It is unclear how many of those were slaves, but undoubtedly they constituted a large percentage. Moreover, it should be pointed out that population figures for the Mahdist and early colonial periods were highly unreliable as they were deliberately inflated or deflated by colonial officials for political reasons.

The Anglo-Egyptian conquest dealt a devastating blow to the population of Omdurman. The battle of Karari resulted in approximately 10,800 dead, 20,000 wounded, and 5,000 prisoners taken.[2] Random killings and execution of Mahdist followers continued for several days after the battle. Undoubtedly, many of those victims were slaves and slave owners. In response, a large number of people fled the city and either returned to their original homes or scattered in different parts of the country. The slaves, in particular, took advantage of the chaotic situation and escaped. Death, flight, and dislocation resulted in a substantial decrease in the population of Omdurman. In 1900 the city's population was estimated at 50,000, representing a two-thirds decline from previous years. Again this estimate must be taken with great caution.

In addition to escape some slaves avenged themselves upon their masters.[3] Revenge was particularly common among soldiers of the Sudanese battalions of the Egyptian Army, most of whom were slaves who served in the Turco-Egyptian and Mahdist jihadiyya. Some of these soldiers defected to the Anglo-Egyptian side during the last years of the Mahdiyya while others were enlisted during the Anglo-Egyptian campaign. After the conquest, some of these soldiers tried to settle scores with their former owners. In one incident, after the battle of Karari a Sudanese soldier went to the house of his former owner, knocked on the door, and as the man came out he pulled his pistol and shot him dead.[4] For several days Sudanese soldiers pillaged the city and seized many female slaves under the pretext that they were their relatives.[5] Another soldier went to retrieve his slave sister and shot the owner when the owner tried to stop him.[6]

Although the collapse of the Mahdist regime provided slaves with an opportunity to escape, flight proved to be a risky option as it was often followed by misery and destitution. Out of desperation many runaway slaves rejoined their owners while others returned to their home areas in the south and in the west. Still, a few found sanctuary with the Christian missions established a few years later.[7]

The large-scale devastation wrought by the Anglo-Egyptian campaign produced a large number of unattached slaves, mostly women, whose owners had either been killed or taken as prisoners. In other words, colonial conquest had unintentionally released many slaves who faced difficult situations. There was a chronic shortage of food and shelter in the capital.[8] While males resorted to banditry or begging, females either attached themselves to soldiers or became prostitutes.[9] The growing number of destitute slaves and dislocated people in the capital prompted some officials to consider the establishment of a sanctuary for the rehabilitation of these victims. However, this was rejected by Wingate who argued that "the time has not yet come" for the establishment of such an institution in the Sudan.[10] The governor-general's reaction was consistent with the government's policy of denying the existence of slavery and minimizing its importance.

Unwilling to assume the additional burden of providing shelter for ex-slaves, the government began to repatriate them to their original homes in the Upper Nile, Bahr al-Ghazal, the Nuba Mountains, and the southern Blue Nile. For instance, between 1902 and 1904, about one thousand slaves were sent to Sinnar, the Upper Nile, and Dar Fur.[11] Some of those repatriated joined the ex-soldiers' settlements in different parts of the country.[12] However, despite massive desertion it appears that many slaves remained with their owners in the city.[13] In 1903 the total number of slaves registered in Omdurman was estimated at 9,000, and there was approximately the same number in the neighboring villages of Jayli, Kadaru, Halfaya, and Jirayf. The slaves constituted between 20 and 25 percent of the population of greater Khartoum.[14]

Unlike their counterparts in the rural areas, slaves in the capital had the advantage of being close to the seat of government. Following the establishment of the new regime, hundreds of men and women flocked into district headquarters and the metropolitan office of the Department for the Repression of the Slave Trade (DRST) complaining about their owners or applying for manumission. But the official oblivion which prevailed in the rural areas also attended the capital. Apprehensive about the social consequences of manumission, municipal administrators discouraged the departure of the slaves and encouraged them to remain with their owners. In fact very few slaves in Khartoum were manumitted through official channels. For instance, between 1911 and 1913 only thirty male and seventy-eight female slaves were liberated by government officials.[15] Realizing the futility of petitioning the government, urban male slaves took matters into their own hands and absconded.

Faced with this situation, the slaveholders made major adjustments. One strategy was to obtain new slaves to make up for their lost manpower. Despite the existence of a metropolitan office of the DRST, slaves were smuggled into the Three Towns and an occasional open sale took place. In 1899 forty-seven people were convicted for slave dealing, and in 1902 fifteen female slaves from Dar Fur were sold in Omdurman.[16] Despite the activities of government officers, clandestine slave dealing continued in the Three Towns and the neighboring villages of Jayli and Soba.[17] However, with the increased vigilance of the metropolitan police, these activities were severely curtailed by the second decade of colonial rule. In the neighboring agricultural villages farmers were forced to mobilize family labor or hire expensive wage labor.[18] However, because of high wages they could not compete with government and private firms. Therefore, they resorted to communal cultivation and crop sharing.[19] In the capital itself slave owners began to hire out their slaves and take significant portions of their earnings.[20]

EX-SLAVES IN AN URBAN MILIEU

The downfall of the Mahdist regime and the diminished authority of the owners removed many constraints from the slaves in the capital. Besides wage employment, the most important feature the city offered to ex-slaves was the opportunity to establish their own neighborhoods and create new communities. This was best exemplified by the Khartoum Daims. This huge slum on the outskirts of Khartoum was founded by runaway and liberated slaves at the beginning of the century.

The roots of the Khartoum Daims can be traced to the period of the Mahdiyya. Although during the Mahdiyya the capital was transferred from Khartoum to Omdurman, Khartoum was not quite deserted. Some of the old residents, including ex-slaves, remained in the neighboring villages of Burri al-Mahas, Burri al-Daraysa, Manjara, and Jirayf. Following transfer of the capital back from Omdurman and the beginning of construction of Anglo-Egyptian Khartoum, people began to move to the new city in search of employment and other opportunities.[21] Gradually a large camp grew up around the site of the present-day Roman Catholic Cathedral. Its inhabitants consisted of ex-slaves, Mahdist remnants, and urban workers. The huts and hovels in which they lived soon developed into a huge slum which attracted an increasing number of people from Omdurman as well as liberated slaves from the rural areas.

This "native" quarter did not conform to the standard of the colonial city that the new regime was trying to establish.[22] One year after the conquest the Town Lands Ordinance was introduced to provide for the settlement of land ownership in Khartoum and other cities. It authorized the government to obtain any land required, either by purchase or by exchange, thus enabling the government to plan towns without interference from property owners.[23] Landowners were ordered to erect buildings conforming to "new standards" within two years. All lands which were not allotted to private owners, or whose owners failed to comply with building regulations, were to become the absolute property of the government.

The replanning of Khartoum was confined to the area within the ramparts which General Gordon had built around the old town. In line with this logic—and using lack of sanitation as a justification—municipal officials decided in 1902 to remove the slums to the south of the old fortification.[24] The residents gave the new site the nickname Tardona ("they expelled us").[25] Later the area came to be known as the Daims (meaning "residential quarter"). According to an official report:

> The population of these deims [sic] consists of Sudanese [slaves] and a minority of Arabs, who supply the daily labor for Khartoum and environs; besides containing the homes of all permanent labor employed by the government departments, contractors, etc., as they cannot be allowed to live within Khartoum itself.[26]

Although ex-slaves formed the core of the Daims' residents, these quarters attracted diverse groups of people. The colonial administration viewed the Daims as entities in their own right in order to disengage itself from any financial responsibility toward them. Since they were considered a "Native Lodging Area" they were outside the official classification scheme and therefore were not entitled to any health or social services such as running water or electricity. Residents lived in small houses of about 30 to 60 square meters. These had low ceilings and the only means of

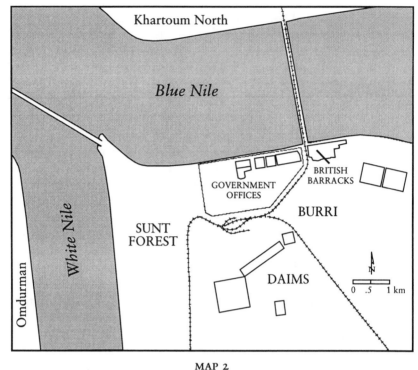

MAP 2

Anglo-Egyptian Khartoum

ventilation was usually one or more small openings stuffed with rags to keep out light and the cold air. The houses had no latrines and inhabitants had no alternative but to use the open area adjoining the Daims.[27] Given these conditions, it is not surprising that the inhabitants of the Daims suffered from outbreaks of diseases such as tuberculosis, which became the leading cause of death in Khartoum in the early years of the twentieth century.[28]

Nonetheless, this pattern of living suited the government. The population of the Daims was viewed as a source of cheap casual labor, which was in great demand during the early phase of the colonial economy. Casual labor meant casual housing. A former colonial administrator summed up the official attitude:

There was, therefore, nothing very strange or reprehensible in allotting only enough space for a single room; it fully served the purpose. It was in no sense a "home"; it was merely a temporary "lodging."[29]

In 1909 the Town Building Regulations were announced. They included detailed instructions as to the type of buildings allowed for each class of land and laid down sanitary regulations. Land holders had to apply to the municipal authorities or to the provincial government to obtain building permits. Three classes of residential areas were recognized according to the size of the plot and the type of building material.[30]

The tenure of these holdings was regulated in 1912 by an ordinance which provided that no title could be acquired by prescription in what was classified as "Native Lodging Areas." It also provided that the land could be recovered at any time with one month's notice and the payment of compensation for the building. Later it was decided that no compensation would be paid if the plot had been in occupation for ten years or more. Consequently, the Daims' residents became tenants of the government and could be evicted at a month's notice.[31]

The most striking feature of the Khartoum Daims was that many of them bear names of ethnic groups from the slave raiding frontiers of Dar Fertit, Dar Fur, the Nuba Mountains, and the Upper Blue Nile. For instance, Daim Banda, Daim Kara, and Daim Jabal, or Kreish, refer to groups whose original home was southwestern Sudan and the eastern part of the Central African Republic. Similarly, Daim Berta was named after the Berta people of the Sudan-Ethiopian border region, while Daim Tegali, or Nuba, alluded to the inhabitants of the Nuba Mountains. Daim Ta'isha and Daim Jawam'a relate to the Ta'isha and the Jawam'a ethnic groups of Dar Fur and Kordofan. The presence of these people in Khartoum amply illustrates the scale of social dislocation and demographic shifts that occurred during the nineteenth century. For example, the presence of the Ta'isha and the Jawam'a in the capital was associated with the khalifa's policy. However, the presence of the Banda, Berta, Kara, Kreish, and Nuba was linked with the nineteenth-century slave trade, which created a vast southern and western Sudanese diaspora.

The prevalence of ethnic labels in the Daims yields significant insights into the history of ex-slaves in the postemancipation period. It sheds light on the way in which liberated slaves tried to rebuild their lives and create new identities. They grouped themselves ethnically, regionally, and occupationally, which was reflected in the names of the various Daims.

The creation of ethnic identities in urban centers, which was common throughout colonial Africa, has attracted the attention of many scholars. In the Zongo of Kumasi, among the Hausa immigrants in Yoruba towns, and in the mining towns of southern Africa, ethnic categories were created and reinforced.[32] They served as a defensive mechanism and a strategy for socioeconomic mobility in the competitive urban environment. Ethnicity helped immigrants to "bring a measure of control to the difficult situation in which they found themselves in their day-to-day life."[33] However, the creation of ethnic identities among liberated slaves served several purposes. Since the slaves were kinless and outsiders in their host societies, their emancipation would entail the redefinition of identity and the construction of quasi-ethnic and quasi-kinship categories. These mechanisms served as remedies for the uprooting that resulted from enslavement.[34]

Persistence of ethnic names such as Banda and Kara among ex-slaves in Khartoum may be viewed as a response to the difficulty of being integrated into the kinship groups of the Arabic-speaking northern Sudanese owners. The quasi-ethnic communities in the Daims allowed newly liberated slaves to find new kin, to reintegrate themselves into communities from their home areas, and to have a sense of belonging. According to oral accounts, once liberated the slave would seek his or her own kinsmen or people from the home area and settle among them.[35] In this manner the slave's status became blurred. Those who did not know their ethnic background adopted the ethnic identity of the communities into which they were forced. Thus, labels such as 'abid Shaiqiyya (Shaiqiyya slave) and 'abid Danaqla (Danaqla slave) were quite common.

However, ethnicity was not the only binding force in the Daims. Shared historical experience, occupational cleavages, and corporate ties also played major roles in the formation of the new communities. For example, former slave soldiers (bazingir) who were employed by the slave traders in the south settled in Daim al-Zubairiyya with their descendants. They named their quarter after Al-Zubair Rahma, the northern Sudanese slave trader under whom they had served. Occupational cleavages were reflected in Daim al-'Attala (porters), Daim al-Gashasha (grass or fodder sellers), and Daim Telegraph, which was inhabited by the workers of the Posts and Telegraph Department.

Other Daims were named after the individuals who founded them. They included ex-slaves, soldiers, and immigrants. For instance, Daim Abu Hashish was founded by Mursal Abu Hashish, a Dinka who served in the personal escort of General Gordon and who was taken by the Mahdi after the fall of Khartoum. He was kept in the Mahdi's and the khalifa's households to drill their slaves. After the reoccupation, he established himself at Muqran and was appointed by the government as the shaykh of the Daims.[36] In 1916 he was replaced by Muhammad Musa. However, Mursal moved and established his own Daim near Burri which is known today as Abu-Hashish. Daim Abu-Hashish was inhabited by ex-slaves from the Upper Blue Nile Province, and the Nuba Mountains, Kara, and Dinka groups, as well as by West African immigrants.[37] Other Daims named after individuals included: Daim Salman, Daim Saʿad, Daim ʿAbd al-Karim, Daim Abu al-Rish, Daim al-ʿAta, Daim al-Nur, and Daim Murjan.[38]

The Daims provided ex-slaves with a place to live and the opportunity to engage in a wide range of economic activities such as petty trading, blacksmithing, barbering, and tailoring. Many people worked as porters, wood and grass sellers, water carriers, etc. In each Daim, there were several marisa (local beer) houses which provided income to many families.

So the Daims were not discrete ethnic units but open communities which absorbed a wide spectrum of people. Although they were pioneered by ex-slaves, their ethnic composition changed progressively. They gradually developed into working-class neighborhoods to which many urban poor gravitated.

Working-class neighborhoods grew in Khartoum North as well, where the government dockyard, stores, and the Egyptian Army barracks were located. Khartoum North was built around the old villages of Khojali, Hamad, and Halfaya. The dockyard workers were drawn mainly from the Danaqla, who had a long tradition of boat building and sailing. They established a neighborhood known as Hillat al-Danaqla. Ex-slaves and immigrants established their own Daims. In contrast, Omdurman maintained its precolonial physical and demographic structure, with little interference from the colonial authorities.[39] In short, the Khartoum Daims remained the largest working-class neighborhood in the capital.

URBAN EX-SLAVES AND COLONIAL WAGE LABOR

Within a few years, the colonial economy began to generate great demand for labor in the capital itself and elsewhere. In the capital the greatest demand was in the construction and building industry. For the new regime, it was important that the government buildings be completed in the shortest possible time so that the seat of administration could be moved from Omdurman to Khartoum. The most urgent task was to clear the site and rebuild Khartoum along "European lines." Some of the most important buildings erected during the first decade included the palace, the army barracks, Gordon College, the Egyptian Army Hospital, residences of senior officials, the Department of Works, the Grand Hotel, the zoological garden, and many other administrative buildings. By 1909 Khartoum extended for several miles along the Blue Nile and for a mile south of the river.[40]

In the early years the government tried to meet labor demands by imposing what amounted to forced labor. Following Kitchener's victory at Omdurman in 1898, a corvée was imposed and thousands of Mahdist prisoners were sent to clear the streets of Khartoum.[41] This coercive measure was also intended to force the ansar to recant their allegiance to the Mahdiyya. Only those who discarded Mahdist dress were spared.[42] About 2,000 jihadiyya prisoners were employed in road building and brick making on the banks of the Blue Nile.[43] They were organized in companies of 400 men, each under its own headman and supervised by a few British noncommissioned officers.[44]

For several years after the Anglo-Egyptian conquest Mahdist prisoners continued to be a source of cheap labor that could be coerced. In addition to construction, ex-jihadiyya were employed by government departments and sent to various parts of the country. For instance, several hundred of them were used to build the telegraph lines to al-Ubayyid and to the southern parts of the country. Since these people were classified as prisoners of war they were given only rations and paid a half piastre per day. However, their daily wage was later increased to three piastres without rations.[45] By 1904 the Steamers and Boats Department had approximately 400 workers, most of whom were dispatched to its wood stations along the Nile.[46]

The government could not depend on this labor indefinitely. Since the early days government departments had turned to urban residents for their labor requirements and many male ex-slaves found opportunities in the growing colonial wage labor. The expanding building activities in the early years absorbed a large number of ex-slaves and other urban residents in unskilled employment. By 1904 about 5,000 people were reportedly employed in brick making, quarrying, and burning of lime.[47]

Moreover, some liberated slaves found sanctuary in the newly established Christian missions where they received an elementary education. For instance, in November 1902, newly arrived Christian missionaries opened a school for young girls in Khartoum. The teacher herself was a former slave who had been sold in Alexandria and converted to Christianity by American missionaries. The first group of students comprised thirteen girls, who received an elementary education and basic training as cooks and servants. They were joined by another 200 whose parents were captured from Ethiopia during the Mahdiyya.[48] It was estimated that in 1903, 20 percent of the school population in Khartoum and Omdurman were liberated slaves.[49]

In addition, many ex-slaves enrolled in the instructional workshops that were established in Khartoum and Omdurman during the first ten years of colonial rule. In 1908 there were about one hundred seventy-nine workers in Khartoum's workshop and fifty-five in Omdurman's, most of whom were ex-slaves.[50] They were trained in carpentry, smith work, cotton ginning, and elementary engineering.[51] By using their educational opportunities, ex-slaves were able to establish themselves as skilled wage laborers and as junior civil servants.

Conversely, the colonial economy offered few opportunities for liberated female slaves. Thus, many of them had no alternative but to work as domestic servants, become prostitutes, or sell local drink. Since the early days of colonial rule, prostitution was a major feature of life in Khartoum.

The involvement of female slaves in prostitution in the Sudan was by no means a twentieth-century phenomenon; it was noted by European travelers such as John Lewis Burckhardt, who visited the Sudan in the early nineteenth century. This was indeed a period of rapid transformation associated with increased commercial activities and the rise of urban centers. Female slaves established brothels in the commercial towns such as Shendi and Berber, which were meeting points for trading caravans.[52]

It is commonplace that prostitution has been a functional consequence of urban society in many parts of the world. In her study of prostitution in colonial Nairobi, Luise White examined this phenomenon in the context of the wage labor market and the socioeconomic transformation of Kenyan society under colonial rule. White emphasizes the role of prostitutes in the reproduction of labor, both in the city and in the countryside.[53] More important, however, is her assertion that prostitution was a logical outcome of the gender bias in the formal wage labor market.

Colonial records in the Sudan stressed the link between female slaves and prostitution. In fact, the fear that liberated female slaves would become prostitutes was one of the main reasons behind the colonial officials' cautious approach to liberating them. However, not all female slaves turned to prostitution; only those who went to live in the cities and had no other alternatives became prostitutes.

The large-scale social dislocation during the last years of the Mahdiyya and the early years of the Anglo-Egyptian conquest created a large number of unattached and destitute women, who had no alternatives for making a living. Unwilling to take on the additional burden of rehabilitating these women and unable to eradicate prostitution, the colonial government tried to regulate it through policy control and medical examinations. As early as 1902 prostitutes were settled in special quarters in the newly emerging

Khartoum Daims where they provided their services to urban workers and other city dwellers.[54] Although the literature on this subject is scant, it appears that prostitution in various Sudanese towns was regulated by pimps.[55] The existence of pimps was evident in the Vagabonds Ordinance of 1905, which will be discussed later in this chapter. Moreover, former slave owners deliberately encouraged their female slaves to become prostitutes and required them to remit part of their earnings to them.

The Three Towns were viewed by the colonial authorities as a labor reservoir from which workers could be deployed to perform unskilled agricultural tasks in different parts of the country. Ex-slaves and the "floating" urban population became the prime target for colonial labor recruitment. But the task of converting this heterogeneous group of people into a stable work force proved to be a difficult one, particularly during the first two decades of colonial rule.

Government failure to attract urban residents to wage employment stemmed from several factors. The urban population consisted of diverse groups of people whose response to colonial wage labor was determined by their particular socioeconomic conditions. While Khartoum began to develop into a colonial town, Omdurman, in which the vast majority of urban residents lived, remained a "native city." Omdurman was a cosmopolitan city with a diverse population including Egyptians, Turks, Syrians, Armenians, Greeks, northern riverain Sudanese, Dar Furians, southern Sudanese, and West African immigrants. Most of these people engaged in trade and nonwage economic activities. The city was laced with markets such as *suq al-Dhura* (grain market), *suq al-Samak* (fish market), *suq al-Jazaryyin* (butchers' market), *suq al-Fallata* (West Africans' market), and so forth.[56] For most of these people there was no compelling need for wage employment. Moreover, land settlement activities in Khartoum during the early days increased land sales. Purchase of land by Greek and other foreign merchants led to a substantial increase in prices, a situation that induced many urban residents to sell their land and live off the proceeds. Officials lamented that unless they were watched, people would "sell every square foot of land they own, and a great deal of that they do not own, for the sake of a few pounds, regardless of the consequence."[57] However, this situation was short-lived, and by 1907 land transactions stabilized.[58]

A significant portion of Khartoum's population was immigrants from the Gezira and the northern riverain regions. Most of these people owned land in their home areas and came to the city to earn cash and return home during cultivation season. Their situation was depicted in the government's annual report: "as soon as the rain set in the Gezira and elsewhere all available men and women proceeded to the rainland and started preparing the ground for cultivation."[59] Rather than become totally dependent on wage employment they combined it with farming. As usual, the reluctance of these people to become steady workers was attributed to their indolence and laziness by the British, who approached the question of labor with certain ethnic notions about Sudanese society and imposed classificatory terms such as "Arab," "Sudanese," and "Fallata." While the so-called Arabs were considered lethargic, ex-slaves were regarded as energetic but requiring discipline.

In order to force ex-slaves to work, the government introduced the Vagabonds Ordinance in 1905 to curb "idleness and vagrancy." Indeed, colonial governments in Africa never failed to apply strategies that they learned from their experience with slave emancipation in the Caribbean and in Europe after the industrial revolution. The working class and urban poor were considered to be dangerous and morally decadent, requiring discipline through some form of coercion.[60]

The Vagabonds Ordinance made a distinction among three categories of people: idle persons, vagabonds, and incorrigible vagabonds.[61] An idle person was defined as anyone who, "able wholly or in part to maintain himself or his family . . . willfully neglects or refuses to do so"; any person who wandered in the streets to beg or gather alms; and anyone who had no settled home and ostensible means of subsistence. The term "vagabond" included any person who, after being convicted as an idle person, committed any of the offenses which would render him or her liable to be convicted as such; any person who was found "in possession of house breaking implements"; any "suspected person or reputed thief who by night frequents or loiters about any shop, warehouse, dock or wharf, with intention to commit robbery"; any person "who knowingly lives wholly or in part on the earnings of a prostitute or in any public places or solicits or importunes for immoral purposes"; and any (male) person who "dresses or is attired in the fashion of a woman in public places, or who practices sodomy as a means of livelihood or as a profession." An "incorrigible vagabond" was defined as any person who, after being convicted as a vagabond, committed any of the offenses which would render him or her liable to be convicted as such, again. Punishment for idleness was one month's imprisonment; punishment for vagrancy was up to five months' imprisonment; and punishment for incorrigible vagabondage was up to one year.[62]

The new law empowered the government to deal with a variety of people who were engaged in activities that were defined by the government as illegal. Idleness, criminality, disorder, and casual labor were all linked specifically to the ex-slaves who lived in the city. "I regret to say," wrote one administrator, ". . . as long as they remain among us we will always have a fine recruiting ground for our prisons."[63]

Coupled with the Vagabonds Ordinance was the establishment of the Central Labour Bureau and the registration system. As pointed out in chapter 2, the main function of the CLB was to discourage the departure of slaves from the rural areas and force those who escaped to the city to seek wage employment. It was in the Three Towns, with the aid of the metropolitan police, that the registration of slaves was most valued. Three years after the establishment of the CLB, it was reported that the registration of ex-slaves and other immigrants in the Three Towns was having "an excellent effect."

Successful registration, however, did not mean successful recruitment. Ex-slaves either withheld their labor or took advantage of the competing demands and sought the best paying jobs. Government departments typically considered wages as an expensive bill and tried to keep them down. In 1908 the average daily wage for an unskilled laborer was three and a half piastres. It should be no surprise that ex-slaves abandoned government jobs and worked for the Gezira cultivators, who offered as much as five to ten piastres.[64]

The limited labor supply in the capital led to competition among government departments, thereby causing a sharp increase in wage rates. As a result, regularly paid workers began to leave permanent employment for casual work. High rates of pay resulted in a decrease in full-time employment, driving wages even higher. Two weeks' work and two weeks' rest became regular practice and provided income to support relatives whose labor was consequently removed from the market.[65] For instance, the population of the Three Towns in 1908 was estimated at 90,000, out of which approximately 30,000 were considered economically active.[66] The problem was that the majority of people who were regarded as economically active did not necessarily work. In order to force these "parasites" to enter the job market tougher registration laws were introduced in 1909. A new law was promulgated on 1 February 1909 according to which all economically active males residing in the Three Towns were required to register and possess an identification paper (labor book).[67] The scheme specifically targeted ex-slaves and other "negroid population" and excluded the Arabic-speaking riverain Sudanese. It was clearly stated that "merchants of Sudanese origin, government officials and landowners, will not be considered to belong to the laboring class and are not required to register."[68] According to the new scheme, no "Sudanese" (slave) would be employed in Khartoum without the registration book or proof of registration. This policy stemmed from British approaches to the question of labor and their notions of ethnicity according to which each ethnic group was assigned to certain types of jobs.

Instructions were given to town magistrates that every "Sudanese" (slave) attending their courts as a witness or in any other capacity should be asked to present an identification. Identification papers were to be carried all the time and were to be presented upon demand by any municipal official. Failure to do so could result in imprisonment under the Vagabonds Ordinance. As a result, it became increasingly difficult for anyone without proof of registration to obtain employment in the capital.

In this way ex-slaves and non-Arab groups were consigned to low-grade jobs and assigned to a particular place in the social hierarchy. British obsession with ethnicity and tribalism can best be illustrated by the lists of the CLB in which the tribal background of workers was clearly identified. Of the sixteen laborers recruited for the Central Experimental Farm in 1912, five were Kara, three Dinka, three Banda, one Kreish, one Feroge, one Binga, one Nuba, and one Borno, most of whom came from Daim al-'Ata.[69] Another list contained the names of twenty workers recruited for a private contractor in 1913. Of those, five were Nuba, five Bergo, four Dinka, three Fertit, two Hamar, and one Kanjara.[70]

By 1911 the CLB had registered approximately 4,525 persons in metropolitan Khartoum, of whom 3,500 were former slaves.[71] However, not all of those registered actually worked. Of this total, 788 were supplied to government departments, and 438 to private employers.[72]

The period after 1913 represented an interlude. In the first place, the completion of the railway line to Sinnar in the south and al-Ubayyid in the west in 1911 facilitated population movement. This period also coincided with severe drought and famine, particularly in the northern riverain areas and in the Gezira, which resulted in large-scale migration. In some districts in the Gezira, entire villages emigrated to nearby towns and elsewhere.[73] At the same time, the number of West African immigrants in the capital began to increase.[74] According to the government's report of 1907, about 1,400 West Africans had settled in Omdurman. Five years later, it was reported that there were approximately 2,440 in Omdurman, 115 in Khartoum, and 130 in Khartoum North.[75] They were welcomed by colonial officials as "an acquisition as they make good work-men and are orderly."[76] The majority of rural immigrants who came to the capital settled in the Khartoum Daims. The new immigrants created a "surplus" population in the capital which became the prime target of the CLB. Provinces that faced serious labor shortages looked to Khartoum for help.

KHARTOUM'S WORKERS IN THE PROVINCES

Workers recruited from Khartoum and sent to provinces called themselves *'ummal jabona* ("they brought us workers").[77] Judging by the labor lists, it is evident that 'ummal jabona consisted of a diverse group of people. They included Arabic-speaking northern Sudanese such as Shaiqiyya, Ja'aliyyin, etc.; West Africans; and many ex-slaves. For example, of the two hundred seventy-three workers dispatched from Khartoum to Kassala in 1913, there were forty-five West Africans, twenty-four ex-slaves, and the rest were Ja'aliyyin, Shaiqiyya, Danaqla, and Mahas. Colonial officials insisted on organizing workers along ethnic lines. Arabic-speaking northerners were employed as *muqqadams* (headmen) and assigned supervisory positions. The government order of 1 February 1909 clearly stated that "Sudanese and Arab laborers will not be employed in the same gang under one Muqqadam."[78]

Although colonial records contain references to women, it is difficult to determine the gender composition of the labor force at this early phase. But it is clear that 'ummal jabona included a substantial number of women who were assigned tasks such as shifting earth and carrying water for which they received less pay. While the daily wage for a man was three to four piastres, women were paid two to two and a half piastres, and boys one and a half to two piastres.[79] Moreover, liberated male slaves moved with their families and assigned women and children to pick cotton.[80]

The overwhelming majority of 'ummal jabona were employed as agricultural laborers on private and state schemes in the Red Sea, Kassala, Berber, and Dongola provinces. In September 1913, for instance, the governor of the Red Sea Province requested the CLB to send 500 workers for cultivation in Tokar, which was facing such a serious labor shortage that the average daily wage for a casual laborer had reached seventeen piastres. The CLB dispatched 273 workers from Khartoum. The arrival of these workers in the area brought wages down to five piastres per day.[81] Urban workers were also sent to Kordofan to pick gum arabic, to the south by the Boats and Steamers Department, and to the Gezira and Kassala. However, employers continued to complain about the "laziness" of these workers. The governor of Halfa Province, for instance, complained that workers sent from Khartoum were unwilling to do piecework at local wages.[82] In 1907 the Public Works Department deployed two hundred men from Khartoum; the Works Department one hundred; and the Lands and Forest Department twenty-nine men, all of whom were sent to the south. However, British officials in the south expressed dissatisfaction with the performance of these workers and with the fact that they were remitting money to the north.[83]

THE CONTRACT SYSTEM AND
WORK CONDITIONS

Since its establishment in 1905, the CLB had issued specific guidelines governing the conditions of employment of casual laborers. It was stipulated that when laborers were employed to do work at a distance from their home, an advance of 15 days' pay would be given until they were in a position to remit money to their families.[84] Dispatched workers were also guaranteed employment for at least four months.

The trouble was that these workers were not willing to subject themselves to the work rhythms that the employers expected, and quite often they became dissatisfied with the working conditions and deserted. In order to ensure the continuous employment of laborers until the work was completed, it was decided that after a laborer had received pay for the first month and a half—including the advance mentioned above—an amount not exceeding ten days' pay would be held from his pay and would be given to him only on the completion of work or on discharge. Workers employed at Port Sudan and in the railways department were given rations and transportation at government expense where facilities for government railways and steamers existed.[85]

With regard to supervision and the settlement of disputes, laborers were to be informed in advance whether they would be supervised by a government official or by a contractor. The CLB's recruits working under contractors had the right to complain to the government officials supervising them. These guidelines were translated into Arabic and circulated among government officials as well as the local omdas and shaykhs, who were required to explain them to the workers.[86]

Quite often contract provisions were disregarded, a situation that led to endless disputes. Employers often ran out of money or offered terms that could not compete with local alternatives, or they could not compete with what was available back in the city. This led to frequent conflicts between workers and employers. One example was the case of the 273 workers who were sent by the CLB from Khartoum to Tokar in 1913. In addition to the contract, these men were "guaranteed" by a merchant in Khartoum who was obliged to refund their railway fare and cash advance in case they did not commence work. However, their arrival at Tokar brought wages down and tenants were able to procure local laborers at the rate of five piastres per day. Given the general perception of the quality of West African and ex-slave labor, the tenants discharged workers from the riverain regions.[87] The stranded workers protested and demanded that they should either be employed or returned to Khartoum at government expense. But the government was not willing to do either. Instead, they were told to "find work" and repay the cost of their trip from Khartoum.[88] Faced with this indifference, the majority of Khartoum workers left Tokar and scattered in the nearby towns of Suakin, Port Sudan, and Kassala. Government attempts to track them down did not succeed. In spite of this, the governor of the Red Sea Province continued to request the CLB to dispatch laborers from Khartoum, but since the rate of pay at the Gezira was twelve piastres, Tokar was of little attraction to Khartoum workers.

The conditions under which casual laborers worked varied considerably. The wood stations on the White Nile route presented one of the most difficult working situations. Workers stayed for months in the stations established by the Steamers Department to provide firewood for the steamers. The work was arduous and involved cutting, stocking, and loading wood on the steamers, a process that could go on day and night.[89] Laborers were paid on a productivity basis. Except for a small cash advance for food, workers were given receipts that they could exchange for cash or credit when they returned to Khartoum.

Like the migrant workers elsewhere in Africa, 'ummal jabona responded to their working conditions in a variety of ways. Under these circumstances, resistance usually took on a covert—although not necessarily disorganized—form.[90] One of the most common forms of resistance was desertion. *Anadi* (drinking houses) in the Daims provided shelter for people who deserted or escaped from work. Colonial police often raided the anadi to return these runaway workers.[91] However, there were numerous occasions of organized resistance. For instance, in 1903 workers from the Forests Department went on strike. A similar action was taken by Egyptian laborers in the Steamers and Boats Department in 1907 in protest over wages. During the same year, young boys in the Fadlab agricultural estate went on strike.[92] Strike actions continued to erupt in different locations. In March 1910 the Central Experimental Farm dispatched a group of workers from Khartoum to its main site at Tayiba. These men were hired on Tuesday, 21 March, and began to work 22 March. The grain provided them was so dirty that the men refused to eat it, and they remained without food until the arrival of their wives from Khartoum.[93] On the third day, they were given five piastres each and dismissed by the clerk. They went to Khartoum to get food and returned in the evening of the same day. After three days of work the men went to the chief engineer requesting that they should be provided with shelter and twenty-five piastres for each man so that they could buy a two weeks' supply of food. Their demands were refused and consequently they stopped working and left. In May 1911 it was reported that all the workers at Tayiba had gone on strike and the government had to send troops from the Camel Corps to assist the civil police in suppressing the strike.[94] The director of works informed the assistant director of intelligence that there was very little to be done to punish deserters. Legally, the government could not do anything, as the majority of laborers were not even aware of the existence of contracts.

Employers responded by enacting rules and penalties for desertion and breach of contract, but most workers were illiterate and consequently contracts remained verbal or signed by the muqqadams. Officials of the CLB sought the opinion of legal authorities who advised that if contracts were to be enforced they should be in writing.[95] The advocate general suggested that laborers be made to affix their seal of thumb marks on the back of contracts or at least be apprised of their existence.[96]

Written contracts stipulated the length of employment, the rates of pay, work load, length of the working day, policies regarding sickness and absences, and penalties for desertion and the breaching of contracts. The contracts followed a standard form. Each would open with the statement: "we the undersigned workers agreed to work for..." and "...do whatever work, whenever, and wherever desired...."[97] The period of employment ranged from two weeks to one year.

Contracts spelled out rates of pay which varied from one employer to another. In most cases, workers would receive an advance which would be deducted from their first pay. In addition, workers were provided with a small amount of rations, blankets, and tents. Transportation was usually provided by the employer, whether it was a government department or private business. Working hours were usually long, averaging ten hours a day. In some cases employers set quotas. For instance, in 1911 the Plantations Syndicate in Zeidab required each laborer to pick a minimum of thirty pounds of cotton per day. The Railways Department set a minimum daily task of three cubic yards of earthwork.

The contracts also spelled out the penalties for breach of contract, desertion, and withdrawal from work. Any laborer who left his work before the end of the contract period would lose a substantial portion of his pay. Absence from work or feigned sickness carried severe penalties, including loss of earnings. However, if the absence was the result of real sickness which occurred during work, the laborer would receive full pay and be treated at government expense. If illness resulted from drunkenness or "immoral practice," a laborer would be responsible for any medical expenses incurred.[98]

The contracts provided the legal framework for the control and disciplining of workers in and out of the work place. For instance, workers were not allowed to make or use marisa or any other intoxicating drinks. The penalty for drinking was a fine of half a piastre; for brewing marisa, one piastre.[99] One of the most serious offenses, however, was disobedience toward supervisors or overseers, which could lead to prosecution under criminal law.

LABOR RECRUITMENT AFTER WORLD WAR I

After World War I the colonial government began to rely on tribal and religious leaders for labor recruitment. In line with this policy, the government tried to establish "tribal" hierarchies in the Daims. Residents were organized "into tribes each of which had its own section under its own sheikh [sic], the whole being under the head sheikh [sic]."[100] The creation of "tribal" chiefs in the city is an interesting aspect of colonial policy. This policy was applied in the rural areas in the 1920s and came to be known as native administration or indirect rule. It was based on the premise that African societies represent a mosaic of "tribes," each immutably living in its own environment. British officials were convinced that the categorization of people into clearly defined ethnic units would make them more manageable. It was thought that the creation of tribal leaders in the Daims would facilitate labor recruitment. In rural areas the authority of leaders was based on a complex web of family, residential, economic, or ethnic ties. However, the exigencies of urban life and its fluid ethnic composition were not conducive to this form of organization. As pointed out earlier, ethnicity was not the only binding link, and the residents of these quarters did not form clearly defined ethnic entities. Moreover, ethnic identities constantly

TABLE 5
Shaykhs of the Daims

Shaykh	Tribal Origin	Residence
Ya'qub Hamid	Berti	Daim Berti
Sulayiman Karrash	Jabalawi	Daim Sa'ad
Allahjabu Mustafa	Jabalawi	Daim Jabal
Bakheit al-Fahal	Jabalawi	Daim No.1
'Ali Bashir	Jawam'a	Daim Jawam'a
Doha Farah al-Dud	Ta'aisha	Daim Ta'aisha
Isma'il Wad Bahar	Tegalawi	Daim Tegali
Nimir Al-Zubair	Feroge	Daim al-Zubayriya
Murjan Garad	Banda	Daim Banda
Ahmad Muhammad al-Soghayir	Kanjara	Daim Kanjara
Al-'Ata al-Mahi	Kara	Daim Kara
Ya'qub Ahmad	Ta'isha	Daim Ta'aisha
Fadallah Salih	Unknown	Daim Silik
Mahmoud 'Abdullahi	Feroge	Daim Salman

shifted in response to changing political and economic conditions. Leaders in the Daims were chosen arbitrarily from the oldest residents. The shaykhs of the Daims in 1917 are listed in Table 5.[101]

The head shaykh of all the Daims was Muhammad Musa, a Ja'afri or West African who was a merchant during the Mahdiyya. After the conquest he was appointed shaykh of a small *hara* (section), and in 1916 he replaced Mursal Abu Hashish as the head shaykh of all the Daims.[102]

In 1917 the assistant director of intelligence met with several shaykhs and asked them to keep an eye on the floating population, who "come and go in the Deims [sic] without reference to any one."[103] It was recommended that "every new arrival should report to the Sheikh [sic] who could ascertain his business and be responsible to him." Those who refused to place themselves under the authority of a shaykh would be liable for expulsion. Nonetheless, these rules remained notional; neither the shaykhs nor the colonial officials were able to control the movement of people in the Daims. In brief, throughout the first two decades of this century the government failed to attract urban residents to wage employment, and labor recruitment required continuous intervention by the colonial officials.

CONCLUSION

Despite the ambivalence of the Anglo-Egyptian regime toward slave emancipation, a significant number of slaves in Khartoum were able to redeem themselves during the first two decades of colonial rule. They took advantage of the chaotic situation after the conquest, the decline of their owners' authority, their proximity to administrative headquarters, and the economic opportunities offered by the colonial economy. Urban ex-slaves pioneered the establishment neighborhoods and communities that became magnets for runaway and liberated slaves. The urban environment provided them with anonymity and an opportunity to overcome their servile past. On the other hand, urban ex-slaves faced increased pressure from the colonial officials who tried to control their mobility and usurp their newly acquired freedom while using arbitrary notions of ethnicity to establish a hierarchy among workers.

In the context of the colonial economy in which agriculture and cash crop production were emphasized, the Three Towns functioned as a labor reservoir. People left the countryside for the city to escape slavery, famine, and other disasters, and found themselves redeployed to the rural areas as laborers. This pattern persisted and was further accentuated by the opening of the Gezira Scheme, whose impact will be discussed in chapter 4.

FOUR

EMANCIPATION AND THE LEGACY OF SLAVERY, 1920–1956

F rom the perspective of this study, the decade of the 1920s was a watershed in the social and economic history of the Sudan. This era witnessed numerous changes that had a direct impact on the institution of slavery and the development of wage labor. These changes include the expansion of cash crop production, namely, cotton in the Gezira Scheme, and the withdrawal of the Egyptian Army (including its railway battalion), both of which created a great demand for technical and agricultural labor. Coupled with this was growing criticism of government policy toward slavery by some administrators and by humanitarian groups in Europe. As a result, the colonial administration began to take serious measures to eradicate slavery. This chapter examines these changes and their impact on slaves, slave holders, and the development of wage labor.

DEVELOPMENT OF THE COLONIAL ECONOMY AFTER WORLD WAR I

In chapter 2, we discussed government efforts to promote cash crop production, particularly cotton in the Gezira and in the central Sudan. Although cotton production fluctuated in the early years, its success after World War I provided a powerful incentive for further expansion. The tenancy system established earlier became a model upon which the Gezira Scheme was organized. A triple partnership involving the Sudan Government, the Sudan Plantations Syndicate, and thousands of tenants was established. The government rented cultivable land from landowners at a nominal rate of LE 1 per feddan, while landowners were given the right to become tenants.[1] The size of each tenancy was limited to forty feddans, of which ten were given to grain and fodder cultivation. The government encouraged landlords such as chiefs and religious leaders to remain on the scheme. These people played a major role in land allocation as they nominated relatives for landholdings.

The tenants were responsible for the cultivation and harvesting of cotton as well as the mobilization of labor. The Sudan Plantations Syndicate provided machinery, seeds, fertilizers, management, and marketing outlets for cotton, while the government provided water and land. The syndicate determined which crops were grown and had the right to terminate tenancy if the tenant failed in his obligation.[2] The arrangement was modified in 1929 when the government increased its share in the profit from 20 to 25 percent, and the tenant's from 35 to 40 percent, while the syndicate was given the right to expand the cotton cultivation area.[3] In 1921 the scheme comprised about 21,000 feddans, and by 1923 it reached 30,000. When the scheme was officially opened in 1925, about 240,000 feddans were irrigated. This rose to 300,000 feddans in 1926, to 682,000 in 1931, and to 852,000 in 1938.[4]

Besides the Gezira, several minor cotton schemes were established in the Gash Delta and in Tokar in Kassala Province, in the Nuba Mountains, and in the Upper Nile Province. Moreover, American cotton was developed as a rain crop in the Gedarif area.[5] The irrigated area of rain cotton increased from 73,000 feddans in 1931 to 161,000 in 1937, but declined to 137,000 feddans by 1939.[6]

In addition to the state-run schemes, the government licensed private individuals to establish pump schemes to grow cotton and food crops. The number of these private schemes rose from thirteen in the 1920s to two hundred forty-four in 1939. Owners included foreign nationals (Greek, Egyptian, Armenian, and Middle Eastern) and local Sudanese notables such as tribal leaders, religious figures, and village heads. The most prominent foreigners in the early 1920s were 'Aziz Kafouri, Muhammad Labib al-Shahid, Victor Hakim, the Fawaz brothers, B. Photinos, S. Izmirlian, Anesti Ketinas, Salim Kafori, and Mu'allim Girgis.[7] Most of their estates were near Khartoum and in the northern riverain areas. As early as 1921 these people formed an association to coordinate their efforts and to defend their interests in the competitive labor market.

Local Sudanese involved in private pump schemes included the three sectarian leaders: Sayyid 'Abd al-Rahman al-Mahdi, Sayyid 'Ali al-Mirghani, and Sharif Yusuf al-Hindi. There were also private businessmen such as Ahmad al-Birayr, Muhammad Ahmad al-Sanhouri, and 'Abd al-Moun'im Muhammad. The most prominent local landowner was Sayyid 'Abd al-

Rahman al-Mahdi, leader of the Mahdist Sect. In an attempt to win his support, the government helped him to create an economic base through land grants and honors. In 1926 he was allowed to establish an agricultural scheme at Gondal on the Blue Nile. Two years later he began a pump irrigation scheme of 200 acres at Aba Island on the White Nile.[8] During the next decade Sayyid 'Abd al-Rahman's agricultural estates expanded considerably. By the late 1930s he had acquired 6,000 acres in the Gezira and several thousand acres in Islang, Um Dom, and Saqqai, north of Khartoum.[9] To a lesser extent Sayyid 'Ali al-Mirghani, leader of the Khatmiyya Sect, followed the same course, acquiring vast tracts of land in the riverain north and Kassala, and collecting considerable dues from his followers. The greatest expansion of private pump schemes took place during and after World War II. During this period the government emphasized food crop production to meet the war demand. The completion of the Jabal Auliya Dam in 1936 facilitated the establishment of several schemes on the White Nile. From 1942 to 1943 a large scheme was opened at Khor Abu Habil in Kordofan, covering 4,000 feddans and increasing to 10,000 feddans in 1945.[10]

The number of private pump schemes increased from 372 in 1944 to 2,229 in 1957.[11] By the time of independence in 1956, the irrigated area covered by the Gezira and private schemes was 2,039,472 feddans, with 115,440 tenants.[12] Private pump schemes operated on the earlier Zeidab model. The landowners were given full control of the schemes. Their responsibilities included provision of water, loans, and 50 percent of the joint expenses. Tenants, on the other hand, were responsible for all agricultural operations, maintenance of canals, clearing fields, and harvesting. After the deduction of joint expenses and other charges, the proceeds were divided between landowners and tenants at the ratio of 60 percent to 40 percent.[13] In addition to these favorable terms, landowners enjoyed considerable power. They evicted tenants at will and manipulated the terms of the arrangements to their advantage. For instance, in order to maximize profits they often inflated joint accounts, thereby reducing tenants' returns.

Since the 1920s cotton has been the backbone of the Sudanese economy. When the Gezira was officially inaugurated in 1925, 7,800 tons of cotton were produced, realizing LE 1,637,000. Production reached a peak in 1929 when 30,500 tons were produced, realizing LE 4,583,000. To promote export, major production areas were linked by railway with Port Sudan on the Red Sea. However, the 1930s' depression coincided with natural disasters such as disease and inadequate rain, which led to a sharp decline in cotton production. The average profit per tenancy fell from

LE 55 in 1929 to nothing in 1930–1931.[14] Recovery began in the late 1930s.

The main export crop after cotton was gum arabic, produced in Kordofan, Dar Fur, and Gedarif. Between 1921 and 1925 production averaged 15,471 tons. The value of the crop in 1923 exceeded LE 1,000,000. Production rose to 19,600 tons between 1926 and 1930, but declined after 1930. Until 1931, gum arabic accounted for 34.8 percent of the Sudan's total exports.[15]

Food crops such as sorghum, sesame, and *dukhn* (bulrush millet) were also sold in export markets. However, production of these crops fluctuated and was affected by climatic factors. In 1920 about 511,000 tons of sorghum were harvested. But sorghum exports were halted in 1925 except for surplus stock from previous years. Since sorghum was the staple diet of the vast majority of Sudanese, the government had to import a large amount from India in 1932.[16]

During World War II, the Sudanese economy occupied a strategic position within a major theater of operations, and the Sudan was an important supply route. In April 1941 a Middle East Supply Center was set up in Cairo to coordinate Middle Eastern and East African imports and to increase self-sufficiency by encouraging local production. Hence the colonial authorities in the Sudan made serious efforts to encourage production of food crops on a large scale, and the government began to play an increasing role in the management of the economy. Imports, exports, and prices were controlled and austerity measures were imposed.[17] Farmers in Kordofan, Gedarif, the White Nile, and other cultivation areas were told to abandon cotton cultivation and to grow food crops. The government purchased all the produce, which led to serious food shortages and famine among farmers, particularly in Kordofan.[18]

After the war, expansion of cash crop production resumed. By 1952 the Gezira Scheme occupied almost one million feddans. New schemes established after the war included the Zande in Equatoria and al-Junaid on the Blue Nile. Between 1946 and 1952 annual cotton contribution to government revenue increased by almost LE 16 million.[19]

While the colonial regime promoted capitalist agriculture in the central and eastern parts of the Sudan, it maintained precapitalist forms of production in other areas. Most government and private schemes were based on the tenancy system. By creating this system, government officials had hoped that agricultural tasks would be carried out by family members, dependents, and followers.[20] They believed that "tribal" heads and religious leaders had access to various forms of labor—extended families,

followers, and slaves—who could be mobilized through non-market de-
vices.[21] However, this type of labor could not meet the heavy demand
during the peak season, and eventually the operation of these schemes
depended on a large supply of seasonal wage laborers. On the other hand,
traditional methods of agriculture and precolonial forms of labor organization prevailed in many parts of the country. In the riverain north, for
instance, agriculture continued to depend on saqiya irrigation, in which
slave labor had played a major role. In brief, the establishment of the
colonial economy did not eliminate slave labor. It is not surprising that
slavery and the slave trade thrived until World War II.

The commoditization of agriculture and the rise of market towns in
central Sudan reinforced the economic position of local elites such as village
heads, religious leaders, and merchants. In the White Nile Province,
Hassaniyya and Hisaynat leaders established cotton plantations, invested
their capital in the grain trade, and began to acquire slaves as laborers and
domestic servants.[22]

Slaves were obtained from the old sources in the Upper Blue Nile, the
Nuba Mountains, and south of the Bahr al-Arab through organized raids,
kidnapping, and purchase. Slave raiding was facilitated by the availability
of firearms and lack of government control of these remote regions. The
Hassaniyya, Hisaynat, and Kawahla raided inhabitants of the Sudan-
Ethiopia border area. They used the preexisting commercial network and
received large supplies of slaves from local leaders such as Khojali al-
Hasan, Sitt Amna, and other northern Sudanese immigrants who had
settled in this area since the nineteenth century.[23]

A similar situation existed in Kordofan and Dar Fur provinces, where
government control was still lax. The Baqqara continued to raid the Nuba
Mountains, Dar Fertit, and Dinkaland, and ventured as far as the Sudan-
Ethiopia border. In short, the endemic traffic in slaves and arms persisted
throughout the 1920s, though it did not reach the extent of earlier decades.
At the same time the institution of slavery continued to thrive, particularly
in Kordofan and Dar Fur. Moreover, in their attempt to appease the
volatile Baqqara, colonial administrators encouraged slaves to remain with
their owners and to return those slaves who ran away.

GOVERNMENT POLICY TOWARD SLAVERY

For a number of domestic and external reasons the Anglo-Egyptian Government began after World War I to change its policy toward slavery and

to take practical steps to eradicate it. The shift was prompted by changes in the colonial economy and by growing criticism of the colonial administration by the British Government, philanthropic organizations in England, the League of Nations, and some members of the administration itself.

After World War I the antislavery and the church missionary societies began to focus their attention on the Sudan in response to numerous reports from some local officials who began to expose government policy toward slavery. The attack was spearheaded by Major P. G. Diggle, an agricultural inspector in al-Bawga (Berber Province) in 1923–1924, and T. P. Creed, the assistant district commissioner in Berber. Creed and Diggle launched a campaign against what they considered the government's contravention of its own expressed policy. In a detailed report submitted to the governor-general, Diggle bitterly assailed the government policy and deplored the hostility of colonial officials who were, in his view, major obstacles to the process of emancipation.[24] According to Diggle, this attitude made the slaves distrustful of the government and hesitant to report their grievances to district headquarters. Diggle questioned the assumption that a sudden abolition of slavery would disrupt the economy. "I firmly believe this to be a false view," he wrote, ". . . but even if I am wrong," he continued, "I do not believe that cultivation in the Northern Sudan or elsewhere is worth the misery and cruelty that slavery involves."[25] Diggle described the plight of slaves and painted a picture totally different from that presented by other government officials. According to him, male slaves were kept working for a whole year for a bare minimum of food and clothes. The argument of administrators that masters looked after their slaves in their old age was "a demonstrable untruth, so far as the locality in which I was established is concerned."[26] Diggle also challenged the notion that, if liberated, male slaves would become idle and females would turn to prostitution. In his view, female slaves were reduced to prostitution because their masters tended to hire them out and live on their earnings. To illustrate his point, he told the story of a local boatman who tried to marry a slave woman with whom he had been living for several years. During that period he paid her master a monthly sum of money. But when he tried to marry her, the grand qadi refused. The man then appealed to the district commissioner, who refused to grant her a freedom paper despite the fact that the woman was not even registered as a slave.[27]

In an attempt to prevent a scandal, A. J. C. Huddleston, governor of the Blue Nile and Diggle's friend, tried to dissuade the latter but failed. Despite attempts to silence and discredit him, Diggle continued his campaign, especially after his departure from the Sudan. His relentless agitation brought the Sudan Government under sharp criticism from humanitarian groups and the British Foreign Office. The controversy revealed the conflict between metropolitan officials who saw slavery as an anachronism and their local counterparts who tried to ignore it. The principal defenders of slavery in the Sudan were provincial governors in the riverain agricultural districts who felt that slave labor was indispensable to the economic well-being of their provinces.

As a result of growing international pressure and internal demands for labor, the Anglo-Egyptian administration began to publicize its previous legislation regarding slavery and declared its intentions to promulgate a new circular which would accelerate the pace of abolition. However, even before the announcement of such legislation, slaveholders began to raise their voices in objection to any change in the prevailing policy. For instance, in June 1924 slaveholders at Abu Hamad mounted an unsuccessful attack on the district's headquarters to free their slaves. Further south in Dar Mali, farmers petitioned the authorities either to stop the flow of emancipation or to grant them tax relief.[28]

However, the most important defense of slavery came from the three sectarian leaders: Sayyid 'Ali al-Mirghani, Sharif Yusuf al-Hindi, and Sayyid 'Abd al-Rahman al-Mahdi. In a joint petition to the director of intelligence the three leaders appealed for caution and tact with regard to abolition.[29] They stressed the "benign" nature of Sudanese slavery, arguing that "those who work for masters were actually partners to the landowners and have many privileges and rights and cannot be called slaves." They said, again using the family metaphor so popular among apologists for slavery worldwide, that slaves were treated as members of their masters' families. The three Sayyids cautioned the government about the social consequences of sudden emancipation. In their view, male slaves would become "useless for any work" while their female counterparts would turn to prostitution. They concluded their petition by urging the government to

consider very carefully the wisdom of indiscriminate issue of freedom papers to persons who look upon these papers as granting them freedom away from any liability to work or to carry out obligations under which they stand.[30]

Despite the sympathy of senior British officials, international pressure and the need for labor were more pressing. On 6 May 1925 Circular

Memorandum No. 60-A-I on slavery was issued, and all previous circulars on the subject were canceled.[31] In the opening statement, the government defended its previous policies and reiterated its position that slavery in the Sudan would, in due course, come to a "natural" end. Furthermore, the document stated that no person born after 1898 was other than free and that no owner had the right to retain a slave against his or her will. Government officials were encouraged not to place obstacles in the way of slaves who applied for freedom, but they were also urged to reconcile owners and slaves whenever possible. District commissioners were asked to make themselves accessible to slaves and to monitor the relationship between slaves and owners. They were told to keep records of complaints and submit annual reports to their superiors.

Yet the new legislation did not satisfy either the British Foreign Office or the League of Nations, which continued to press the Sudan Government to respond to Diggle's allegations. Once again the colonial administration defended its previous policy, making a distinction between "slavery" and "domestic slavery."[32] In its attempt to rebuff allegations the Sudan Government appointed C. A. Willis as a special commissioner to collate information on slavery and pilgrimage.[33] He was authorized to examine all records and obtain all relevant information and to make recommendations that could speed the demise of slavery. Willis sent questionnaires to provincial administrators about the state of slavery in their provinces, and he visited most of the northern provinces. The findings were compiled in a long report submitted to Sir John Maffey, the governor-general, in 1926.

Willis recommended that special attention be given to Kordofan, Dar Fur, and the Abyssinian border region where slave raiding was still rampant. Most important, however, was his recommendation to reform the Islamic courts, which placed great obstacles in the way of female slaves seeking their freedom. Nevertheless, Willis echoed his colleagues' fear of freed slaves moving to towns and becoming idle or involved in crime. "Manumission by itself," he wrote,

> is often of little value, and some "follow up" system is needed to ensure the establishment of the manumitted person in conditions which will not involve either a descent into a life of crime or a lapse back into servitude.[34]

As a result of continuous pressure from the League of Nations and the Anti-Slavery Society, toward the end of the 1920s, the Sudan Government began periodically to publicize its legislation and submit reports to the league.

At the same time the government began to take active measures to suppress rampant slave trading and arms smuggling. A massive campaign was launched in 1928 in the Upper Blue Nile, the White Nile, and the Bahr al-Arab regions through the mobilization of police and the monitoring of the trade routes. Hundreds of slave dealers were convicted and imprisoned, including Sitt Amna, who was sentenced to fifteen years' imprisonment in Wad Medani.[35] Similar actions were taken in the Nuba Mountains. In 1928 over 1,000 slaves were retrieved, 200 slave traders were convicted, and 200 firearms were confiscated.[36]

Coupled with this was the enforcement of the Passports and Permits Ordinance, which had been introduced in 1922 and was used to declare many parts of the Sudan closed districts to nonresidents. These areas included parts of Dar Fur, Kordofan, Kassala, and the Blue Nile provinces as well as the south, and the Nuba Mountains.[37] Although the measure was intended to check the spread of Islam and the Arabic language, it became a useful tool in the government campaign against the slave trade.

In 1929–1930 the Anglo-Egyptian regime announced its "southern policy." A brand of native administration, southern policy aimed at curtailing the spread of Islam and the Arabic language in the southern Sudan. Measures were taken in the early 1930s to evict northern Sudanese administrators and traders from the south and to control population movements between the north and the south.[38] The task of rolling back northern influences from the south involved total demographic, political, and social restructuring. It resulted in the eviction of a large number of people who were perceived as major vehicles through which "alien" influences were disseminated. This category included northern traders as well as Hausa, Borno, Dajo, Sara, Bergo, and Wadaians. In order to prevent any further spread of northern influences, the region had to be sealed off from Dar Fur and Kordofan, and physical contact between its inhabitants and those regions was prohibited through the creation of a buffer zone between Bahr al-Ghazal and Dar Fur. Finally, the remaining population of the western district of Bahr al-Ghazal was moved further south and settled along government roads.[39] Such measures enabled government officials to have some control over these volatile regions and to curtail slave dealing.

While government antislavery campaigns greatly reduced slave dealing activities, they did not eradicate them completely. Occasional kidnappings and abductions continued. In 1932, for instance, ninety-three freedom papers were issued in the Funj Province to children kidnapped from Ethiopia and the upper Blue Nile. In 1940 eleven cases of kidnapping were reported. In another case two men were arrested, one of whom was sentenced to five years' imprisonment and a fine of LE 15.[40] During the same year a boy was kidnapped from French Equatorial Africa, which led to the conviction of five people. The perpetrators were nomadic Arabs from Kordofan who had habitually attacked the caravans along the pilgrimage routes between the Sudan and West Africa.

SLAVES, SLAVE OWNERS, AND EMANCIPATION

The response of slaves and slave owners to the colonial economy and to government measures varied considerably. This variation was an outcome of the uneven impact of colonial economic policies. In this respect northern Sudanese provinces may be divided into three broad categories. The first category consisted of the Gezira, Gedarif, and Kassala, where cash crop production was promoted. The second category consisted of the northern riverain provinces of Dongola and Berber. The last category included Kordofan and Dar Fur provinces.

By the 1920s the Gezira region emerged as the economic hub of the Sudan. Expansion of cotton production created an unprecedented demand for agricultural labor and attracted many people (slaves and free) from other parts of the country. By 1921 it was estimated that ex-slaves constituted one-third of the unskilled labor force on the scheme. They worked as woodcutters, canal diggers, and cotton pickers.[41] The scheme opened many opportunities for slaves in the Blue Nile Province, as many of them either became tenants, established crop sharing arrangements with their former owners, or became wage laborers.[42] Still, many others joined the ex-soldiers' settlements in the province, where they became a source of labor.[43] At the same time some slave owners hired out their slaves to other tenants and appropriated their wages.[44] In short, establishment of the Gezira Scheme accelerated the pace of emancipation of male slaves in the Blue Nile Province. For example, in Rufa'a District, 1,082 slaves were registered in 1912. By the mid-1920s the number of people in servitude had declined by about 70 percent.[45]

In the riverain provinces of Dongola and Berber, land shortages and poor economic conditions continued to drive people out of those areas. The majority went to the Gezira, Kassala, Tokar, and Gedarif regions. For instance, by the mid-1920s the slave population in the Halfa area was less than 500, as against an estimated 9,000 at the turn of the century.[46] In Dongola, the massive exodus of slaves threatened agricultural production and alarmed provincial officials, who tried to stop labor recruitment in the province.[47] Loss of slave labor forced farmers to make adjustments by mobilizing family labor or establishing sharecropping arrangements with their former slaves.[48]

Farther south in Berber Province, Diggle's campaign and the introduction of mechanized pump irrigation accelerated the pace of emancipation. Moreover, because of its proximity many slaves from Berber drifted to Atbara, the headquarters of the railway, particularly after the departure of the Egyptian Army Railway Battalion in 1923.[49] By the mid-1920s only a small percentage of the slaves—mainly women—remained in the province.

While socioeconomic transformation accelerated the pace of emancipation in the Gezira, Kassala, and the far north, Kordofan and Dar Fur lagged far behind. A combination of economic and social factors ensured the continuation of slavery and slave raiding. Kordofan's population consisted of a multitude of ethnic groups who pursued various economic activities. The southern part of the province was inhabited by several groups of Baqqara cattle herders such as the Missairiyya and Humr, who also practiced cultivation. The northern part was settled by the nomadic groups such as the Kababish and the Kawahla. The eastern part was inhabited by the Nuba who were a major source of slaves for local inhabitants and outsiders. Among the Baqqara the slaves were left in charge of cultivation while their owners pastured cattle. Among the Kababish and the Kawahla nomads the slaves were used mainly as cattle herders.

Baqqara social customs guaranteed the continued dependence of former slaves. It is important to point out that manumission was not uncommon among the Baqqara. The slave among the Humr was usually freed through ceremonies in which the owner would verbally proclaim him free. He would then be escorted on horseback around the neighboring camps, and be given presents and livestock. Once freed, the male slave and his offspring would be regarded as members of the clan. Moreover, the prevalence of concubinage created a permanent bond between ex-slaves (especially females) and former owners.[50] Yet the integration of ex-slaves into the kinship groups of their former owners remained superficial. Former slaves were still considered inferior members of the lineage and still found it hard to marry freeborn women.[51]

The existence of blood ties between slaves and slave owners led colonial administrators to believe that "the conditions of slaves in Kordofan is [sic] on the whole better than elsewhere, they have their own house and family life, and get clothing and the like from the master."[52] Hence, these officials invariably returned runaway slaves and pressured those who gained manumission to remain where they were.[53] The official attitude was reflected in the number of freedom papers offered to slaves between 1912 and 1925. During this period, only 364 slaves were officially freed in the northern district and 429 in the western district.[54] It is not surprising, therefore, that in 1925 there were still 25,000 slaves in Kordofan as against an estimated 40,000 in 1900.[55]

The existence of many ex-soldiers' settlements in the province attracted a large number of runaway and liberated slaves. In the mid-1920s there were several ex-slave settlements in the Eastern District and at Melbis, south of al-Ubayyid.[56] During the 1920s many slaves from Dar Missairiyya settled on vacant lands or on lands given to them by their former owners. Other slaves left Dar Missairiyya altogether and settled as farmers around Talodi in the southeastern part of the province.[57]

Despite the fall of 'Ali Dinar in 1916, farther west in Dar Fur slavery remained an integral part of life, particularly among the Rizaiqat, the Ta'isha, and the Habbaniyya in the Bahr al-Arab region. Despite growing discontent and streams of applications for manumission by slaves, colonial officials continued to discourage manumission. As in Kordofan, social and economic ties ensured continuous dependence of ex-slaves.

In summary, while cash crop production opened many opportunities for slaves in the Blue Nile Province and attracted many others from the riverain north, their counterparts in Kordofan and Dar Fur would remain in bondage for many years to come.

ARMY EMPLOYMENT AND COLONIZATION SCHEMES

As we have seen in chapter 2, many ex-slaves were absorbed into the Sudanese units of the Egyptian Army and were settled in agricultural colonies after their discharge. These settlements continued to be magnets for many runaway and liberated slaves. However, the transformation of these quarters was viewed by officials as a sign of social decadence that would lead to prostitution and criminal activity. Consequently, the colonization scheme was reevaluated in the early 1920s and some modifications were introduced. The revised scheme was based on the same principles as the previous one. However, admission into the colonies was limited to soldiers who had completed eighteen years of service. Moreover, the selection process would take place at the beginning of the cultivation season in April so that the settlers would commence cultivation immediately after their discharge.[58] The new scheme also included a free trip from the place of discharge to the colony, a new tax remission system, and free medical treatment. To ensure discipline and control, the colonization schemes were linked with local auxiliary military units.[59]

Following the governors' meeting in February 1920, the civil secretary wrote to all provincial governors inquiring about the possibilities of settlements in their provinces.[60] On the basis of their responses new sites were selected in Kordofan, Kassala, the Nuba Mountains, the Blue Nile, the White Nile, Sinnar, the Upper Nile, and Bahr al-Ghazal Province. The choice of these sites was based on the availability of freehold agricultural land. For this reason, the Red Sea, Khartoum, and Dongola provinces were excluded. By 1923, there were about twenty-three colonies with about 2,000 ex-soldiers.[61]

However, by the late 1920s settlement of ex-soldiers was abandoned. It was during this period that the government began to apply the system of native administration. According to the official view, the effective application of this principle in the southern Sudan, the Nuba Mountains, and other non-Muslim areas entailed checking the spread of Islam and preserving local cultures. Therefore, it was hoped that ex-soldiers who came from those areas would return rather than settle in "detribalized" colonies. Most important, however, was the changing political climate in the Sudan in the early 1920s and the mutiny of the Sudanese units of the Egyptian Army in 1924.

The influence of Egyptian nationalism in the Sudan was manifested after World War I. Among the various political organizations that emerged was the White Flag League which was founded by 'Ali 'Abd al-Latif, an ex-army officer of slave parentage. His father had been in the Mahdist jihadiyya, had escaped to Egypt, and returned to the Sudan with the Anglo-Egyptian Army. The White Flag League raised the slogan of "Unity of the Nile Valley," and began to call for the Sudan's independence and unity with Egypt. The organization established branches in several Sudanese towns and attracted Sudanese officers and civil servants. In 1923–1924, the White Flag League held demonstrations in various towns, the most important being that of the Military School's cadets in August 1924. These protests convinced the British that the evacuation of the Egyptian Army was an urgent matter. Although this goal had been on the agenda for several years, the opportunity occurred after the assassination of Sir Lee Stack, the governor-general of the Sudan and sirdar of the Egyptian Army, on 19 November 1924 in Cairo. This was followed by the British ultimatum to the Egyptian Government which demanded the immediate evacuation of the Egyptian Army units from the Sudan. Subsequent events have been dealt with elsewhere in detail and need not be repeated here.[62] Suffice it to say that in reaction to the ultimatum, the Egyptian Army units in Khartoum North refused to carry out the evacuation orders. In solidarity with their colleagues, Sudanese battalions in Khartoum, Omdurman, and Talodi decided to rise up against the government and stage a mutiny. It was eventually suppressed and the ringleaders were executed. By the end of November the evacuation of Egyptian troops was completed, and shortly after that the Sudan Defence Force was created. While the mutiny of the Sudanese battalions has been considered an expression of nationalist sentiment,[63] there were indeed other factors at work. Most prominent among those were occupational grievances. Since the early 1920s senior British officials had begun to raise questions about the cost of the army, and many of them had expressed their desire to disband the Sudanese battalions and limit the promotion of Sudanese officers to a rank no higher than warrant officer.[64] Another factor was the lack of financial security for discharged officers. Their only options after being discharged were manual labor or unemployment. This had become a major source of discontent that pushed them toward the White Flag League. During the disturbances, discharged officers provided the link between officers on active duty and the civilian population.[65]

Viewed from another angle, the 1924 incidents involved the question of allegiance, which was a major factor in the system of military slavery. Officers of Sudanese battalions tried to remain loyal to their patron, the king of Egypt, and against the British.[66]

Sudanese units paid a price for their loyalty to their Egyptian patrons. Immediately after the mutiny, the Eleventh Sudanese Battalion was disbanded and the remaining units were absorbed into the Sudan Defence Force. However, even these units were gradually eliminated, and by 1927 they had been completely phased out.[67] The new Sudan Defence Force was organized on a territorial basis as the country was divided into five military areas: Northern, Eastern, Central, Southern, and Western. Recruits were obtained locally from each area. In 1926 the Sudan Defence Force had an establishment of 127 British officers, 41 British noncommissioned officers, 188 Sudanese officers, and 7,963 Sudanese in the ranks. The Sudan Defence Force was designed to be a small force that would be responsible for the maintenance of internal security. Hence, the process of reduction continued and by 1936 its total strength was 4,854 men.[68]

The disbanding of the Sudanese battalions of the Egyptian Army and the subsequent reduction created an enormous problem of unemployment. The demobilized soldiers and officers began to petition the authorities for employment. While the uneducated elements were employed as messengers, ghafirs (watchmen), gatekeepers, and janitors with government departments, their educated colleagues had great difficulty finding jobs.[69] As a result, a military labor bureau was established in 1927 and entrusted with the task of finding employment for discharged soldiers. In view of the demand for technical labor, most of the officers and skilled soldiers were employed in the Sudan Plantations Syndicate, The National Bank of Egypt, and the Sudan Light and Power Company. Fearing that the unemployed ex-servicemen might organize themselves and cause further disturbances, the government created reserve units in which these men could be absorbed. Twelve companies were raised, each consisting of 130 reservists under the command of a retired officer.[70] The reservists were called up annually for two weeks' training. They received a small retaining pay, which was increased during the training period. The combined pay varied from LE 3 per annum for soldiers, to LE 5 per annum for noncommissioned officers. The units were stationed in Singa, Kassala, Gedarif, Kosti, al-Ubayyid, Talodi, Wau, and al-Fashir. By doing this, the government intended to establish a measure of control over discharged soldiers and provide them with an income.

While the majority of the people from the lower ranks in the Sudanese units were dispersed in different Sudanese towns, the officers tended to congregate in the Three Towns, particularly in Omdurman. Their preference for Omdurman can be attributed to the fact that most of them had relatives in the city since the days of the Mahdiyya.[71] For example, following the 1930 retrenchment scheme that involved eighty officers who had been part of the Sudanese battalions of the Egyptian Army, forty-eight expressed their desire to settle in Omdurman. Most of them were of Dinka, Shilluk, and Nuba origin, or were from other southern and western Sudanese groups.[72] They established their own quarter in the city, which came to be known as *hay al-Dubbat* (officers' quarter), as well as their own club. In view of their training and close association with Egyptian officers, these Sudanese ex-officers were easily assimilated into the Egyptian culture and way of life. This is evident by their speech, dress, life-style, and political orientation. Many of them later joined pro-Egyptian political organizations.

The recruitment of ex-slaves into the army continued after the formation of the Sudan Defence Force. As mentioned earlier, the new force was organized on a territorial basis and each unit was recruited from the local population of the area in which it was stationed. This arrangement was more convenient for ex-slaves who wished to enlist in the army but who did not want to travel long distances. Yet the size of the army remained very small until the late 1930s when it expanded considerably as a result of the Italian presence in Ethiopia and the outbreak of World War II. The Sudan Defence Force had risen from 4,582 men in 1939 to 30,000 men in 1944. A military school was opened in Omdurman in 1936, thereby creating a greater degree of professionalism. One of the most important developments, however, was the creation of mechanized units in the Sudan Defence Force. By 1937, six companies had been mechanized. The mechanization process was particularly important, for it facilitated the training of local soldiers and helped them to acquire technical skills that proved to be useful after their discharge.

A significant portion of the new recruits were ex-slaves who were able to take advantage of government policy toward slavery. Sudanese troops fought against the Italians in Ethiopia and were sent to Libya, Palestine, and Egypt. Through their travel and association with people of different nationalities, they were exposed to political ideas and attitudes which had many implications. In the first place, through military training, thousands of these servicemen acquired trades. They became motor drivers, fitters, telegraph operators, etc. Following demobilization many ex-soldiers joined the labor force, filling jobs that required technical skills. Most important, some of those most active in the trade union movements that emerged in the postwar era were demobilized soldiers, especially those who had obtained technical skills.[73]

Ex-slave soldiers were responsible for the dissemination of many cultural traits from their home areas into the northern Sudan. It has been suggested that the introduction of *zar* (spirit possession) in North Africa was associated with southern Sudanese who were recruited into the Turco-Egyptian Army.[74] Zar is both a category of spirits and the cult associated with possession by those spirits. Such possession can cause problems or illness, usually a form of mental illness. Many of the rituals of the zar ceremonies are directed at controlling such disorders. Healing is enacted through possession of certain distinct spirits under the guidance and leadership of a shaykha. Patients become actively possessed by a defined spirit; while in this state they impersonate the supposed characteristics of the possessing spirit in behavior, dress, movement, and sometimes, speech. The whole procedure is carefully controlled and orchestrated by the leader, who derives his or her knowledge and power from traditions. Many of the recurrent themes and terms in zar, such as *sanjak* and *brigadir*, appeared to have been derived from the army. Ex-slave soldiers made significant contributions to the growth of urban popular culture in various Sudanese towns, particularly in the field of music. According to Juma'a Jabir, these ex-servicemen pioneered the performance of indigenous music using Western instruments.[75] While in the army, many of them had been trained in brass instruments commonly used in military bands. In order to understand the contribution of ex-soldiers to the development of modern Sudanese music, it is important to trace the origin of military bands.

Military bands were an integral part of the Turco-Egyptian Army in the nineteenth century. The best known were *al-Musiqa al-Bahriyya* (Naval Band), *musiqa al-Bolis* (Police Band), and Beringi and Kingi musiqa.[76] Before the British occupation of Egypt, military bands were trained by an Italian instructor named Boba Bey. However, when these bands were reorganized after the British occupation, Boba was replaced by a British instructor, and two schools of music were established in Cairo.[77]

The first Sudanese military band was created in 1897 when two infantry staff bands were sent from Halfa and Suakin to Cairo to receive instruction. However, the British felt that members of these units were too old and discharged them. Shortly after that, thirty-eight young Sudanese boys were sent from the Wadi Halfa area to Cairo for training. These boys formed what came to be known as the Sudanese Frontier Band. They were trained in brass instruments, and within one year they were able to play various musical instruments. Their performance impressed British officers who described them as "the best in the Egyptian Army."[78] Sudanese bands continued to receive training in Cairo until 1912 when a school of music was established in Omdurman. At the same time, several musical bands were created within the Sudanese Battalions of the Egyptian Army.[79]

Colonial policies of military recruitment resulted in the concentration of people from the same ethnic group in each unit. Hence, each unit performed a march based on musical tunes or songs from its home area. This led to the emergence of, for example, a Shilluk March, a Banda March, a Binga March, a Baqqara March, and so forth.[80] After their discharge, these ex-servicemen lived in the Radif settlements. From the Radif quarters and ex-slave settlements a form of dancing known as the *Tum Tum* emerged and became popular in many Sudanese towns. The Tum Tum can, therefore, be regarded as a blend of folk tradition and martial music. The contribution of these ex-slave soldiers involved a process of modernization and indigenization. The Radif quarter in Kosti, for example, produced performers such as 'Abdullah wad al-Radif and the Tomat (the first female performers in Kosti). Also among these pioneers in Kosti were Adam Rayhan and Sabt.[81] Retired soldiers also taught music classes and formed the backbone of the orchestras that dominated the performing arts in many Sudanese towns after World War II.

EMANCIPATION OF FEMALE SLAVES

While the colonial economy and postwar reforms had created many opportunities for male slaves, they had little effect on female slaves. Indeed, only a few slave women took advantage of legislation and gained manumission by bringing their cases before civilian administrators. These fortunate few happened to live in districts such as Berber, where officials were more sympathetic to their cause. These were exceptions; the vast majority of female slaves remained in bondage for many years to come. Unable to stop the departure of male slaves, owners devised several strategies to prevent the emancipation of female slaves. If a slave woman who had children was granted freedom by a district official, a male owner might simply take the case to a Shari'a court and claim paternity of the children, and the qadi would often grant him custody. This practice was one of the main issues that Diggle and Creed in Berber Province had raised in their protest. But senior administrators continued to warn against indiscriminate manumission of slave women, arguing that such action would create a class of bastard children. They also emphasized the "tangible benefits" of Muslim law with regard to concubines.

However, the period of the late 1920s witnessed a great deal of debate among senior administrators over the issue of concubinage and child custody. It was agreed that conflicts between officials and Shari'a judges regarding slaves should be referred to the legal secretary and the grand qadi.[82] Moreover, the grand qadi agreed to modify the rules with regard to the children of slave women. Since, theoretically, no person (male or female) born after 1898 was legally in a state of bondage, all children must, therefore, either be born in wedlock or be considered illegitimate. Thus, no master could claim the child of his slave woman unless he claimed her as his own wife.[83]

This was followed by legislation of which the most important was Shari'a Circular No. 34 of December 1932. This circular authorized the Shari'a courts to raise the maximum age of *hadana* (the right of the mother, grandmother, or other female relative, to the care and custody of the children) beyond the age of seven for a boy and nine for a girl. It is important to point out that this legislation had already been introduced in Egypt a few years earlier. However, the Sudan reform went further and instead of raising the maximum age by only two years, it followed the Maliki school, which makes the age of hadana puberty for a boy and marriage for a girl.[84]

In another attempt to limit the jurisdiction of Shari'a courts over slavery cases, the government began to refer some of these cases to native administrative courts. These courts were created in the early 1930s to apply customary law. The Native Courts Ordinance of 1932 created several categories of courts: a native court, with a shaykh (tribal head) as president sitting with members; a shaykh's court comprising a shaykh and a *majlis* (council of elders); a village court; and a shaykh's court of one shaykh sitting alone.[85] These courts were empowered to administer the customary law prevailing in the area or within the ethnic group over which the court exercised its jurisdiction, provided that such native law and custom were "not contrary to justice, morality, or order." It was assumed that the jurisdiction of these courts did not normally include the application of Shari'a law, unless the Shari'a might have influenced or replaced customary law in any particular locality. However, the warrants and orders establishing some of these courts, situated far from any Shari'a courts, expressly authorized them to deal with matters of personal status under Islamic law, provided that they had an *'alim* (a learned man) sitting as a member of the court.[86] As it turned out, the procedures of these courts became a combination of the Shari'a and customary law, and the former was invariably applied in slavery cases. Thus, this legislation did not bring any improvement in the status of female slaves.

As late as the mid-1930s, slave women were unsuccessfully petitioning local authorities for their freedom, particularly in Kordofan and Dar Fur. This can best be illustrated by the case of Amna bint Ahmad, a Bergo woman from Dar Fur Province. Amna had been kidnapped in 1916 by Kababish Arabs and sold to 'Abdallah Adam of the Majanin tribe in the neighboring Kordofan Province. While she was away in the desert looking after her master's camels, she met a male slave, became his mistress, and bore him three children—one daughter and two sons. Owing to harsh treatment by her master, Amna decided to run away to al-Ubayyid in 1932, where she submitted her complaint to the Omda (Native Administrator). However, when her master found out that she was living in al-Ubayyid, he called upon the Omda to return her. As she refused to return, her master, with the help of the Omda, took away her children. Amna then took the matter to the district commissioner who ordered the return of her children. With the Omda's help, the owner was able to bring the matter before the Shari'a court, alleging that Amna was his wife and the children were his.

The court ruled in his favor and granted him the custody of the children.[87] Amna had no alternative but to bring her case before the authorities in Khartoum. In March 1934 she wrote to the civil secretary pleading for the return of her children. The civil secretary requested the governor of Kordofan Province to investigate the matter. The governor replied that as long as the Shari'a was immutable, there was very little he could do. In his opinion,

> The shari'a law is the law of the country in these cases and the only way to avoid conflict between administrative decision and shari'a decision was for administrative authorities not to give decisions which are likely to conflict with shari'a law.[88]

The civil secretary told Amna that if she wished to pursue her case, she should appeal to the grand qadi.[89] Official records do not mention how the case was finally resolved.

Another tragic case occurred in 1934 in Kassala Province where the district commissioner refused to allow a liberated female slave to reside in town, fearing that she would become a prostitute. He returned the woman to her Rashaida owners who killed her as a deterrence to others who might seek their own freedom.[90]

Perhaps the most daring step by the government to erode the authority of the Shari'a courts was the promulgation of Shari'a Circular No. 46 of 25 April 1936. Section 1 of this circular stipulated that certificates of freedom given by administrators to slaves should have no effect on a prior marriage, although a woman to whom such a certificate was given was to be regarded as thenceforth free, with all that this involved, by the Shari'a courts. Section 2 stated that neither the courts nor the *madhun* (marriage officer) was to register a marriage contracted on behalf of a woman by anyone in the capacity of her owner unless she was herself present, willing, and a party to the contract.[91] Section 3 stated that the courts should not entertain any plea about the marriage of an ex-slave woman to her former master, to his children, grandchildren, or former slaves, or to any other relative unless the marriage was proved by an official certificate, and the woman concerned was present, willing, and participant in the contract. And in just the same way the courts should not entertain any plea of marriage contracted by a man on behalf of a woman in the capacity of her owner except as provided in Section 2. Similarly, Section 5 decreed that the courts must not entertain any claim of inheritance on the grounds of ownership, but that any such claim lay in the exclusive competence of the province governor. Section 7 decreed that if any dispute arose regarding slavery in the Shari'a courts it should be referred to the competent authority, namely the district commissioner, and the Shari'a court should rule on the basis of his decision. Section 8 stated that the Shari'a courts should administer the rules applicable to freeborn people in every case concerning the following matters: dowry; restitution of conjugal rights; custody of children and the mother's right to take her children from one town to another; wages for custody; suckling and maintenance; proof of divorce; judicial divorce or failure of maintenance; fear of adultery; cruelty or disease; appointment of an executor; legacies and gifts; requests for decrees of putative death; or inheritance.[92] Section 9 stipulated that where the subject of a suit was anything other than the above, and one of the parties was formerly a slave, the court must refer the matter to the grand qadi before it gave its decision. These provisions represented a departure from the prevailing policy and provided safeguards against the exploitation of slaves, particularly females. Nonetheless, they had little impact in the rural areas. As late as the 1940s and even the 1950s, masters in remote provinces continued to defy these rules and to devise strategies to retain their female slaves.[93]

While the vast majority of male slaves gained manumission by the Second World War and found opportunities in wage employment or moved to towns, many female slaves remained in bondage. For instance, in Berber Province in the mid-1920s, 70 percent of the female slaves remained with their owners, as opposed to 45 percent of males.[94] Even those who gained manumission had limited choices: they could move to another village; they could migrate to towns and engage in prostitution or sell drink; or they could remain in their villages and maintain close ties with their former owners, who continued to be their patrons. As elsewhere, manumission did not end the ex-slaves' needs for membership in the society that enslaved them. Undoubtedly the majority of former female slaves, who lacked education and the skills to find wage employment, had no option but to remain near their owners' families. In the riverain north they earned their living by performing hard menial jobs such as grinding and threshing wheat and sorghum during harvesting season, in return for a small percentage of the produce.[95] Some of them hired out their children to work for local farmers, while others lived on the outskirts of the villages where they sold drink. However, a few ex-slave women received formal education and embarked on pioneering careers such as teaching, or nursing. In this respect, these fortunate few were better off than freeborn women who faced great difficulties in gaining access to education and employment.

MANUMISSION AND THE LIMITS OF EQUALITY

One of the most important questions that faced former slaveholding societies in the West in the postemancipation period was the economic and social status of ex-slaves and their descendants. For former slaves in the Sudan, as elsewhere in Africa, abolition did not automatically lead to social and economic equality. A central question to be raised, then, is what *did* freedom mean to ex-slaves in economic and social terms?

Ex-slaves did not form a separate class, but were scattered across the social and political spectrum. Some moved to the cities and became part of a heterogeneous working population, while others remained in the rural areas and engaged in farming or pastoral activities. Still, a few gained educational skills, joined the civil service, or enlisted in the army. In other words, ex-slaves became involved in relationships with other groups in the lower rung of the social hierarchy.

The status of former slaves depended on the political and social structures of the slaveholding society and the degree to which outsiders had been integrated into it. In this regard the condition of ex-slaves and their descendants varied from one part of the Sudan to another. A fundamental issue is the extent to which ex-slaves gained access to land and other resources.

In the riverain areas north of Khartoum, arable land was limited. As pointed out earlier, all saqiya-irrigated land was privately owned. It was inherited by family members according to Shari'a rules. This meant that outsiders such as nomads and ex-slaves could not have access to saqiya land. The only option these groups had was crop sharing.

Social stratification in the riverain areas was reflected in residential patterns. For the most part, villages consisted of kinsmen (extended families, distant relatives, and affines), while those not kin such as nomads, *halab* (gypsies), and ex-slaves lived on the periphery.[96]

Each village community had a hierarchy within the *ahl al-balad* (village residents) who were considered *ahrar* (free). The original owners of the land were at the top, and below them were the "Arabs" (nomads). Below the Arabs were the halab who specialized in blacksmithing. At the bottom were the *'abeid* (slaves) and their descendants, as well as the *khalit* (racially mixed). The ahl al-balad were the dominant group on the grounds of their *asl* (origin). A central element in social differentiation was land ownership. It is worth mentioning that land had lost most of its economic value but until now it remains a symbol of prestige and of "good" origin.[97]

In certain villages, such as Nuri and al-Qurair in Meroe District, physical separation of those not kin to each other is quite evident. The ahl al-balad built their houses directly adjacent to the Nile River; beyond them were the dwellings of those living on saqiyas, or waterwheel-irrigated lands. Next to the saqiyas were the slave houses, followed by the shacks of the nomads who lived on the fringes of the village. The majority of ex-slaves congregated in their *ruwakib* (straw huts) at a distance from their former owners. However, the Nile flood of 1946 destroyed houses and forced residents to move farther away from the riverbanks. Yet the same residential pattern continued. For example, in al-Qurair ex-slaves settled in a separate quarter called Dakkam. At neighboring Mussawi Island, ex-slaves moved across the river and established a separate community in Nagazu. In his study of Nuri, Ahmad al-Shahi has described the conditions of ex-slaves and their descendants.[98] In the early 1970s Nuri had a total population of 4,104 out of which 287 were ex-slaves and their descendants. The majority of the 'abeid in Nuri lived on the *jabal* (hill) on the outskirts of the village. A few individuals owned land or had date palm trees that were given to them by their masters. Ex-slaves continued to maintain social obligations toward their former masters. On social occasions such as marriages, naming ceremonies, circumcisions, or funerals, the former slaves rendered help and their presence was expected. Publicly and directly, Nuri people do not refer to the 'abeid as such, but in private they may refer to an individual as *'abidna* ("our slave").

The official abolition of slavery did not alter the social and ideological structure that produced and supported servitude, although it perhaps made status distinctions more subtle. As mentioned previously, many people in the northern Sudan have adopted an Arab identity and have constructed genealogies tracing their origins to an Arab ancestry. They devised strategies to distinguish themselves from ex-slaves and, for that matter, from other groups such as the "Arab" and the halab.[99]

Since the criteria of color and wealth sometimes lost validity, the villagers defined slave status in terms of behavior. To them slaves were the purveyors of immorality and the worst human traits, which to this day are usually referred to as *akhlaq al-'abid* (slave manners). Although the majority of slaves and their descendants are Muslims and speak Arabic, they are still considered as merely displaying a veneer of Islam. This is reflected in folklore and popular culture. For instance, in one of the zar songs, a slave accompanies his owner to Mecca and Medina, but the effects of this pilgrimage are lost upon him. Moreover, the 'abid spirit was considered to cause a most serious and prolonged zar-inflicted ailment.[100] Indeed, the portrayal of slaves as vicious, untrustworthy, and dishonest is common in classical Arabic literature.[101] In northern Sudanese schools, children learn the poetry of Al-Mutannabi (915–965 A.D.) about Kafur al-Ikhshedi, the Nubian eunuch who became the regent of Egypt in the tenth century. Al-Mutannabi described slaves as mean, immoral, and submissive. He wrote:

> The slave is no brother to the Godly freeman, even though he be born in the clothes of the free. Do not buy a slave without buying a stick with him, for slaves are filthy and of scant good.[102]

In the central and eastern parts of the Sudan where land was abundant, ex-slaves occupied vacant lands and built viable agricultural communities. This was particularly the case in the Nuba Mountains and in the Gedarif area.

Slaves among the Humr of southern Kordofan were manumitted through ceremonies and were given a small number of livestock. However, in many parts of Kordofan ex-slaves found it hard to establish their economic independence. Following the introduction of cash crops, the Missairiyya and the Humr tried to deny their former slaves access to fertile land. For instance, when the Missairiyya moved from the northern part of their territory to the fertile south in the 1920s, they left their land in the hands of their former slaves. However, a few decades later, the Missairiyya decided to return and began to cultivate sesame and groundnut as cash crops. In the process, they tried to expel their former slaves from the land they had been cultivating for many years.[103] Similarly, the Humr tried to monopolize gum trees and denied their ex-slaves access to this crop.[104]

On a social level, despite the existence of blood ties between slaves and their owners, ex-slaves and their descendants did not become full members of Humr society.[105] The Humr do not distinguish between slaves and other non-Arab and non-Muslim groups such as the Dinka, their neighbors across the Bahr al-Arab. The term ʿabd (singular of ʿabeid) was used to refer to a wide range of people such as slaves, pawns, and any Dinka or Nuba. However, when a Dinka adopted Islam, or had been living among the Humr, he would be referred to as *jengayi*, to distinguish him or her from a non-Muslim Dinka.[106]

Further west in Dar Fur, ex-slaves of the Rizaiqat and the Habbaniyya were known as the "Bandala" or "Mandala." The Bandala lived in independent communities on both banks of the Bahr al-Arab. In Dar Fur they were known as Mandala and in the Bahr al-Ghazal as Bandala, both terms referring to a particular kind of dance.[107] Their presence in the Bahr al-Ghazal dates to the eighteenth century, when a few groups of slaves had escaped from their Rizaiqat owners and sought refuge with the Feroge and the Nyagulgule. In the Bahr al-Ghazal the Bandala eked out a living by fishing and hunting and acquired a reputation as excellent elephant hunters. They were organized in semiautonomous settlements under their own headmen who were controlled by the Feroge shaykhs. The Bandala paid half of their tusks to the Feroge sultan in return for protection and patronage. The Feroge could not demand any work from the Bandala, for the latter could always threaten to cross the river into Dar Fur. Using the same tactic against the Rizaiqat, the Bandala were able to maintain their autonomy. On the other hand, the Feroge made arrangements with the Baqqara by which the latter agreed to recapture and return runaway Bandala, while the Feroge promised to return any slave who might escape from the Rizaiqat.[108] Despite living in autonomous colonies at some distance from the Baqqara, the Bandala continued to recognize their ties to former masters. A modified, if loose, social and political connection was maintained between the two groups.

Following the announcement of southern policy, provincial officials in the Bahr al-Ghazal and Dar Fur made relentless efforts to evict the Bandala from the Bahr al-Ghazal and settle them with their former owners. Because they were Muslims, their presence in the south was undesirable. But the mobility of the Bandala and their ability to conceal their identity rendered the application of these measures impossible.[109]

The most important area in which ex-slaves and their descendants are still handicapped is marriage. Although marriage within the same ethnic group is encouraged throughout the Sudan,[110] ex-slaves and their descendants still find it hard to marry freeborn women, particularly in rural areas where people are expected to marry within the paternal line, preferably from the family of a father's brother, though the marriage of matrilineal parallel cousins is also desirable.[111]

Although marriage across ethnic and class lines has become common in urban centers and among educated groups, intermarriage with ex-slaves or their descendants is still considered undesirable by many Arabic-speaking northern Sudanese.[112] This prejudice is supported by Shari'a rules, which insist on *al-kafa'a fil zawj* (equality of standard in marriage). According to the Hanafi school of jurisprudence, the groom must be equal to the woman's family in religion (both Muslims), occupation, asl (family genealogy), property, and freedom from bondage. The Maliki school, on the other hand, maintains that equality in religion is the sole criterion.[113]

One of the most publicized cases of marriage across social lines occurred in 1973.[114] It involved a young educated couple. As her legal guardian the woman's father objected, arguing that the fiancé was of slave origin, and, therefore, he was not equal to his daughter. Furthermore, the father and his relatives threatened to kill the woman if she insisted on marrying him. The woman applied to the Khartoum North Shari'a Court asking the court to give her permission to marry, to remove her father as guardian, and to restrain him.[115] She insisted that the fiancé was equal to her in every respect. However, her father's lawyer claimed that the fiancé was of slave origin; therefore, he was not *kufu'* (equal) to her family. The court then rejected her application and upheld the father's right as guardian to withhold his consent to the marriage.

Through an advocate, the woman appealed to the Province Court, which overturned the lower court's decision. However, informally the court tried to convince the woman to withdraw her appeal to remove her father as guardian, and urged her not to marry a man who was rejected by her family. When she refused both, her father appealed the court's decision to the Shari'a High Court, emphasizing the lack of kafa'a. Although the High Court upheld the Province Court's decision and allowed the couple to marry, the court deliberation was intriguing. The principle of kafa'a was not challenged. Rather, the decision was based on the fact that the woman's father could not prove that her fiancé was of slave origin. The court maintained that since the fiancé had a university degree, he was equal to her. Furthermore, the judges cited the Prophet Muhammad's saying which stressed the equality of all Muslims regardless of their race or ethnic origin. Finally, the court maintained that slaves in the Sudan were obtained through purchase, kidnapping, and raiding. Since these methods were not sanctioned by the Shari'a, slavery in the Sudan was illegal.[116] In general, though, manumission did not change the social status of liberated rural slaves who continued to be regarded as socially and culturally inferior.

Of particular importance is the way in which the term 'abeid persisted. This term is used in a much broader sense than the literal meaning of enslaved persons; it also implies a quasi-racial category referring to all non-Arab groups. In other words, the term 'abd seems to be in continual flux. This illustrates the changing nature of the ideology of slavery in the northern Sudan. In chapter 1, we have seen how this ideology emerged among the Arabic-speaking northern Sudanese. It was closely associated with the adoption of an Arab identity and the creation of certain notions about non-Arab groups. Enslavement occurred, in part, from the imbalance in political, military, and economic power between the two groups. This imbalance persisted under colonial rule. Economic and educational resources were concentrated in the central and northern Sudan, while the southern and the western parts of the country were neglected. In precolonial times these areas functioned as slave reservoirs for northern Sudan and the outside world. In the twentieth century, they became a backwater and a source of cheap labor. Hence the conditions that produced the ideology of slavery were maintained under colonial rule.

This raises a question: How did ex-slaves react to this situation? Unfortunately the available evidence does not provide an adequate answer. In general, in the rural areas, where ex-slaves suffered most from the badge of slavery, the younger generation tended to leave the localities altogether. As a result, the number of ex-slaves and their descendants in many parts of the riverain north is diminishing rapidly.[117] In some cases ex-slaves tried to organize themselves and defend their interests. For instance in Nuri (Meroe District), ex-slaves organized themselves in the early 1950s under the leadership of Sa'id al-Mahi. Sa'id established a *khalwa* (Quranic school) and brought a *faki* (teacher) to teach their children. After his death, the khalwa was abandoned and the movement ended. However, in the urban centers ex-slaves established more advanced political organizations, a subject that will be examined in chapter 6.

CONCLUSION

The interwar period was a time of momentous socioeconomic changes in the Sudan that accelerated the pace of slave emancipation and the development of wage labor. These changes included the expansion of cash crop production, the growing international pressure on the Anglo-Egyptian Government, and the withdrawal of Egyptian civilian and military personnel. These changes prompted the colonial government to take active measures to abolish slavery. While many male slaves were manumitted, their female counterparts remained in bondage for many years.

Although slavery persisted, its demise was eminent by World War II. Nonetheless, official abolition neither changed the prevailing social values, nor did it improve the social status of ex-slaves and their descendants.

FIVE

THE DEVELOPMENT OF THE LABOR FORCE, 1920–1956

～

Two important developments during the interwar period had a critical impact on the growth of the wage labor force. The first was the opening of the Gezira Scheme in the mid-1920s and the expansion of cash crop production. The second was the withdrawal of the Egyptian military and civilian personnel from the Sudan in 1924. While the former generated an unprecedented demand for agricultural laborers, the second accelerated the growth of the industrial work force, particularly in the railway department. This chapter examines these developments and focuses on colonial labor recruitment policies; the character of the labor force that emerged, particularly its segmentation along occupational and ethnic lines; and the development of the labor movement after World War II.

COLONIAL LABOR POLICIES: PRECEPTS AND PRACTICES

Chapter 2 examined the conceptual framework through which British officials approached the question of labor. From the beginning, colonial administrators conceived of economic roles in ethnic terms. In vain they tried to sort Sudanese people into distinct ethnic categories, each with specific qualities pertaining to labor. Accordingly, the Arabic-speaking northern Sudanese were viewed as lazy and averse to heavy manual labor. On the other hand, non-Arabs were considered energetic and suitable for hard menial work. With these convictions, administrators proceeded to recruit laborers. Their approach was best described by Jay O'Brien's phrase: "if one knows a person's ethnic identification, one could fairly reliably predict what form her or his incorporation would take, including type, pattern, and intensities of work."[1]

In reality, ethnicity and economic roles did not correspond neatly. In the first place, ethnic boundaries and ethnic identity were so fluid that they defied any rigid classification.[2] The degree to which each group participated in wage employment depended on its social and economic conditions and the need for cash. While some groups became dependent on wage labor, others did not seek it except on certain occasions such as crop failures, famine, or to meet special expenses. However, colonial officials explained these differences in cultural and ethnic terms. To illustrate this point, it is useful to examine the case of Nuba workers in the sanitation service.

In the absence of modern sewage facilities in many Sudanese towns during the early years of this century, waste was gathered in buckets which were removed from latrines by conservancy workers at night. Buckets were taken away on large lorries to collection stations outside the towns where they would be transferred to tram trucks and then taken to trenching grounds. It was a hazardous job involving a great deal of risk.[3] Bucket removal usually took place between 6:00 P.M. and 6:00 A.M. Clearance usually took about twelve hours, but during rains the men worked for twenty-four hours.[4]

In the early days of colonial rule, workers for the conservancy were recruited from released and runaway slaves. However, this source began to evaporate as many ex-slaves shied away from it. The government then resorted to prison labor, meaning that the collection took place during the day, which was a nuisance.[5] In order to attract workers, municipal authorities in Khartoum increased the daily wage to nine piastres but this did not have the desired result. The labor shortage was so severe that the authorities seriously considered abolishing the whole system. However, sanitation officials were relieved when Nuba immigrants in the capital (particularly the Tira and Nima groups) began to take these jobs. This led to the assumption that only Nuba people could perform this task. They were described as "young, strong, and quick with the result that the system was run by a small number."[6] However, the continuous supply of Nuba workers for the conservancy was threatened when the government announced its Southern Policy in 1929. In theory, the essence of that policy was to check the spread of Islam and the Arabic language into the non-Muslim parts of the Sudan which included the south, some parts of Dar Fur, and the Nuba Mountains. This required limiting contacts between them and northern Sudanese Muslims, and prohibiting their immigration to the north. Indeed, the Nuba figured prominently in this scheme. In line with the new policy, their presence in the north was considered undesirable and

TABLE 6

Ethnic Origin of Sanitation Workers

Sudanese [slave] and southern "Negroid"	35
Fur and western non-Arab tribes	28
Arabs [nomads]	19
Fallata	8
Danaqla	6
Ethiopians	1

the government began to draw up plans to repatriate them. The governor of Kordofan Province wrote:

It is our policy here, with which you [governor of Khartoum Province] are generally in agreement, to build up a Nuba civilization on Nuba cultural lines. I am convinced that the authentic Nuba has a future before him, while the detribalized Nuba is in general neither a credit to his stock nor to the government.[7]

The governor went on to suggest that departments should not recruit Nuba laborers, and that governors of northern provinces should endeavor to "round up" and repatriate Nuba who were out of work.[8] The civil secretary wrote to the governors of the Blue Nile, Berber, Funj, Kassala, Khartoum, and White Nile provinces requesting them to discourage Nuba settlements in their provinces and send back to Kordofan any unemployed Nuba they could find.[9] However, as it turned out, the Nuba presence in these provinces was not vital to their sanitation services. Consequently, the civil secretary inquired about the number of Nuba as well as non-Nuba employed by the sanitary services, their rates of pay, and whether or not they had a supply of non-Nuba potential workers.[10]

According to the returns, in the Funj Province there were no Nuba in the sanitary service; the conservancy was carried out by prison labor. The only potential recruits were the Gumus, a non-Arab group who lived east of the Rosayris district.[11] In Berber, only twelve Nuba were employed in the sanitary service out of a total of one hundred nine workers. The ethnic origins of these workers are listed in Table 6.[12]

The rate of pay was 120 to 170 piastres per month. In Kassala Province the total number of Nuba employed in the conservancy was seven (two in

Kassala and five in Gedarif).[13] There were twenty-nine non-Nuba, most of whom were Halenga, Beni 'Amir, Borno, and Fur. In the White Nile Province there were three Nuba out of a total of eight workers. The rest were Dinka, Fur, Fertit, Hamaj, and Bergo. However, the strongest objection came from the governor of Khartoum Province who responded:

> In theory we are in complete accord as regards policy but as the natives of Khartoum will not undertake that part of conservancy work dealing with bucket cleaning and as Nubas are at present the only source of labor supply for it, my agreement can only be in theory and I cannot take any practical steps to dispose of Nuba labor.[14]

On previous occasions, the chief sanitary inspector in Khartoum had explored the local labor market for this job but found that while people were willing to take up other types of jobs in the Sanitation Department, they avoided the conservancy. Even the depression of the early 1930s and the high rate of unemployment in the Three Towns did not convince people to seek work in the conservancy. They were willing to take up other jobs which paid three or four piastres per day rather than the twenty piastres in the conservancy. The inspector cautioned that if immigration from the south and the Nuba Mountains was halted, the entire conservancy system in the capital would collapse.

After a great deal of discussion among senior officials, and in view of the acute shortage of conservancy workers particularly in Khartoum, pragmatism prevailed and the authorities decided not to pursue the repatriation of Nuba. J. A. Gillan informed the governor of Khartoum:

> For the time being we must leave it that you will do everything you can not to increase the proportion of tribal Nuba laborers in the sanitary service, and to replace it by other labor whenever possible. Detribalized Nuba of course do not matter, except in as far as they may form a nucleus for fresh immigrants.[15]

Although the Nuba sanitation workers were allowed to remain in the north, British administrators remained faithful to the official policy and continued to discourage migration from the south, including the Nuba Mountains and other areas to the north.

FORMATION OF AGRICULTURAL LABOR

The operation of the various agricultural projects established during the interwar period required the creation of a reliable supply of wage laborers, so that the Gezira Scheme exacerbated a shortage of skilled and unskilled labor that had been a problem for many years. The construction of the scheme involved two gigantic operations. The first was the building of a dam at Makwar, the digging of canals, the erection of buildings, and the leveling and development of 300,000 feddans. These tasks were entrusted to the Sudan Construction Company which was later responsible also for the construction of the Jabal Auliya Dam. The second operation (the irrigation phase) was to begin in 1925 and was undertaken by the Sudan Plantations Syndicate. Hence, these two companies began to compete for the limited labor supply.

Labor recruitment during the first decade of colonial rule was conducted through the Central Labour Bureau which became dormant by World War I. In 1921 the CLB was superseded by a Labor Committee, chaired by the director of agriculture. Unlike its predecessor, the Labor Committee did not intervene directly in the recruitment process. Rather its role was limited to the coordination and provision of general guidelines.[16] The labor market conditions that had prevailed in the prewar years continued to persist as the majority of the rural population was still reluctant to enter the wage labor market. The southern provinces were excluded from recruitment for political reasons, while the available manpower in Kordofan, Kassala, the Blue Nile, the White Nile, and the Red Sea provinces was absorbed locally. What remained were the Dongola, Halfa, and Berber provinces. However, colonial administrators in these food-producing areas were not willing to lose their vital agricultural labor force to the Gezira. Moreover, the demand for labor in the Gezira coincided with the harvesting of the largest grain crop ever known in the country. At Tokar, owing to a record crop of cotton, there was also an exceptionally heavy demand for cotton pickers. Another factor that strained the supply was the cheapness of dura in the 1921 season and, therefore, there was little incentive for the people to earn cash.

In the beginning, the Sudan Construction Company was given a free hand to recruit labor from the northern provinces. However, the Sudan Plantations Syndicate maintained that the work on the Makwar Dam and the main canal should be done by imported labor so as "to leave Sudan labour for other subsidiary works."[17] It further argued that since the Gezira Scheme was "an undertaking designed essentially for the benefit of the Sudan," and the Jabal Auliya dam was constructed "almost entirely in the interest of Egypt," the former should be given priority in labor recruitment,[18] a position that was supported by the Labor Committee. Then the question of the respective claims of the construction company and the syndicate for local labor was raised. In the committee's view, the completion of the Gezira Scheme was an urgent task, but it cautioned that "it is against everyone's interest that there should be competition between these two parties for a supply which is insufficient to meet the requirements."[19] The Labour Committee lamented the fact that the two companies did not discuss with each other the problem of supply and the rates of wages. Moreover, there was strong evidence that the Gezira's works were attracting essential labor from the food-producing areas north of Khartoum. In 1921, for instance, the Nuri agricultural station in Meroe District reported that a large number of men were drifting from the area to Makwar where they were paid ten piastres per day as well as being given free transportation.[20] Similar complaints were voiced by the governor of Berber Province and private employers in Khartoum.[21] As a result, the Labor Committee strongly recommended that recruiting in Khartoum and the northern provinces, including the Red Sea Province, should cease—a recommendation that was typically unenforced. But the committee conceded that the drift of people from the north to the Gezira was inevitable, but that it could be "restricted to a certain extent by providing that wages paid in the Gezira, though sufficient to attract local and southern labor, should not be high enough to draw in large numbers from the northern provinces."[22] On the question of wages in the Gezira, it was suggested that they should be based on current wages in the northern Sudan and should not exceed seven piastres per day. Finally, the Labor Committee proposed that a permanent conference or a joint committee should be set up, to include representatives from the government, the Irrigation Department, the Sudan Construction Company, and the Sudan Plantations Syndicate, to deal with the question of labor and wages. These suggestions were never implemented. The construction company continued to offer higher wages on the grounds that the cost of living in the Makwar area was higher than in Khartoum. Yet even if wage control had succeeded and the methods of recruitment had been improved, the labor shortage would have remained. The vast majority of the population were still reluctant to enter the wage labor market. The Labor Committee saw no prospect of improving the supply and conceded that "for the next five years, until the dams were completed, labor shortage will be a dominant factor in the economic situation" and that the "Sudan must reconcile itself to a permanent labor

TABLE 7

National and Ethnic Origin of Laborers at Makwar, 1921

Europeans	406
Egyptians	9,525
Yemenis	868
Sudanese:	
Danaqla	854
Ta'isha	240
Fallata (from Kordofan)	787
Local Fallata	611
Local Sudanese	4,786

difficulty."[23] In the meantime, it was hoped that private contractors in the Gezira would import their own workers from Egypt.

Despite the belief that foreign labor was expensive, Egyptian, Yemeni, and Ethiopian laborers were used extensively on various government projects during the first two decades of British rule. In 1921 there were more Egyptian workers than Sudanese at Makwar. European labor was also used, especially in technical positions. In the early 1920s, the contractors of the Sudan Construction Company made relentless attempts to recruit Ethiopian laborers as well as Italian artisans. But the importation of European workers had its own drawbacks: when an agent of the company approached the British Government to facilitate the recruitment of 300 stonecutters from Italy, there was a fear that "men with dangerous Bolshevist and socialist tendencies" might be introduced into the Sudan.[24] Hence, a British consul in Italy was instructed to make "enquiries about each man before granting visas." Tables 7 and 8 detail the nationalities of workers employed by the Sudan Construction Company at Makwar and Jabal Auliya in 1921.

TABLE 8

Ethnic Origin of Workers at Jabal Auliya, 1921

Europeans	49
Egyptians	2,667
Fallata (from Kordofan)	320
Local Sudanese	290

However, this official classification must be read with caution. For example, the term Dongolawi sometimes refers to people from Berber Province and other districts in the northern Sudan. There could be many Shaiqiyya, Ja'aliyyin, Manasir, etc., among them. In 1921, 2,000 people reportedly left Berber Province and some 11,000 left Dongola Province for Tokar and the Gezira.[25] Poor economic conditions in the riverain provinces continued to drive both the slaves and freeborn farmers out of these provinces. Hence it is safe to assume that the 4,786 workers classified as local Sudanese and Dongolawis included runaway and liberated slaves.

The company adopted differential wage rates and made a distinction between native and foreign workers. The daily wage for an Egyptian worker was fifteen piastres, for a Yemeni fourteen piastres, for Sudanese ten to twelve piastres, and for women seven to eight piastres.[26] These differences were justified on the grounds that foreign laborers were more efficient than locals. Sudanese workers were used in cutting, brick making, fetching, carrying for masons, and various low-grade jobs. They also worked under different conditions. Their contracts were usually for seven months, and if they left on their own accord or for reasons of disobedience or poor health, they were required to pay the contractor the amount advanced to them and the railway fare. They were also expected to bring food sufficient for forty-five days from the date of their arrival, and after that, they were to buy their supplies from the company's stores.[27]

The company's dependence on expensive Egyptian labor could not continue indefinitely. The bill for importing Egyptian labor was LE 150,000 in 1921, LE 153,000 in 1922, LE 147,000 in 1923, and LE 144,000 in 1924.[28]

From the government's perspective, what was needed was a landless Muslim population that would become totally dependent on wage employment. In this regard, West African immigrants and settlers were perceived as the ideal solution. These landless immigrants were considered more industrious than local Sudanese.[29]

THE WEST AFRICAN SOLUTION, 1925–1955

West Africans appeared as laborers on the Gezira Scheme during the early decades of colonial rule. Following the opening of the scheme in the mid-1920s, colonial officials engaged in a heated debate over West African immigration and settlement. While some officials such as Arthur Huddleston, governor of the Blue Nile Province, and officials in the Gezira, favored their settlement on the scheme, C. A. Willis vehemently opposed it, arguing that it would arouse the hostility of the Arabic-speaking landowners.[30] It was decided that West Africans would be settled in separate colonies under their own shaykhs.

Figures for West African immigrants in the Sudan were based on estimates. As mentioned in chapter 2, the oldest of these settlements was Mai Wurno on the Blue Nile. This settlement's population increased from 4,000 in 1912 to 42,000 in 1937.[31] Continuous immigration gave rise to several settlements in the fertile regions of Gedarif, Gash, and Kassala.

West African communities were by no means homogeneous. There was a distinction between the old established settlers and newcomers. Most of the old immigrants were members of the Sokoto nobility. Some of them had resided in the Sudan for several generations and were known as *mawalid* (born in the Sudan). Newcomers were settled on vacant land and engaged in cultivation of maize and groundnut. During the slack period they supplemented their income with fishing or sought wage employment on the scheme.[32] Social distinctions among West Africans proved to be useful for labor recruitment. It was from the old residents that tribal heads, village shaykhs, and labor agents were selected. For instance, in the 1920s, Mai Wurno's political and economic position was strengthened by the colonial government. Like Sayyid 'Abd al-Rahman al-Mahdi, Mai Wurno was given land and titles and became a major collaborator with the regime.[33]

While the West African immigrants were welcomed by relieved government officials, they faced increased hostility by local tenants. This was due to the fact that officials used them to discipline tenants. Any tenant who failed to meet his obligation would be replaced by an immigrant. Indeed, this happened during the depression. As cotton profits declined, many local tenants either abandoned their plots or left them to hire agents or relatives and returned to their previous farms where they grew food crops. The scheme's authorities responded by evicting such tenants and replacing them with West African immigrants who did not hesitate to fill these vacancies.[34] However, because of local hostility toward them, many of the West Africans were given small plots on the peripheries of the scheme.

The tendency of the Gezira tenants to hire workers to perform agricultural tasks has generated an endless scholarly debate. A number of scholars considered this attitude a vivid manifestation of the legacy of slavery in Sudanese society. They argued that the Arabic-speaking tenants still have a "slave-master mentality" and an inherent distaste for heavy manual labor.[35] Accordingly, West African migrant workers were seen as natural replacements for slaves.[36] However in a recent study, Abbas Abdelkarim rejected this view and offered a different explanation for the attitude of the Gezira tenants. He argued that, in view of the low yields and fluctuations of farming income, the tenants engaged in nonfarming activities such as trading and wage employment in towns. Furthermore, the large size of the tenancies and the labor-intensive cotton production required additional labor resources that could not be met by the tenant household.[37] As pointed out earlier, the attitude of various Sudanese groups toward wage labor was determined by their local economic conditions, and, above all, by the uneven pattern of capitalist development in the country. Mark Duffield has argued that the comparison between the "Fallata" and slaves is misleading since the "Fallata were slaves not to any person but only to their dependence on wage labor."[38] The high productivity of the Fallata had little to do with innate qualities or physical characteristics but can be explained by their social and economic conditions. These landless immigrants had no choice but to become wage laborers. The immigrant worker had to work hard to earn a certain sum of money in the shortest possible time so that he could proceed on pilgrimage to Mecca or return home to get married or settle down.[39]

Besides West Africans, the sedentary and nomadic populations in the White Nile Province came to form an increasingly important part of the migrant labor system. In addition to nomadism, White Nile Arabs practiced cultivation during the rainy season for subsistence purposes. The opening of the Gezira Scheme provided them with opportunities to earn cash. They were induced by tenants who offered them fodder plots as part of their wages. This meant that the nomads could earn cash without jeopardizing their nomadic activities. However the vast majority of the nomads preferred to cultivate their own land if the rains were good rather than become laborers.[40] Therefore, from the government perspective, the nomads were unreliable and less productive than West Africans. It was reported that while the nomad would not work after ten or eleven o'clock in the morning, the West African would continue working until two or three o'clock in the afternoon. Moreover, the West Africans' implements were more efficient for weeding, especially during the rainy season in the Gezira.[41]

Nonetheless, local tenants continued to prefer nomads to West Africans. In addition to being subject to racial prejudices, West Africans were considered to be a source of criminal activity and a menace to public security. Tenants preferred to hire less hardworking locals with whom they could establish patron/client relations and create long-term obligations.

The government also tried to establish a monopoly over the labor supply. In this regard other economic activities that might compete with the Gezira were suppressed and attempts were made to curtail recruitment activities of private estate owners. The most important of the latter was Sayyid 'Abd al-Rahman al-Mahdi. As the leader of the Mahdist Sect, he commanded a virtually unlimited supply of free labor from his followers, who believed that working for the Sayyid would bring them baraka (blessing). For example, during the winter of 1939 it was reported that the Sayyid employed 170 workers on his schemes in Islang, Um Dom, and Saqqai, north of Khartoum. These workers received no pay and lived in squalid conditions. Government officials complained that this gave the Sayyid an "unfair advantage in competition with other pump schemes."[42] They urged that he should be instructed to limit this type of labor and provide decent accommodations for laborers. The Sayyid was told to release all his laborers with the exception of technicians.[43]

During World War II, the Gezira enjoyed an abundant supply of laborers, prompting colonial officials to comment that Western labor was almost "a drug on the markets in the Gezira."[44] By that time many Sudanese groups sought wage employment. The promotion of capitalist agriculture and the integration of the remote parts of the country into the cash nexus created massive dislocation. In Kordofan, for instance, the introduction of cash crop production increased competition for land, consolidated the position of local elites, and displaced many people. Cash needs increased as more and more people began to depend on markets for their subsistence. Moreover, the establishment of agricultural schemes reduced grazing areas for the nomads. Poor rains in 1940 and 1941, and the government policy of purchasing and storing grain during the war, created famine in parts of the west.[45] As a result many people began to migrate in search of wage employment. Gradually a system of labor migration between the Gezira and the western Sudan emerged.[46] The cotton picking season, between January and April, coincided with the slack period of grain cultivation in the central Sudan. It was during this period that the vast majority of immigrants flocked to the Gezira from Kordofan, the southern Blue Nile, and Gedarif, by lorries, railway, and on foot. In moving to the Gezira during the picking season, farmers would leave their land to relatives or their immediate families. As the demand for work in the Gezira began to decline in late April, immigrant workers would return home to cultivate their land.[47] As Mark Duffield has pointed out, the entry of the western Sudanese into the labor pool changed popular conceptions of the term Fallata. Gradually the term was applied to a wider category of people and was no longer limited to West Africans.[48]

However in 1943, the situation began to change and the Gezira experienced its most serious shortage of labor on record. Successful grain crops in the Blue Nile Province, and high wages, gave laborers a good bargaining position. The number of daily laborers dropped from 136,000 in 1942 to about 83,000 in 1943.[49] The labor shortage can also be attributed to demand elsewhere, particularly in Kassala and Gedarif.

In an attempt to attract laborers, the Labour Board suggested that the government should allocate additional quantities of consumer goods to the areas of agricultural production to stimulate the need for cash. Additional recommended measures included the use of "local coercion" and the utilization of the Local Government Ordinance which permitted compulsory labor on works of public utilities for a maximum of ten days a year. Provincial governors were empowered to remove surplus workers from their provinces and send them to the Gezira.[50] Railway facilities were to be provided to encourage West Africans and other western Sudanese to settle in the Gezira. In this regard the Sudan Railways expressed a desire to reduce the 50 percent surcharge for a period of six months and reduce fares to the Gezira stations. The Labour Board recommended the establishment of low rates, for large parties of workers in special coaches, to be taken and distributed to tenants provided that they could be prevented from getting off the train at "unauthorized" stations en route. Licenses were given to civil and military recruiting agents through their provincial headquarters.[51]

After World War II, West Africans began to face increasing hostility, which was expressed in the Sudanese nationality laws enacted in the late 1940s. According to the 1948 ordinance, "Sudanese" was defined as any person who had been a resident, or whose ancestors resided, in the Sudan before the conquest in 1897. The 1956 law empowered the minister of the interior to naturalize any person who had resided in the Sudan for the previous ten years, provided that he or she was of "good character" and spoke adequate Arabic.[52] Various groups of Sudanese nationalists opposed granting citizenship to West African residents, particularly in the Gezira. The main motive behind this opposition was to deny them access to tenancies. Colonial officials in the Blue Nile Province also discouraged the naturalization of these people. In 1952, the Gezira Board, which took over the management of the scheme, decided that non-Sudanese tenants would be allowed to retain their tenancies only until they died, deserted the land, or were evicted, after which tenancies would be given to local Sudanese.[53] These restrictions resulted in the outward migration of many West Africans from the Gezira, and their migration to the Sudan declined greatly in the postindependence period.

The decline of West African immigration happened at a time when cash crop production in the Sudan expanded considerably, particularly between 1950 and 1975. The growing demand for labor was met by participation of various Sudanese groups who had not been previously incorporated.

CASH CROP PRODUCTION AND
CLASS FORMATION

The promotion of capitalist agriculture brought about a spectacular social transformation in rural areas. Indeed, the process of class formation and relations between tenants and agricultural laborers in the Gezira and elsewhere has generated a great deal of controversy.[54]

A central element in the debate over the process of class formation in the Gezira was the economic position and political role of tenants. According to some scholars, tenants were small employers who appropriated surplus value and exploited seasonal laborers.[55] These scholars point out that despite their precarious position, tenants were better off than seasonal workers who occupied the lowest rung on the ladder of social hierarchy. The wages of migrant workers varied from year to year and from season to season. Their pay was low and they lived in squalid conditions.

Recent studies, however, have emphasized the heterogeneity of tenants and argued that only a small percentage of them derived the bulk of their income from surplus value.[56] These studies divided the Gezira tenants into three broad categories on the basis of tenancy size. Big tenants owned 30 feddans or more. The vast majority did not work on their plots but relied on hired labor and pursued other economic activities such as trading and providing credit to smaller tenants.[57] In addition to hiring workers, big tenants could mobilize kin and exploit former slaves by paying them low wages.[58] The second category included middle tenants, who owned between 11 and 30 feddans. They usually worked on their plots but hired labor during the peak season. They constituted 41 percent of the Gezira tenants. The third category were small tenants who owned between 2 and 10 feddans and did their own work through family labor. Many of them supplemented their income by working as wage laborers in towns during the slack period.[59] Although Abbas Abdelkarim has rejected the categorization of tenants on the basis of the size of their plots, he nonetheless has emphasized the fact that most of the Gezira tenants drew their income from nonfarming activities.[60] The bulk of the tenants worked for the scheme's management and the colonial state. They were required to perform certain tasks and had no say in production or financial management of the scheme.

At the same time, their return was fixed at a certain percentage and was affected by fluctuations of cotton prices.[61] As Norman O'Neill put it:

> The principal contradiction is not between tenant farmers on the one hand and migrant laborers on the other, but between all these producers of surplus-value and the small class of wealthy tenants and commercial capitalists who utilize the neo-colonial state to exploit them.[62]

Conflict between the Gezira tenants and the colonial state culminated in the 1946 strike, which grew out of the tenants' frustration and suspicion over the financial management of the scheme. Following the strike, and with the help of the Sudanese Communist Party (SCP), a tenant union was created in the early 1950s.[63] The union waged a political campaign against the colonial government and the incipient agrarian bourgeoisie to get more favorable terms for the tenants. It continued to maintain close links with the SCP and engaged in fierce battles against the postindependence Sudanese governments until the early 1970s, when its radical leadership was suppressed by Numeiri.

THE DEVELOPMENT OF THE INDUSTRIAL LABOR FORCE

Throughout the colonial period, the Sudanese economy was dominated by agrarian production, and any activities that might compete with the Gezira Scheme were discouraged. Hence, little attention was given to industrialization. With the exception of a few government departments such as the railway and public works, the size of the industrial work force was insignificant. The greatest expansion in this segment of the labor force occurred after World War I, mainly in the Railway Department.

Until 1924, the Railway Battalion of the Egyptian Army provided most of the labor at its headquarters in Atbara and on the railway line. The rationale behind the use of military personnel in the railways was that it was much easier to staff the stations in the desert with soldiers than with civilians, who would require married quarters.[64] In addition to their wages, Egyptian soldiers were provided with uniforms and rations free of charge. They were trained in telegraph work, plate laying, blacksmithing, and other technical skills.[65]

In 1913 the Railway Battalion had 27 officers, 19 clerks, and 2,429 men. By the end of World War I, the number had declined to about 2,000. Table

TABLE 9
Egyptian Railway Battalion

	Officers	Men
Headquarters	10	261
Traffic	3	461
Engineering	11	996
Workshops	3	285
Civilian clerks (watchmen)	3	123
Total	27	2,126

9 shows the distribution of the workforce among the various railway departments in 1923.[66] The last major undertaking by the engineering division was the Haiya-Kassala line which was completed in 1924.

The cost of Egyptian labor was too high, as each Egyptian conscript cost about twice as much to maintain as a Sudanese civilian. Total cost of the Egyptian Railway Battalion was LE 67,767 in 1923, or LE 16,000 more than the cost of comparable civilian labor.[67] Yet in the official view, the "superior" physical strength and military discipline of the Egyptians was worth the cost. However, as pointed out earlier, the presence of Egyptian personnel in the Sudan was considered to be undesirable as they were viewed by British officials as nationalist agitators. Hence, beginning in 1923, steps were taken to reduce Egyptian personnel in the railways. During the same year, the 385 Egyptian engineering troops working in the Mechanical Department at Atbara were reduced to 285. In the wake of the 1924 incidents the British decided to dispense with the service of the Egyptian Railway Battalion altogether.

The removal of the Egyptian Railway Battalion created a great demand for labor, especially in Atbara. This provided an unprecedented opportunity for released and runaway slaves from the neighboring areas such as Berber, Darmali, Abu Hamad, and in faraway areas such as Karima and Dongola.[68]

However, the filling of skilled posts—especially in the Traffic Department—which were abruptly vacated was not an easy task. Until the mid-1920s organized training for technical labor was given by the Department of Manual and Technical Training at Gordon College and the Omdurman School for Stone Masons, founded in 1907. In 1924 a school for metal-workers was established at Atbara and eight years later the remainder of the class was amalgamated with the Omdurman school which became a building trades school for masons, carpenters, joiners, bricklayers, and tinsmiths.[69] In 1924 the Railway Department opened a school for various metalworking trades. There was also an engineering school, where instruction was given in Arabic by Sudanese and British locomotive inspectors. A school of marine engineering at Khartoum North Dockyard and an electrical engineering school with a branch at Port Sudan were also opened. These schools aimed at producing enginemen, electricians, and chargemen. Later on, new trades such as chromium plating and tool-and-press works were introduced. The Traffic Department of the railways also established a school devoted to the theory, practice, and demonstration of railway traffic operation.[70]

One of the most urgent tasks was the training of Sudanese train drivers. In this regard, the railway officials gave preference to those whose parents were railway employees, on the grounds that trainees were familiar with the railway atmosphere.[71] At the beginning, British engineers had a low opinion of local recruits and were apprehensive of their ability to learn. According to a British engineer,

> One is confronted with a number of young natives who begin with a fundamental horror of hard or sustained effort of any kind, little idea of discipline, complete ignorance or indifference to the most obvious signals of mechanical distress, and a temperament unfitted to anticipate danger.[72]

Because of this perception, local recruits went through a rigorous training program.

The first step was to train them as engine cleaners. The usual age for entering this service was between seventeen and twenty. At this stage recruits were given a grounding in safety regulations and were introduced to the various parts and workings of the locomotive. They were kept in the workshops receiving frequent instruction, individually and in classes. The period of training for engine cleaning was one of probation and instruction. Transfer during this period was avoided as much as possible to maintain stability. When the cleaner was ready for promotion to fireman, he would be tested. If his three months' probation was satisfactory, he would be certified by the locomotive inspector and would be promoted as soon as a vacancy opened. He would then spend several years as an engine-shunting fireman, and again as a main-line engine fireman. While the cleaner's training was more general, the fireman's training was more specialized and directed toward encouraging the individual fireman to get the best results from his own engine.[73] As the fireman became due for promotion to engine driver, his training would be broader and more theoretical. He would have, at that stage, already mastered most of the General Rule Book of the Engine Drivers. There were, in all, no fewer than 313 rules occupying 171 pages, and the prospective driver was required to know them thoroughly and be able to apply them. When the fireman passed his test, he would be ready for promotion to shunting driver, and finally main-line driver. At each promotion he would qualify for a higher scale of pay. The first group of Sudanese engine drivers was produced in 1930. Their performance was hailed and there were virtually no accidents.[74]

Training skilled workers also required familiarity with the technical vocabulary. The prevalence of foreigners in the Railway Department had shaped the language used in the work place. The official language of the railways and the steamers administration was Arabic. All internal accounts and all correspondence, except with non-Arabic-speaking foreigners, was conducted in Arabic. Almost all the administrative and technical staff used English as a second language. In the railway posts, where almost all of the senior officials were British (of whom only a few were literate in Arabic), many internal rules and regulations were printed in English and Arabic.[75]

At the end of 1931, the Railway and Steamers Department had about 11,857 workers, of whom 10,996 were Sudanese.[76] However, of the 1,147 clerical and technical staff, there were 457 Egyptians, 396 Sudanese, 254 British; the rest were Greek, Syrian, Maltese, Armenian, etc.[77]

Another government establishment which was affected by the withdrawal of the Egyptian Army was the Military Works, responsible for construction of all government buildings throughout the country. In 1924 it was abolished and its remains were absorbed into the Public Works Department.

Despite government attempts to change the situation, foreign skilled workers were still dominant. After World War I, the number of foreign artisans increased, particularly after the collapse of the Ottoman Empire. Some skilled workers from Asia Minor, Greece, and Armenia came to settle in the Sudan, especially in the Three Towns.

The slow progress in the growth of skilled labor was also seen in the development of clerical employees and civil servants. Between 1925 and 1929 the number of Sudanese employed by the government increased by 50 percent, and in 1930 their total exceeded that of all other nationalities combined. Sixty-four percent of their total of 2,750 were employed in technical and semi-technical departments. Of the total number of so-called classified staff (clerical and civil servants) in 1930, including the army, 50 percent were Sudanese, 23 percent Egyptian, 18 percent British, and 4 percent Syrian and other groups. The increase was far greater in the government's departments than in provinces due to the policy of "indirect rule," which gave more power to tribal leaders.[78] However, the task of creating local artisans and clerical staff was hampered by the government's antipathy toward and distrust of the educated class, an attitude that prevailed after the 1924 crisis. The depression of the early 1930s, which prompted the colonial administration to retrench, was another major blow to this process. As of June 1931, 93 of the 1,032 British posts (or 9 percent of the total), 152 of 1,464 other foreigners, and 43 of the 2,760 Sudanese (or 1.6 percent) had been retrenched.[79]

The Railway and Steamers Department also bore their share of the retrenchment. The full impact of the crisis fell during the winter of 1931–1932. A reduction in the number of staff amounted to 31 percent of the British, about 33 percent of Egyptians, and almost all the Greeks. Train and steamer services were reduced, several stations were closed, workshops went on short time, and many men went on unpaid leave.[80] At Port Sudan the stevedoring was largely the work of Yemenese porters who were brought by contractors. In 1932 these contracts were discontinued and the government began to recruit porters from the Nile Valley and the Beja from the hills behind the port.

The departure of many expatriate staff in supervisory and technical grades made the training of local Sudanese an urgent task. Hence financial stringency had quickened the pace of the Sudanization process, particularly in the Railway and Steamers Department. However, the creation of local technical skills required a more vigorous educational program, a task that was not undertaken until the mid-1930s. Official policy toward education and the educated class in general began to change during the governor-generalship of Sir Stewart Symes who took office in 1934. Unlike his predecessors, who tried to rely on traditional leaders, Symes considered the intelligentsia a vital force that could be co-opted and utilized by the colonial regime. A committee under the chairmanship of G. N. Loggin was set up to review the educational system in the country. The committee's report stressed the importance of technical, engineering, agricultural, and veterinary training. Between 1935 and 1939, the number of Sudanese in senior administrative posts increased. For example, their number in Division I of the senior posts increased from one in 1930 to six in 1935, and to twenty-eight in 1939. In Division II and Division III, the number of Sudanese increased from 2,735 in 1930 to 3,225 in 1935, and to 4,612 in 1939.[81]

WORKING CONDITIONS AND WAGES

Among the most important characteristics of the labor force created under the colonial system were the marked distinctions between the unskilled and skilled workers, and between these two categories and the white collar workers. These distinctions were reflected in the system of pay, residential patterns, and lifestyle of these groups.

Government employees in the Sudan were divided into two categories: classified and unclassified staff. The term classified referred to civil servants. Unclassified employees referred to those who were employed permanently on monthly rates of pay, temporary employees on monthly salaries, and day laborers. Classified scales and rates of pay were left in the hands of the individual government department to determine.[82] In 1937 the government introduced a system known as the Block Grant to create uniform wages.[83] According to this system, the head of a government department was given an appropriation to cover the cost of wages and other expenses, and was allowed to determine the rates of wages in his department. This resulted in great variations in wage rates for similar jobs within each government department and different pay scales for unskilled and skilled laborers.[84]

Taking the Sudan Railways as an example, by 1948 there were no fewer than 372 job categories; they were divided among departments as shown in Table 10.[85]

Typically the colonial government considered wages an expensive bill and made every possible effort to keep them down. The rates of pay in the Railway Department were subjected to a series of revisions between 1924 and 1935. But in 1935 the department adopted rates of pay for workers at the bottom of the pay scale, thus setting the basic wage for the lowest paid

---
TABLE 10
Grade System at the Railway
Departments, 1930s

Mechanical Department	200 categories
Traffic	46
Catering	40
Engineering	31
Public health	21
Stores	16

TABLE II

Railway Department Pay Scales

	Monthly salary	*Cost of living*
General laborer	LE 1.350	LE 1.800
Fitter mates	1.800	3.600
Laborers, engineering	1.050	1.350
Plate layers	1.200	1.650
Tulba	1.350	2.700
Shunters	1.800	3.000
Oilers	1.800	3.000
Points men	1.500	2.700
Line burners	1.200	1.650

worker at less than 150 piastres per month.[86] The Railway Department did not provide housing for workers except in desert stations.

There were remarkable differences in wages between various government departments. In the Public Works Department, skilled artisans received from LE 4 to LE 9.4, with an increase every other year; in the Irrigation Department, artisans' pay ranged from LE 4 to LE 6.5; and in the Agriculture and Forests Department, the rates of pay for artisans ranged from LE 4 to LE 14 per month.[87] A daily laborer in the Gezira Scheme could make as much in eight months as he could in one year as a railway worker. Artisans in private firms earned much higher wages, though they did not have paid leave and other benefits that government workers had.

The Committee of Inquiry that reviewed these pay scales in 1948 revealed an astonishing situation: an artisan was paid up to five times as much as an unskilled laborer; the clerk was earning a salary twice and even four times the wage of the artisan, and fifteen times the basic wage of the laborer. A middle school boy at the age of sixteen or seventeen could enter Scale K-1 at LE 3.5, and reach a maximum of LE 9.5 at the age of forty. In reality, he would probably pass the Civil Service Examination and move to Scale J-1 at the age of twenty-two or twenty-three, and earn LE 6.5 with a ceiling of LE 17. A secondary school boy who passed the Civil Service Examination would enter J-1 with a salary of LE 6.5 and could expect to attain the maximum of LE 36 in Scale G. If he was good, and a vacancy existed, he could reach Scale F, with a maximum pay of LE 50.[88]

In response to these conditions and to the rising cost of living, workers in various sectors of the economy began to organize themselves and demand improvements. Although workers' resistance reached a climax in the post–World War II period, its roots can be traced to the 1930s. In addition to their low pay, Sudanese workers resented the continuing employment of foreign artisans at a time when many Sudanese were unemployed. A stream of articles in *Al-Fajr* deplored this policy and suggested that the government should stop the immigration of foreign artisans.[89] Strikes occurred in the late 1930s and during the war years. In 1941 and 1942 various groups of workers went on strike no less than fourteen times in different parts of the country.[90] Despite the sporadic nature of these strikes, they demonstrated the workers' growing consciousness and their ability to act collectively.

THE EMERGENCE OF LABOR ACTIVISM

The Sudan had at one time one of the best organized and one of the most radical labor movements in Africa and the Middle East. Although this movement has received substantial scholarly attention, several aspects of its history deserve further exploration.[91] Prominent among those was the relationship between the union leadership and the rank and file, and the roles of family, kinship ties, residence, and ethnicity, in the development of workers' solidarity and mobilization. These issues fall beyond the scope of this study and would require extensive research, particularly in the field of oral history. The recently published memoirs of Al-Tayyib Hasan al-Tayyib, a prominent labor leader in the 1940s, have many anecdotes which reveal a great deal about the workers' experience.[92]

As elsewhere in Africa, transportation workers took the lead in establishing working-class organizations and in staging labor protests. The vital role of the railways and docks in communications, exports, and imports gave their workers a strong bargaining position. The growth of a sense of community and solidarity among them stemmed from their shared work experience, communal residences, and the close-knit networks both inside and outside the work place. This was particularly the case of Atbara, where the headquarters and the main workshops and stores of the Railway Department were located. About 90 percent of the city's population were railway employees. The vast majority of Atbara workers were immigrants from the northern province which was inhabited by the Ja'aliyyin, Shaiqiyya, Manasir, Rubatab, and Danaqla. Most of them were peasants who migrated to Atbara to escape the poor economic conditions in the province. With the exception of the Danaqla, almost all of these immigrants were Arabic speakers who belonged to the Khatimiyya Sufi order. In other words, the railway workers of Atbara had a homogeneous ethnic, regional, and cultural background. Immigrants from particular villages congregated in certain neighborhoods such as Umbakoul, thereby combining preexisting ties with new forms of urban solidarity. The railway workers of Atbara developed a strong sense of urban identity and created a dense web of social networks.

As early as the mid-1930s, the railway workers at Atbara formed working-class associations, the most important of which was workers' clubs. These clubs facilitated interaction among the workers and became major tools for mobilization. In 1938 the graduates of the Atbara Technical School requested permission from railway management to establish a society. Permission was granted but with several conditions attached. For instance, the railway management insisted that the principal of the Atbara Technical School be the president of the workers' club and approve its cultural and social activities.[93] In 1940 the club was moved from the small house in which it had been established to a new building which comprised a general assembly room, a library and reading room, and three classrooms. An essential part of the association's activities was the provision of adult education for its members. Continuing education classes were held in technical subjects in English and Arabic. The society also organized lectures and debates as well as theatrical activities. Egyptian newspapers, magazines, and novels were widely circulated among the workers. The association also published a magazine called *The Atbararian*. This magazine became the main forum through which workers expressed their opinions. The Railway Department itself also ran a boardinghouse to provide food and lodging for newly appointed boys who came straight from school, and a welfare fund for staff.[94] In addition to cultural activities, workers began to discuss the need for unity and for labor unions.

Labor activism increased after World War II as a result of inflation, deteriorating living conditions, and the growth of the nationalist movement. In 1946, a stream of articles written by workers began to appear in *al-'Aamil al-Sudani*, which was published by Khartoum workers, and in *The Atbararian*, demanding the establishment of trade unions. In June 1946, the graduates of the technical school took a further step and formed the Workers' Affairs Association (WAA). The WAA would not only fight for higher wages and fewer hours of work, but also for the social and educational improvement of its members. Its program included the establishment of cooperative societies and voluntary savings. Membership was open to any railway worker, provided he was Sudanese. The WAA's council was to consist of twenty members to be elected for two-year terms. Council members were to elect an executive committee consisting of a president, two vice-presidents, a secretary, an assistant secretary, a treasurer, and an accountant. The first committee included Sulayman Musa as president, Al-Tayyib Hasan al-Tayyib as vice president, 'Ubaid Bardouli as secretary, and Qasim Amin as assistant secretary.[95]

On 16 July 1946, the WAA informed the railway management of its existence and demanded recognition, which was denied. At the time, the colonial administration had begun to formulate a labor policy and to consider the question of labor unions. Until then, the government had had no clear labor policy. The Labour Board, established in 1936, was an advisory body concerned with the Gezira Scheme. In 1945 a labor officer was appointed by the government, while the British Foreign Office appointed Mr. M. T. Audsley as a labor advisor to the Cairo embassy. He was dispatched to the Sudan in 1946 to examine the conditions of workers and to make recommendations.

It is common knowledge that trade unions were introduced in European colonies in Africa after the Second World War to channel growing labor protests and to control workers. The British Colonial Office came to see trade unions as an essential means to create a "reliable and disciplined work force." The 1930 Passfield Circular set the pattern for all later treatment of the colonial trade unions.[96] It urged colonial governments to bring trade unions inside the law, giving them "supervision and guidance" and thus smoothing their "passage into constitutional channels."[97] The establishment of trade unions was part of the larger effort to keep labor disputes within certain boundaries and to contain the growing discontent.

In the Sudan the British seemed to be in no particular hurry to introduce labor unions. James Robertson, the civil secretary at the time, wrote:

> The factories, workshops, and departmental staffs seen by Mr. Audsley comprise a negligible element of the working population of the Sudan, the vast majority of whom are agricultural peasantry or West African or Southern Sudanese negro laborers, or men of mixed negro and Arab blood, all of whom in the eyes of the dominant "Arab" leaders of the unstable "intellectuals" of the towns, have no right nor liberties but a predestined status of permanent inferiority. . . .[98]

The Labour Board recommended the formation of committees (joint labor-management consultative councils) in government departments and private firms. The declared objective was that "the artisans and the laboring classes should be encouraged to take an intelligent and constructive interest in the internal running of their business or departments."[99] However, the government made it clear that it did not want the committees to concern themselves with the question of pay or conditions of employment. In other words, the scheme was to develop workers' organizations that concerned themselves only with economic issues through slow and careful evolution.

These proposals were swiftly rejected by the WAA, which insisted on its recognition as the sole representative of the railway workers. In response to the management refusal, the WAA immediately began to mobilize the railway workers and led a large demonstration in Atbara on 12 July 1947 which was broken off by the police, and the WAA leaders were arrested.[100] The WAA launched a successful strike which had the full support of the workers and won the sympathy of the population of Atbara. Al-Tayyib Hasan recalls that men and women cheered in the streets as the labor leaders were taken to the prison in al-Damir.[101] The generous donations from the local community, from railway workers in the rural areas, and from the Egyptian Railway Workers Union helped sustain the strike.[102] Following mediation, an agreement was reached, whereby the government would recognize the WAA, subject to referendum of all railway workers. This was held in August, and the executive committee of the WAA was confirmed in office almost unanimously.[103]

Recognition led to further militancy. Railway workers came to constitute the active core of the working class. The WAA became the main voice of the railway workers and launched a campaign to improve their wages and living conditions.

After the war, the cost of living continued to rise, while wages remained low. About 26,500 government employees received a monthly salary of less than LE 3.[104] For an employee with a monthly income of LE 12, the cost of living index (1938=100) was 770.2.[105] Yet the government was not willing to spend money on wages and continued to build financial reserves and reinvest in revenue generating projects such as expansion of cotton production and communications.

In January 1948, the WAA demanded higher wages, shorter hours, and further improvements. The railway management referred these demands to the central government arguing that they were beyond its jurisdiction. The WAA launched a three-day strike, which won unanimous support and shut down the communication system in the country. As a result, a committee of inquiry was established to investigate the working conditions and to make recommendations. However, British officials attributed the growing workers' militancy to communist activities and Egyptian propaganda. Faced with this ambivalence, the WAA called for an indefinite strike, which began on 16 March 1948. The committee of inquiry finally submitted its report, which was accepted by the WAA after some modifications, and the strike ended on 18 April 1948.

A series of strikes between 1948 and 1952 led to pay increases, the legalization of trade unions, and the introduction of labor laws. The most important of those were the Workmen's Compensation Ordinance, the Employer and Employed Persons Ordinance, the Regulations of Trade Disputes Ordinance, the Trade Unions Ordinance, the Workshops and Factories Ordinance, and the Wage Tribunal Ordinance.[106] Although these concessions were limited, the broader implications of the strikes were far reaching. Independent unions sprang up in various government departments and private firms. By 1951 there were sixty-two registered unions. Frequent mass meetings and demonstrations were held in urban centers, as strikes and unrest spread throughout the country.

Trade unions became an effective tool for the workers. In 1949 the WAA began to focus its attention on the establishment of an umbrella organization. However, the government wanted separate unions for each establishment and resisted the idea of a union for all workers. In 1949 a Workers Congress comprising fifteen unions was formed, and in 1950 it became the Sudan Workers Trade Union Federation (SWTUF).[107] From the beginning the federation was dominated by the railway workers. Its leaders included prominent communists such as Muhammad al-Sayyid Sallam and Al-Shafi' Ahmad al-Shaykh. By the early 1950s, the labor movement had become intertwined with the nationalist movement. Of all the nationalist organizations, the communists had the strongest link with the labor movement.

The birth of the Sudanese communist movement coincided with the rise of the labor movement. In 1945 a group of Sudanese students who had studied in Egypt formed the Sudanese Movement For National Liberation (SMNL).[108] After early uncertainties, the SMNL came under the leadership of 'Abd al-Khaliq Mahjoub. The movement attracted a significant number of Sudanese intelligentsia and was closely linked with the labor movement.[109]

The SWTUF enjoyed remarkable success during the early 1950s. However, it had become increasingly isolated from the rank and file of workers. A major rift between the federation and other unions occurred in 1953, when the federation, together with the communists, opposed the Anglo-Egyptian Agreement for self-rule. In their view the agreement gave excessive powers to the governor-general during the transitional period and to the colonial officials in the south.[110] But the federation failed to mobilize workers for a general strike against the agreement. It misjudged the mood of the great majority of workers who supported self-rule. In the 1953 elections, the railway workers in Atbara gave their overwhelming support to the Khatimiyya candidates and elected an anti-SWTUF executive committee.[111]

Sectarian parties, on the other hand, evinced little interest in the labor movement. This attitude was consistent with their vision of Sudanese society and their political philosophy. These parties represented the interests of the traditional establishment—religious heads, tribal leaders, and big merchants—who sought to maintain the existing class structure and rejected the existence of inequalities. However, after the unions gained recognition and became powerful, the sectarian parties changed their strategy. Realizing that unions represented an important constituency, they tried to influence them through financial help.[112] They also made concerted efforts to control the Railway Workers Union and to create a wedge between it and the communist-dominated SWTUF. The National Unionist Party, which came to power in 1954, was active in installing an anti-federation executive committee at the top of the powerful railway union.

The hostility of the sectarian parties toward the labor movement became more pronounced after the establishment of self-rule in 1954. By using the state apparatus, the parties tried to control the labor movement and to limit the influence of the unions. It required all unions to register and be supervised by the minister of social affairs. In the spring of 1954 the government reduced the cost of living allowance. The weakened federation could do very little to oppose this. Yahya al-Fadli, minister of social affairs, launched a campaign against the SWTUF, harassing, dismissing, and detaining its leaders. In 1956 he declared the SWTUF illegal. Citing the 1948 law, the minister decided that workers in one enterprise had the right to form unions, but that a federation of unions including more than one enterprise was forbidden.[113] The Railway Workers Union accepted the decision and broke away from the SWTUF. The government grew more adept in dealing with grievances (through manipulation, division, propaganda, and so forth), and strikes receded considerably. Finally, in 1958, the parliamentary government was overthrown by the army and a military dictatorship was established. Political parties were dissolved, labor unions were forbidden, and their leaders were detained. Nevertheless, the military regime failed to eradicate workers' activism, and labor unions played a major role in the downfall of the junta in 1964.

CONCLUSION

The interwar period witnessed the greatest expansion in the wage labor force in the Sudan. This labor force was segmented along regional, ethnic, and occupational lines, a logical outcome of colonial recruitment policies and the manner in which various Sudanese groups were integrated into the colonial economy. Yet, despite its segmentation, this work force gave birth to one of the most militant trade union movements which has become a powerful force in Sudanese society.

SIX

EX-SLAVES AND WORKERS IN KHARTOUM, 1920–1956

By the mid-1920s the majority of slaves in Khartoum had redeemed themselves and were joined by ex-slaves from the rural areas. As we have seen in chapter 3, since the turn of the century urban ex-slaves and immigrants established their neighborhoods and created communities in the capital. This trend continued after World War I and was accentuated by postwar slavery policy, the opening of the Gezira Scheme, and the growing demand for labor. Khartoum residents found employment either in the city itself, or in the Gezira when conditions in the capital were not favorable. Although the depression of the 1930s had greatly reduced employment, the situation was reversed during the Second World War. Once the war ended, unemployment ensued. Moreover, the postwar period witnessed a massive influx of rural immigrants to the capital, a situation that increased the anxiety of colonial officials. Large-scale immigration, unemployment, and a "floating" population engendered intensive debate among administrators on the broader questions of migrant labor, social policy, and urbanization. Colonial officials tried to halt the flow of immigration into the capital and initiated a new urban policy. In addition to these themes, this chapter will examine the social and economic conditions of ex-slaves and workers, labor protests, the structure of working-class neighborhoods, and the development of popular culture.

EMANCIPATION AND WAGE LABOR IN
KHARTOUM, 1920–1939

The fast pace of emancipation in Khartoum can be attributed to a host of factors. Among these was the proximity of Khartoum slaves to the seat of power and the small size of the province. Availability of wage employment and of other economic opportunities in the capital allowed urban male slaves to establish their economic independence. Even before the promulgation of the 1919 and 1925 circulars, a great number of Khartoum's slaves redeemed themselves, largely through their own initiatives. For example, the number of papers issued in Omdurman between 1922 and 1925 was about thirty, but approximately 150 slaves were freed annually without freedom papers.[1] Owing to anonymity and the availability of various sources of income in this urban complex, slave owners could do little to force the return of discontented slaves.

By the mid-1920s, the decline of slavery in the capital was obvious. According to official estimates, there were approximately 3,000 to 4,000 slaves in Omdurman in 1926 compared to an estimated 10,000 in 1900.[2] In Khartoum North and the rural district, there were about 2,000 as opposed to 8,000 to 9,000 at the turn of the century—a decline of 75 percent.[3] However, the majority of liberated urban slaves settled in the Daims. According to the district commissioner of Khartoum, by 1926 about 15,000 ex-slaves had established themselves in the Daims.[4]

For ex-slaves and other dislocated persons the city provided an opportunity for economic and social mobility. Unlike the rural areas where customary values prevailed and servile origin was a handicap, the exigencies of urban life gave ex-slaves greater mobility and the ability to overcome the stigma of slavery. In the urban environment social barriers disappeared gradually. The presence of people from diverse ethnic backgrounds and intermarriage between various groups allowed ex-slaves to blend in and blur their servile past.

Moving to the city was another phase in the ex-slaves' struggle for freedom. As they settled in the capital, they became part of a mass of dislocated people who competed for limited opportunities. In addition to the challenges of urban life, liberated and runaway slaves had to contend with colonial vagrancy laws, registration, and other forms of coercion. They devised several strategies to cope with these problems. They moved between city and countryside, and between wage employment and other economic activities.

Unfortunately there are no figures on wage employment in Khartoum during this period. The urban wage labor market offered a limited number of permanent jobs, mainly in government departments. The majority of urban workers were employed on a casual basis. Hence, urban residents took advantage of their proximity to the Gezira and the competition between various government departments for labor. It is necessary, therefore, to examine how the expansion of the agrarian economy and the establishment of the Gezira Scheme affected the plight of ex-slaves and other immigrants in the capital.

The expansion of the agrarian economy created a huge demand for labor and spurred competition for the limited supply in the country. This led to a rise in wages and gave workers a favorable bargaining position. From the early 1920s the impact of the Gezira Scheme was felt in the capital. The construction of the Makwar Dam and the main canal attracted a large number of urban residents. While the daily wage for an unskilled laborer in the capital was fixed at six piastres, the Gezira was offering ten piastres. The drift of urban workers to the Gezira prompted municipal authorities in Khartoum to prohibit contractors from the Gezira from recruiting in the capital.[5] In addition to the Gezira, urban residents found employment on private pump schemes around the Three Towns.

Throughout the 1920s, the Gezira peak season offered seasonal relief for Khartoum residents. However, the 1930s' depression dealt a serious blow to the wage labor market. As cotton production and prices fell, the demand for labor in the Gezira diminished. Therefore, the early 1930s was a time of unemployment, misery, and destitution for the vast majority of Khartoum residents. Many who had gone to the Gezira returned to the capital and joined the growing army of unemployed.[6] Moreover, as revenues fell, the government reduced its expenditures, enforcing a retrenchment program in 1931 in which hundreds of permanent employees lost their jobs. In 1932 about 7,000 ex-slaves and other immigrants were reportedly unemployed in the capital.[7] The rampant poverty became a subject of newspaper editorials and was made evident by the increase in crime and the spread of diseases such as tuberculosis and leprosy.[8] The government provided a certain amount of relief to the urban poor and a number of alms houses were established in Khartoum to provide shelter for the poor and for orphans.[9]

By the mid-1930s, however, employment opportunities began to improve following the resumption of work on the Jabal Auliya Dam and the expansion of irrigation in the Gezira. In 1935 the Jabal Auliya Dam employed between 7,000 and 10,000 workers, of whom 4,431 were Egyptian.[10] As the demand for work in the Gezira and at Jabal Auliya remained seasonal, Khartoum workers moved back and forth between these sites.

LABOR CONDITIONS IN KHARTOUM DURING WORLD WAR II

Economic expansion during the war created cash earning opportunities for many urban residents. Prospective workers could choose from a wide range of jobs in the capital itself and in the Gezira and other agricultural districts. In 1940, approximately 4,000 people were employed on a daily basis in various military establishments. The main employers of labor in the capital in 1940 and wage rates are shown in Table 12.[11]

Demand exceeded supply during the war years. According to official estimates an additional 700 to 800 workers were required.[12] A labor shortage was caused by the drift of urban workers to the Gezira and other agricultural districts during the peak season, where they could sell their labor for much higher wages. This, in turn, resulted in serious shortages in the capital and created competition among government departments. As a result, work conditions and wages varied from one employer to another. Government attempts to establish uniform wages failed.[13] Municipal

---

TABLE 12

Workers Employed in Khartoum in 1940

Employer	Number of workers	Daily wage (in piastres)
Public Works Department	3,030	6
Sudan Railways (Engineering Division)	300	5
Municipal engineer	200	5
Egyptian Irrigation Department	158	5
Royal engineers	100	6
Royal Army Service	100	6
Royal Army Air Force	200	6

officials suggested that West African and Nuba workers should be offered free transportation to encourage them to move from the Gezira, Funj, and Gedarif areas to Khartoum.[14]

In 1941 about 4,562 workers were employed in the capital, while the number required each day was about 5,860.[15] The shortage of daily laborers continued in 1942 and government departments had great difficulty obtaining laborers at the prevailing rate of wages (six piastres per day). Government departments complained that artisans as well as technical and clerical employees had begun to leave their posts at military and civil departments and were immediately offered employment at better terms by other government establishments.[16] Despite their conviction that the existing rate was "barely a living wage," officials opposed an increase on the grounds that they would lead to inflation.[17] They suggested that rations of sugar and flour should be offered instead. The Labour Board further recommended that the following rates should be applied in Khartoum as an experiment: six piastres per day for an unskilled laborer, seven piastres for slightly skilled, and eight piastres for semi-skilled.[18]

Once the war ended the situation reversed. The demand for casual labor in Khartoum fell. By 1943 the Sudan had ceased to be a theater of operations. Government departments laid off employees and soldiers were demobilized. At the end of the war, public and private employment in the Three Towns dropped and rampant unemployment resulted. According to official estimates, between six and seven thousand daily laborers were discharged in 1943, the vast majority from the Sudan Defence Force, the Royal Air Force, and the Public Works Department.[19] To municipal officials, "the presence of a large number of unemployed and de-tribalized [casuals] of diverse origins in the capital and other towns would be an embarrassment."[20]

While the Three Towns enjoyed abundant labor, the Gezira experienced a severe shortage. In January 1943 the shortage of pickers, porters, and daily laborers in the Gezira reached critical proportions. Seasonal workers took advantage of high wages, built savings, and returned home.[21] Municipal officials therefore decided that these people should either return to their homes or be redeployed to the Gezira.[22]

In 1943 provincial administrators took steps to purge the capital of the so-called "parasites." Between April and November 1943, 3,500 urban residents were rounded up and sent off to cultivation areas. Kassala and the Blue Nile Provinces received 1,500 and 1,000 respectively, while the Forests Department absorbed 1,000.[23] However, low productivity and high rates of desertion were reported. Of the 1,000 men taken by the

Forests Department, about 600 to 700 deserted between July and October, while a quarter of those sent to the Gezira left within one month of their arrival. In other words, the postwar era resembled the early decades of this century, when urban workers were dispatched to various public work projects in the countryside. To prevent their return, the governor of Khartoum Province was asked to apply coercive measures including police roundups and the establishment of quarantines.[24] But implementation was hindered by insufficient police and the availability of alternatives to wage employment in the urban complex.

Discharged soldiers had great difficulty in finding employment. Many worked as ghafirs (watchmen) outside the Sudan. By November 1943, 1,895 men had enlisted as ghafirs in the Middle East (mainly in Egypt and Palestine) and Eritrea. Only 604 returned after the completion of their contracts.[25] To prevent this, the Labour Board recommended that the number of recruits for this occupation should not exceed the number of those who returned. Meanwhile, absorption of demobilized noncommissioned officers and men into civilian departments presented a serious problem. Most lacked education and technical skills.

Despite the labor shortage, wages in the capital remained high. In Khartoum, the daily wage for an unskilled laborer in 1945 was six piastres, and in Omdurman was as much as twelve piastres.[26] A laborer could earn enough in three or four days' work to keep him for a week or so. So according to official estimates only one-third of the available casual labor was employed at any given time.[27]

URBAN MIGRATION AND LABOR AFTER WORLD WAR II

The period after World War II witnessed a massive influx of rural immigrants to urban centers, a logical outcome of the major socioeconomic transformation taking place in the countryside. This change included the commercialization of agriculture, which impoverished rural producers and concentrated administrative, commercial, and industrial activities in the urban centers, particularly in the capital. War rationing and price controls led to shortages of basic commodities in the rural areas. Moreover, in 1946 the riverain provinces north of Khartoum were struck by the worst Nile flood in many years, which prompted people to flee the region. In 1948–1949, famine conditions prevailed in many parts of the country. Poor rains affected food production and reduced grazing areas for many nomads. As a result grain

TABLE 13
Regional Origin of Immigrants in Khartoum

Origin	Khartoum	Omdurman	Khartoum North
West	65%	70%	37%
North	25%	20%	50%
South	10%	10%	10%

prices rose sharply. In Dar Fur for instance, the price of dukhn in 1949 was twice the price of dukhn in Omdurman. This crisis prompted the government to establish a famine relief committee and to import large quantities of grain.[28]

The postwar migration to the Three Towns brought people from diverse ethnic, linguistic, and regional backgrounds. Table 13 lists the regional origins of immigrants to the Three Towns.[29] Although the percentages in the table are rough estimates, the preponderance of immigrants from the west and remote parts of the country is confirmed by the 1955 census.[30]

Within the Three Towns there were marked variations in the pattern of settlement, the nature of the labor market, and economic conditions. The greatest attractions for new immigrants were Omdurman and the Khartoum Daims. According to official estimates (which were far from accurate), Omdurman's population grew from 76,000 in 1926 to 105,000 in 1944, an increase of 40 percent.[31] Unlike Khartoum North and Khartoum, which can be considered typical "colonial" cities, Omdurman remained a "traditional" African city; it was mainly a residential town. Most residents engaged in petty trading and made traditional handicrafts. Omdurman attracted retired government officials, craftsmen and petty traders from the neighboring rural districts, the northern riverain provinces and Kordofan, and West Africans. Since the Mahdiyya western Sudanese had constituted the bulk of the city's population, the new immigrants joined their kin and were attracted by freehold land, which was unavailable in Khartoum and Khartoum North where leasehold prevailed.[32]

Khartoum also received a significant portion of immigrants and demobilized soldiers. The population of the city rose from 44,311 in 1939 to 55,933 in 1944.[33] In Khartoum North, the increase was from 15,063 to 25,100 or two-thirds.[34] The main attraction of Khartoum North was the availability of wage employment, especially in the Steamers Department and in the workshops of the Sudan Railways.

———————————— TABLE 14 ————————————
Ethnic and Regional Origin of Immigrants

	Group	Numbers	Group as % of total
1.	Arab	65,087	27.4
2.	Miscellaneous	11,540	4.85
3.	Nuba	6,457	2.72
4.	Beja	2,715	1.14
5.	Nubian	24,625	10.38
6.	Central Southerners (Nilotic)	3,700	1.56
7.	Eastern Southerners (Nilo-Hamitic)	548	0.23
8.	Western Southerners (Sudanic)	2,091	0.89
9.	Westerners	102,478	43.00
10.	Foreigners with Sudanese status	2,337	0.99
11.	Foreigners with non-Sudanese status	15,474	6.51
	Total	237,052	100.00

One of the most important postwar trends was the large-scale arrival of people from the south and the Nuba Mountains. During the prewar era, the Closed District laws and the British Southern Policy restricted the migration of Southerners and Nuba to the northern Sudan. However, after 1947 these restrictions were eased. Southern Sudanese and Nuba poured into the capital, prompting one colonial official to comment that many "came under the impression that the streets are paved with gold."[35] Their presence in the capital was viewed as constituting a "real and growing problem" and the government made serious attempts to repatriate them.[36]

According to the 1955–1956 census, the capital's population was divided into the ethnic and regional categories shown in Table 14.[37]

However, such classifications can be misleading, for ethnic labels and ethnic identity fluctuated constantly. For instance, the term Westerners referred to people from Dar Fur, Kordofan, and West Africa. Arabs might have included several groups who did not identify themselves as Arabs. For our purpose, what is important is the fact that the urban population became more diverse in ethnic and regional origin. The question then, is: what is the significance of this? How did these people earn their living in Khartoum and under what conditions did they live?

TABLE 15
Economic Profile of the Three Towns Population

Town	Total	Males	Females
Khartoum			
Persons 5 years and over	79,418	47,364	32,054
Gainfully employed	36,554	33,857	2,697
Unproductive occupations	42,864	13,507	29,357
Khartoum North			
Persons 5 years and over	32,932	18,543	14,389
Gainfully employed	13,671	12,938	733
Unproductive occupations	19,261	5,605	13,656
Omdurman			
Persons 5 years and over	97,076	51,226	45,850
Gainfully employed	35,548	32,591	2,957
Unproductive occupations	61,528	18,635	42,893

Wage employment was scarce after the war. While a few people held permanent jobs, the vast majority worked as casual laborers or engaged in nonwage activities such as petty trading, domestic services, tailoring, and barbering. Unfortunately, there is little information on the so-called "informal sector" in Khartoum during the colonial period. It appeared that the majority of the urban population was male. According to the 1955–1956 census, the population of the Three Towns was estimated at 245,736, distributed as follows: Khartoum, 93,103; Khartoum North, 39,082; and Omdurman, 113,351.[38] The population figure above included 135,328 males and 110,408 females. This may be attributed to the fact that most immigrants were either bachelors or married men who left their families behind.

According to the 1955 census, the number of economically active persons was small, constituting about one-third of the population in Khartoum and Khartoum North, and less than that in Omdurman.[39] The number of economically active persons in the capital was 85,781. The census takers considered any person five years of age and older economically active.[40] The categories of employment cited by the census are listed in Table 15.[41]

From this economic profile, it is evident that the number of people on wage employment was very small. Hence, the great majority of urban residents engaged in nonwage activities such as petty trading, tailoring, blacksmithing, prostitution, etc., and they fell under the rubric of the so-called "informal sector."

Informal activities figure prominently in the works of Richard Sandbrook, Jeff Crisp, Luise White, Claire Robertson, Frederick Cooper, and others.[42] These authors question the validity of this term and challenge the notion that "informal" economic activities were parasitic. On the contrary, they argue, the informal sector offered employment to a wide range of people who could not enter the official labor market and provided goods and services cheaply for low-paid urban workers. The presence of these "parasites" and their activities defied the official concept of an orderly city and a clearly defined labor force.

In the Sudan, colonial records show rough estimates of what officials termed "parasites" such as petty traders and shopkeepers. In 1945, there were 3,000 licensed shopkeepers in Khartoum, 2,000 in Omdurman, and about 300 in Khartoum North.[43] However, these figures excluded unlicensed traders and a host of other economic activities. According to the 1955–1956 census, the Three Towns had 7,397 shopkeepers of whom 4,408 were in Omdurman. Small-scale entrepreneurship was therefore widespread in the capital. This sector of the economy deserves description.

Commercial life in the urban area centered around the *suqs* (markets) which were scattered throughout the Three Towns. These were divided into central suqs, small suqs, open-air suqs, and isolated shops in the residential areas. The central suqs were the largest and most congested, and displayed a wide range of both local and imported goods. The Arab markets in Khartoum and Khartoum North were similar to the Omdurman suq in that they were old and had retained an older character as opposed to European markets or *al-suq al-Afranji*. In these suqs, shops selling identical items were grouped together. For instance, there were markets for vegetables, meat, hides, skins, beds, and so forth. A number of shopping streets in Omdurman stood out: *shari' al-Saqha* (goldsmith street), *shari' al-'Anaqreib* (beds street), and *shari' al-Munajidein* (mattress and pillow-makers); *shari' Abu Rof* was known for its perfume sellers.[44] The northeastern corner of the Omdurman suq specialized in the selling of locally made shoes and leather goods, hides and skins, cloth, confectioneries, tea, coffee, sugar, and fruits. The northwestern section was famous for the sale of meat, vegetables, grain, onions, spices, and so forth. The southeastern section dealt with imported items such as footwear, ready-made cloth, clocks, watches, and electrical goods. The difference between the traditional markets and the European markets was quite noticeable. The latter provided services mostly for foreign communities and highly paid Sudanese, while the former drew most of their customers from low-income groups. The majority of merchants in the European markets were foreigners—mainly Greeks, Egyptians, Syrians, Italians, and Indians.[45]

In addition to the main markets there were many smaller ones, usually within walking distance of residential quarters. They represented smaller versions of the main suqs, concentrating mainly on groceries such as sugar, tea, coffee, salt, spices, vegetables, and meat. The open-air suqs specialized in livestock, fodder, firewood, and charcoal. These open markets supported the majority of the population with their daily needs. Hundreds of small grocery shops scattered throughout the residential areas, occupying in most cases strategic corners at the intersections of streets, also supplied daily needs. These shops represented over 50 percent of all shops in the 1960s. In addition to the retail traders with fixed locations, there were many hawkers, street sellers, barbers, and shoeshine boys. Some of these hawkers came from the farming communities of Kadaru, Jailyi, Halfaya, and Jiraif. They sold vegetables and milk in the capital.

Another important category of small entrepreneurs was craftsmen and mechanics. The capital had 21,620 craftsmen and mechanics employed in woodworking, building, and the textile industry; 6,509 machinery operators including drivers of commercial vehicles; and 6,639 domestic servants of whom 869 were females.[46]

From the perspective of this study, brewing local drink and prostitution deserve attention. As pointed out earlier, colonial officials associated these activities with ex-slaves. Making alcoholic drinks in a Muslim society raises a number of issues. It is well known that Islam prohibits the use of alcohol. But the brewing and consumption of alcohol is an old tradition in the Sudan, common among Muslims as well as non-Muslims. The most common drinks in the Sudan were *marisa* (local beer) and *'araqi*. Recipes varied from one region to another. In the riverain north, marisa-making was a regular part of a woman's work. It was provided for marriages, circumcisions, and village work parties. A stigma was attached to brewing only when women did it commercially or in urban areas, where it was closely associated with prostitution. Among non-Muslims in the south and west, marisa was a staple. In the urban centers marisa and 'araqi became major cash earning commodities and provided income for many women, particularly liberated female slaves.

The illicit marisa and 'araqi trade created a home industry dominated by women, which was central to the social and cultural life of many urban dwellers. Drinks were sold at the *anadi* (singular: indaya) or drinking house. The owner of the indaya was called a *shaykha*, who was responsible for making the drinks and running the indaya. In each indaya a number of people, both male and female, served drinks.

The anadi were found in almost every Sudanese town and were usually located in the so-called "native quarters." In Khartoum they were concentrated in the Daims. According to oral informants, the most famous indaya owners in the Daims in the 1940s and 1950s were Makka Sandal, a Nuba who lived in Daim 'Abd al-Karim; Um Darbayn, a Berti; Um Hagayn, an ex-slave of unknown origin; and Al-Zayn Fogi, a Bergo.[47]

The anadi served as social clubs for urban workers and low-income people who provided the owners with a steady stream of customers. Barmaids and prostitutes attracted male customers to the establishments and increased consumption. In the Khartoum Daims, there was a bus called *abu ta'rifa* (because it cost one-half piastre) which carried customers from one indaya to another.[48] Some workers spent all their earnings and ended up in debt. The anadi became refuges for runaway workers. They attracted criminals, thieves, pimps, and idlers to the Daims.

In southern Africa, consumption of alcohol by mine workers was encouraged by mine owners who realized that wages spent on liquor lengthened the tenure of the migratory labor force.[49] In the Sudan, however, colonial officials seemed more concerned with moral and social decay. Their attitude toward drinking typified their image of Sudanese society and tradition. Sudanese were expected to behave as "good" Muslims and to refrain from drinking.

From the beginning, brewing of local drinks was considered illegal by the colonial state in the Sudan. In 1899, the government introduced legislation which prohibited the importation and the sale of alcohol without a license.[50] This law did not apply to marisa. However, the Native Liquor Ordinance of 1903 forbade the manufacturing and the sale of all drinks, including marisa, without a license.[51] Colonial officials were convinced that drunkenness was responsible for the spread of criminal activities in the rural areas. But the government had no means of enforcing these rules. The Native Liquors Act of 1919 prohibited the manufacture, sale, or possession of 'araqi or marisa without a license. Punishment for violation was imprisonment for up to one year, a fine, or both.[52] These laws did not have any effect. In fact, sale of local drinks increased in the urban centers, particularly during the depression, and was bitterly attacked in the local press. In 1934 *Al-Fajr* magazine deplored an incident in which a woman in Omdurman was caught hiding 'araqi in a handbag for the purpose of selling it on the streets.[53] At the official level, however, government officials lamented the fact that even middle-class civil servants drank 'araqi. In 1930, the civil secretary deplored this and contended that government employees should be prosecuted if found drinking 'araqi.[54] The governor of Khartoum Province mobilized native authorities to eradicate 'araqi drinking.[55] The district commissioner of Omdurman enlisted the support of the 'ulama against 'araqi drinking. The president of the board of 'ulama promised to speak on the subject in the mosque.[56] Municipal authorities launched a campaign against women who manufactured or sold local drinks. In 1934 the usual sentence imposed on women found manufacturing 'araqi, or in possession of it, was two months' imprisonment and a fine of LE 4 for manufacturing, or one month imprisonment and a fine of LE 2 for possession.[57]

Another activity that involved liberated female slaves was prostitution. Prostitution had been a major feature of urban life in Khartoum since the early years of colonial rule. Owing to the continuing migration of single men to the Three Towns, the demand for prostitutes grew and the capital was laced with brothels. Everywhere their presence contravened government laws and raised the wrath of the traditional Muslim establishment. Between 1923 and 1925, the total number of women convicted under the Vagabonds Ordinance was 555; of those, 319 were reportedly female ex-slaves.[58]

Despite the vagrancy laws, prostitution persisted and was tolerated by postindependence Sudanese governments. This activity was no longer limited to former female slaves but included freeborn women as well as Ethiopian immigrants. It remained an integral part of urban life in most Sudanese cities until the introduction of the Shari'a laws under Ja'far Numeiri in 1983.

NEIGHBORHOOD, COMMUNITY, AND CULTURE

The experience of urban ex-slaves and workers cannot be fully understood without an examination of their neighborhoods and the kind of communities they created. These were essential elements of workers' lives and played a crucial role in shaping their consciousness. Ex-slaves, migrants, wage, and nonwage workers lived in the same neighborhoods, engaged in a dense web of social networks, and created a vibrant popular culture.

By the late 1940s, Khartoum had become the home for a multitude of people from diverse ethnic, cultural, and regional backgrounds. The vast majority of these people lived in the Khartoum Daims and other working-class neighborhoods in the capital, where they established viable communities and shared the urban experience.

The postwar urban migration produced startling changes in the Daims. The continuous influx of people from the rural areas into the Daims created several layers within the population of these quarters. The old residents had become firmly rooted in the urban environment. They lived with their families and became well-integrated into the economic and social patterns of the city. The new immigrants, on the other hand, left their families behind and devised their own strategies for survival. They sought people from their home areas and developed several kinds of associations for help in times of need.

The first problem that faced any immigrant in the city on arrival was to find accommodation, which was mostly provided by relatives and "home people." Since most of the immigrants were single men, they usually stayed with bachelors from their home area. After finding work, they arranged to share a room or a house with friends and home people. The links with home people also played a major role in finding employment. The process of finding employment through personal connections naturally led to a concentration of workers from the same region or ethnic group in one quarter.[59]

In addition to links with kin in the urban environment, most of the immigrants retained significant connections with their home areas. The accommodation of visitors coming from home and looking after them constituted an essential part of migrants' social obligations. Failure to meet these obligations would severely damage the social standing of an individual both in town and in the rural areas. Links with home areas were also maintained through occasional return visits and money remittance to relatives.

Maintaining links with home areas was also related to different rights in land ownership and access to land. Immigrants, particularly from the riverain regions in the north, resorted to the institution of *amana* (trust), and arranged for their land to be cultivated by others (family members or trustworthy neighbors) and seldom considered selling it. Rather, savings accumulated while they were away would be invested in a waterwheel or in the purchase of more land.[60] Immigrants continued, therefore, to keep an eye on their land. However, the shortage of land along the banks of the Nile, and the application of the Shari'a law of inheritance, resulted in great fragmentation of land into small holdings. As time passed, interest in land and agriculture gradually declined and the vast majority of migrants became totally committed to urban living.

By the 1950s the two streams—the earlier and the new—converged to produce a growing ethnic diversity among the inhabitants of these quarters. Despite their ethnic diversity, the Daims' residents were welded together by social and economic conditions and the exigencies of urban life. There was a great deal of intermarriage between residents. Besides ethnicity, other social bonds such as neighborhood became important. People of the same *hay* (quarter) formed friendships and supported each other during social occasions such as weddings and funerals. The most important venues for social interaction were the social clubs, the anadi, the soccer teams, and the mosques.[61]

One of the most important examples of social networks that developed in the poor neighborhoods in the capital was the *sanduq* (box) or rotating savings association. Such groups, common in Africa, operated on the principle of tontine, in which a number of individuals would contribute a sum of money at specific intervals to such a savings group; at each interval one of the contributors would take the whole amount. Such associations first appeared in the Three Towns in the 1940s.[62] The sanduq included both males and females, bachelors and married couples. It was usually based on localities, although members from outside were often allowed to participate. It was the main way for working-class families to achieve a surplus so they could meet important expenses incurred such as house repair, and ceremonies surrounding birth, circumcision, engagement, and marriage.

Early residents, many of whom were ex-slaves, gave the Daims a distinctive character. Unlike other immigrants who maintained links with their home areas, some ex-slaves became deeply rooted in the urban environment. In many ways they were pioneers who made significant contributions to urban popular culture.[63]

Because of their background, mobility, and the nature of the urban environment, ex-slaves played a crucial role in the emergence of a vital popular culture. Since the vast majority of these people had come from non-Arab and non-Muslim groups in the south and the west, their culture had strong elements of resistance, synchronism, and adaptation. The first generation kept the traditions of their home areas alive in the urban environment. Drawing upon their own experience, old residents in the Daims still describe many of the activities that took place on Fridays in these neighborhoods. They included traditional dances from Dar Fur, Dar Fertit, the Nuba Mountains, and the southern Sudan.[64] In this manner cultural traits from the southern and western hinterlands survived for many decades in the Sudanese capital. According to informants, until the 1940s the Dinka, Kreish, Banda, and Nuba languages were widely spoken in the Khartoum Daims and Omdurman, and indigenous African religions were practiced throughout these neighborhoods.[65] However, ex-slaves were gradually assimilated into the cultural norms of the society which enslaved them. Indeed cultural uprooting and assimilation were two of the most fundamental features of slavery.[66] The conversion of ex-slaves and other non-Muslim groups in Khartoum was facilitated by the *khalawi* (Quranic schools), which were dominated by West African immigrants such as the Hausa, Borno, and Fulani fakis. Many ex-slaves of Dinka, Fertit, and Nuba origin became prominent religious figures in Khartoum.[67]

It was in the Daims, Mawrada, and 'Abbasiyya that people from different cultural backgrounds encountered each other and produced a new dynamic urban popular culture. Among the most significant aspects of this culture were music and singing. Since this subject has received little attention in popular and scholarly writings, the following analysis remains tentative.

Until World War I, Sudanese music and performance were limited to folk songs and traditional dances from different parts of the country. The most common type of singing in the northern Sudan was the *madeih*, a religious chanting that praised the Prophet Muhammad and local holy men. Another type was the *dobait*, vocalized singing in which a romantic theme or praise was communicated. Following the establishment of colonial rule and the rapid growth of urban centers, new forms of music and new styles of performance began to emerge in different Sudanese towns. The Three Towns took the lead in cultural activities.

The period after World War I saw the development of a new style of singing called *haqiba* (from the Arabic *hiqba*, or epoch), which incorporated the madeih style. According to the Sudanese musician and musicologist Jum'a Jabir, this new style first appeared in the Three Towns in the early 1920s.[68] The haqiba singing was performed by individual vocalists accompanied by a chorus, and the main musical instrument was the tambourine. However, in this particular form of singing the main emphasis was on the lyrics rather than the tunes.

Just as in southern Nigeria where new musical forms were pioneered by urban workers, the first generation of haqiba singers was drawn from the working population of Khartoum. They included artisans, tailors, mechanics, and many ex-slaves. It is important to mention that, at the height of Islamic civilization, professional musicians had come mainly from the *mawali* (medieval Arab term referring to clients or manumitted slaves) class as well as from non-Arab groups such as Persians and black Africans. Hence, singing and performance became associated with servile origins and low social status. The Arabized northern Sudanese held similar perceptions despite the fact that their traditional dances have distinctive African elements which were deeply rooted in their traditions. However, it is important to stress that the great majority of singers were Arabic-speaking northern Sudanese. The main concern here is the way in which ex-slaves introduced new styles of singing and dancing that had a lasting effect on Sudanese music.

The first generation of Sudanese musicians faced many challenges but were able to overcome tremendous social pressures. This was particularly the case with female singers, who had to contend with the additional burden of gender discrimination. During the 1920s and 1930s, there were at least thirteen well-known female Sudanese singers of whom the most popular was 'Aysha al-Flatiyya, a Sudanese of West African origin. The hostility she faced as a female performer and as a Fallata prompted her to consider seriously returning for good to Nigeria, her original homeland.[69]

At the beginning, haqiba singers performed mainly at weddings and other social occasions. However, the first commercial recording appeared as early as 1921, when an Egyptian record company opened a branch in Omdurman.[70] A few years later, two other Egyptian companies—Audion and Misiyan—established branches in Omdurman. The production of phonograph records played a major role in popularizing haqiba songs, as did the political climate of the early 1920s. Slogans of the White Flag League and pro-Egyptian groups—such as "Unity of the Nile Valley"— became major themes of haqiba songs.

However, the most important role in the dissemination of urban music was played by the Omdurman radio station, which was established in 1941.[71] This was accompanied by the introduction of new musical instruments such as the mandolin, violin, accordion, trumpet, and piano. This represented a major shift in haqiba singing as many performers began to rely on these instruments rather than on a chorus. As pointed out in chapter 4, discharged soldiers had played a major role in popularizing Western musical instruments. These instruments and urban stylistic influences were combined with the Sudanese rhythms and dance to lead to the rise of a new form of music which set the standard for urban music.

By the end of World War II, however, a new form of popular culture in the Three Towns began to appear in working-class neighborhoods such as the Daims and Mawrada, where people gathered for social recreation. The new means of mass communication such as radio, television, and newspapers exposed all segments of the urban population to European and American popular music, including jazz. Electronic instruments became a common feature of Sudanese music. By the 1960s and 1970s a blend of Sudanese, European, and Afro-American music began to emerge in Khartoum. This was best exemplified by the music of the late Osman Alamo and Sharhabil Ahmad. The latter is a Sudanese of West African origin who is still considered the doyen of "Sudanese Jazz." Sharhabil's music is a blend of jazz and indigenous musical idioms and lyrics. Once again, ex-slaves, and people of southern and western Sudanese and West African origin, were in the vanguard, followed soon by others. In Sharhabil's footsteps, jazz bands began to emerge in different parts of Khartoum and Omdurman. Of these, the most prominent was *Firqat Jazz al-Dium*, which was founded in the Daims. Professional musicians found that their art was in great demand in the urban area and provided entertainment for its residents. In wedding and naming ceremonies, on the streets, and in drinking houses, several styles of music were played.

The Khartoum Daims, 'Abbasiyya, and Mawrada not only became the homes of many musicians and performers who had a lasting impact on Sudanese urban music, but they also produced many athletes who became stars in al-Hilal, al-Mareikh, and Mawrada soccer clubs. Residents of these quarters were highly cosmopolitan. They developed unique styles of dress and attitudes which distinguished them from other urban residents. Arabic-speaking northern Sudanese associated residents of the Daims, 'Abbasiyya, and Mawrada with social deviance and servile origin. These quarters remained enclaves in which the cultures of ex-slaves and non-Arab Sudanese groups thrived and became integral parts of Khartoum popular culture.

Urban ex-slaves were pioneers in several other ways. They took the lead in articulating the grievances of all non-Arab groups in the Sudan and established political organizations to defend their interests.

EX-SLAVES AND THE STRUGGLE FOR EQUALITY

In order to understand the response of ex-slaves, it is essential to locate them within the Sudanese social structure.

Half a century of colonial rule brought about profound changes in Sudanese society with far-reaching implications. It created a number of social forces that developed different forms of consciousness and collective action as well as various visions of society and identity.

It is evident that the main beneficiaries of the colonial economy were tribal heads, religious leaders, and big merchants. The latter included the

Mahdi and the Mirghani families. In urban centers, a small class of commercial and industrial bourgeoisie, consisting mainly of foreign nationals, dominated the import and export trade. Below these groups was a small class of salaried civil servants and professionals. At the bottom was the mass of farmers, nomads, urban workers, and agricultural laborers, who constituted the overwhelming majority of the population. Tribal heads, religious leaders, and big merchants, the vast majority of whom were Arabic-speaking northern Sudanese, came to express their class interests through the political parties that came to power after independence.

Since educational services were concentrated in the central and the northern parts of the country, most of the educated elements who later dominated nationalist politics came from these regions. In other words, the vast majority of the Sudanese elites were Arabic-speaking northerners who embraced an Arab identity. This identity became a major criterion for distinction and exclusion. In the late 1930s these elites formed the Graduates Congress, the antecedent of the major political parties. Although the nationalist movement in its origin was secular, its leaders soon realized that the only ones who could mobilize people beyond the tribal level were the sectarian figures. Hence, nationalist leaders sought the backing of Sayyid 'Abd al-Rahman al-Mahdi of the Ansar, and Sayyid 'Ali al-Mirghani of the Khatimiyya. The alliance between the intelligentsia and the religious establishment determined the character of the political parties. In this manner the Umma Party became the political voice of the Mahdists. Its support came mainly from the traditional followers of the Mahdiyya in Kordofan, Dar Fur, and the White Nile Province. The National Unionist Party (NUP), on the other hand, initially had the backing of the Khatimiyya Sect, but later the Khatimiyya shifted its support to the People's Democratic Party. Although the NUP had no particular ideology, it was known for its pro-Egyptian sentiment. In brief, the political parties that were founded under colonial rule and came to dominate Sudanese politics afterwards, represented the interest of the traditional establishment.

The lower strata of the social hierarchy consisted of an array of disparate groups such as workers, agricultural laborers, poor peasants, and nomads. Although ex-slaves were scattered across the lower rung of the social hierarchy, they continued to suffer from the badge of slavery and were regarded as socially and culturally inferior. It is not surprising that the language in which they expressed their identity and articulated their grievances took an ethnic form. In this regard, urban ex-slaves, particularly in Khartoum, took the lead in articulating these grievances and tried to create a united front embracing ex-slaves as well as all non-Arab groups in the Sudan.

The first known political organization that squarely began to address the conditions of ex-slaves and their descendants was *al-kutla al-Sawda* (The Black Block) which was founded in 1938 by the thirty-year-old medical assistant, Muhammad Adam Adham, who came from a Dar Fur slave family. Muhammad's father was an army officer of Daju origin. After his graduation from the Kitchener School of Medicine, Muhammad joined the Sudan Medical Service in 1936 as a medical officer. However, his career was marred by troubles relating to excessive drinking and neglect of his duties, which forced him to resign.[72] With financial assistance from his family, he opened a private clinic in Omdurman.

The Black Block began as a social organization. It was preceded by the Black Co-operative Society, which was founded in the late 1930s as a philanthropic organization mainly concerned with the social conditions of discharged soldiers and ex-slaves in the Three Towns. In 1948, the Black Co-operative Society became the Black Block, which was officially launched by Adham in the Three Towns of Khartoum, Khartoum North, and Omdurman.

Although the block's main concern was improvement of social and economic conditions of people from the southern Sudan and the Nuba Mountains, in order to elude the government, the organization adopted broad and less militant slogans. Its declared objectives were:

1. Strengthening national unity by national reforms

2. Social betterment, improvement of the conditions of the poor, fighting crime, etc.

3. Elimination of social distinctions between Sudanese citizens

4. Institution in the Sudan of a free democratic government to maintain social justice and equality and develop the country in all respects

5. Building of a strong national army, equipped with modern weapons.[73]

The Black Block gradually became more vocal in its political objectives. At the time, the British administration in the Sudan was setting up the Legislative Assembly which was boycotted by the pro-Egyptian unionist parties but was supported by the Umma Party, whose opposition to unity with Egypt was a position favored by the British authorities. The Black Block supported the establishment of the Legislative Assembly and participated in its elections, winning two seats in Khartoum and Omdurman.[74]

The Black Block developed close contacts with the Umma Party because of the latter's opposition to the Sudan's union with Egypt and its support for the idea of the "Sudan for the Sudanese." One of the leading figures of the Black Block was 'Abd al-Qadir Ahmad Sa'id, who was also a member of the Umma Party. He advocated the position that the block should serve two purposes: to look after the interests of the "blacks" in the Sudan; and to support the Umma Party in the elections to the Legislative Assembly. In 1948, he approached the secretary general of the Umma Party for financial support. A few days later, Osman Mutwali met 'Abdalla Khalil, a prominent leader of the Umma Party who later became prime minister, and requested financial support (LE 500) for propaganda purposes. Some members of the Umma Party were apprehensive about the block, fearing that it might begin to call for the separation of the south from the rest of the country. After further consideration and consultations with leaders of the Umma, a sum of LE 300 was given to the block, with a promise that the balance would be paid in due course.[75]

A general meeting of the Black Block was held at Dr. Adham's house in Omdurman on 18 October 1948 and was attended by several hundred people, most of whom had come from the Khartoum Daims.[76] Speeches were made emphasizing that the objective of the organization was to safeguard and promote the interests of blacks in the Sudan. An administrative committee comprising forty-five members and a fifteen-member executive committee were formed. Besides Adam Adham, who was the treasurer of the organization, leading members included: Osman Mutwali, originally a Daju from Dar Fur, who was the vice-president; Zayn al-'Abdein 'Abd al-Tam, a retired army officer who had been a leading figure in the White Flag League; 'Abd al-Nabi 'Abd al-Qadir, an ex-army officer of Shilluk origin who was the general secretary; and Hasan Murjan, a civil service employee of Dinka origin, who was vice-secretary.[77] Following the meeting in Omdurman, a delegation comprising Dr. Adham, 'Abd al-Qadir Ahmad Sa'id, Ahmad 'Ajab, and Ramadan 'Azzam, proceeded to Atbara to rally the support of the black workers of the Railway Department. Another delegation headed by Osman Mutwali went to Kassala where they found a great deal of enthusiasm. They then proceeded to Port Sudan where they received conditional support, the condition being that the block should not be subservient to the Umma Party and should back the policy of the colonial government to establish a Legislative Assembly.[78] Other towns in which the campaign was successful were Kosti and Sinnar. In Wad Medani, however, the delegation was met by strong opposition from a more militant group called the "Black Liberals." This organization had been founded and led by 'Abd al-Jalil Faraj Abu Zayd, his brother 'Abd al-Qadir, Gindeil Effendi, Bakheit Mustafa al-Tayyib, and Ibrahim 'Abdalla.[79] Apparently, the objective of the Black Liberals was to discredit the leaders of the Black Block because of their support of the Umma Party. When elections to the Legislative Assembly were held in Wad Medani, the Black Block worked hand in hand with the Umma Party. After the elections, the Black Liberals continued their opposition openly.

The most prominent figures of the Black Block in Wad Medani were 'Abd al-Nabi 'Abd al-Qadir Mursal and 'Abd al-Rasul 'Abd al-Jalil. It was reported that 'Abd al-Rasul had persuaded Ahmad Fattah al-Bishari, a prominent businessman in Wad Medani, to assist black soldiers discharged from the Egyptian Army and their families as well as any other blacks who needed assistance. According to official reports, money was actually given to some families in Omdurman under the pretext that it was coming from the "Officers' Fund."[80] Despite continued opposition of the Black Liberals, the Black Block continued to command an overwhelming majority.

The Black Block expanded rapidly and attracted an increasing number of people from the Nuba Mountains and Dar Fur and from among West African immigrants and ex-slaves. Social clubs were established in the main Sudanese towns and Adham began to edit a biweekly journal called *Africa*, which addressed social and cultural subjects. In order to undercut profiteering by northern Sudanese merchants and build a financial base, the block established its own shops in different parts of Khartoum.[81]

Northern Sudanese political parties dismissed the Black Block as a racist organization and the colonial government refused to license it as a political party. Many of its social clubs were closed down, but later were allowed to reopen on the condition that they confine their activities to social affairs. As a result, the Black Block never became a full-fledged political party and suffered from poor organization. No names of its members had hitherto been registered. Printed subscription forms were prepared but never distributed. Moreover, the organization continued to experience financial difficulties. It was reported that in 1949 it had a credit balance of about LE 80.[82] As a result of all this the activities of the block diminished and by 1954 it had become an underground organization.

The Black Block represented the first attempt to form a broad front comprising ex-slaves and other non-Arab groups in the Sudan. Following its collapse, these groups fragmented into a number of regional movements. In 1954 a Nuba Mountains General Union was formed by people who had been active in the block; a Beja Union was established again by former members of the Black Block; and similar organizations were also formed in Dar Fur.

The rise and fall of the Black Block was significant in many ways. Its rise underlined the contradictory elements of incorporation and marginality which slavery involved.[83] Its failure, on the other hand, was a manifestation of the complex class structure that had begun to take shape. The conditions of ex-slaves and their descendants in the northern Sudan were different from those of non-Arab groups in the south and the west. Indeed, what is common between them is that they were both victims of northern Sudanese racial attitudes. But for the ex-slaves and their descendants, the redefinition of identity was more complex.

In his study of ex-slaves on the East African coast, Frederick Cooper has argued that during the time of slavery, the social identification of slaves pointed in two directions. On the one hand, they became Muslims and learned about Islam to assert their moral equality. On the other hand, they held on to their traditions in order to assert the validity of their own culture. In the postemancipation period, they were more likely to identify with the owners' culture, which would provide them with social and economic stability.[84] Ex-slaves and their descendants in the northern Sudan were assimilated into northern Sudanese culture in crucial ways. The vast majority of them became Muslims and spoke Arabic. This was part of the process of uprooting which enslavement involved. Assimilation of ex-slaves into northern Sudanese cultural norms "conferred" upon them a rank higher than that of southern Sudanese and other non-Arab groups who were regarded with great disdain, on racial as well as cultural grounds. So, if social discrimination was the common factor between ex-slaves in the northern Sudan and other non-Arabized groups, cultural factors divided them. These differences can be illustrated by examining the relationship between the two groups.

Several attempts were made by leaders of the Black Block to form an alliance with southern Sudanese political organizations in the Three Towns. For example, when the Southern Sudan Emergency Political Committee was formed by southern Sudanese immigrants in Khartoum in the early 1950s, a group of ex-slave soldiers (who had formed an organization called the Sudan Union Party) approached them with the idea of forming a joint political party. However, this was flatly rejected by Southerners on the grounds that these ex-soldiers had pro-Egyptian views.[85] The southern Sudanese strongly believed that the Sudan Union Party was simply a branch of the National Unionist Party, which called for unity with Egypt. They further alleged that the Sudan Union Party had received a sum of LE 4,000 from Major Salah Salim, the Egyptian minister, during his visit to the Sudan in the early 1950s.[86] It is not clear whether or not these allegations were true. What is clear, however, is that these ex-servicemen continued to harbor an unwavering loyalty to Egypt and continued to embrace the slogan of the "Unity of the Nile Valley."

Southern Sudanese were decidedly apprehensive of the ex-slaves who were living in the northern Sudan. In their view, these people had lost their identity and were assimilated into the northern Sudanese cultural norms. For example, the membership of the Southern Social and Political Club, which was established in Khartoum, was confined to "genuine southerners" whose homes were south of the 14th parallel.[87] This reflected the nature of the social structure that emerged during the colonial period and of the polarization of Sudanese society along regional and ethnic lines. By independence, political conflicts in the Sudan were clearly drawn along ethnic and regional lines.

LABOR PROTESTS IN KHARTOUM AND POSTWAR SOCIAL REFORMS

The bulk of the literature on the Sudanese labor movement has focused mainly on industrial workers employed in large factories and the transportation sector. Little attention was given to workers in small factories as well as nonwage workers.[88] This bias stemmed from the belief that the environment in which small factory workers and self-employed persons worked did not foster the growth of working-class consciousness and activism. It is not surprising that Khartoum workers have received little attention despite the fact that they engaged in various forms of labor protests before and after World War II.

The Three Towns had the largest concentration of workers and civil servants. The capital was also the political hub of the country and the headquarters of the various nationalist organizations. Khartoum workers took the lead in establishing working-class associations. The first workers' club in the country was established in Khartoum in 1935. It published a magazine called *Al-'Amil al-Sudani* (The Sudanese Worker). Moreover, workers were instrumental in the establishment of soccer clubs such as Hilal, Mareikh, Mawrada, Burri, and so forth. These clubs gave workers an opportunity to gather for social and cultural purposes.

As early as the 1930s, Khartoum workers engaged in collective actions and demanded better working conditions. Urban workers were hit hard by the depression. In addition to low pay, these workers resented the continuing employment of foreign artisans at a time when many Sudanese were unemployed. A stream of articles in *Al-Fajr* deplored this policy and suggested that the government should stop the immigration of foreign artisans.[89] Labor unrest in Khartoum was best exemplified by the strike of the tram workers of the Sudan Light and Power Company.

The first tramway in the Three Towns had been inaugurated in 1904.[90] By 1906 it carried over a million passengers a year. Another line was established in Omdurman in 1906. Twelve trains a day were running from Abu Ruf in the north to Mawrada in the south. From there a steam ferry carried passengers to Khartoum. By 1910 the Khartoum tramline had been extended to Khartoum North. Expansion of this service continued, and by the late 1920s many parts of the Three Towns were linked by tramlines which became the main means of transportation for urban residents.

After 1925 the tramway was managed by the Sudan Light and Power Company, in which the government held 49 percent of the shares.[91] The company employed over two hundred workers and technicians on a permanent basis. The drivers and conductors of the trams went on strike to protest low salaries, lack of fringe benefits, and the continuing employment of foreigners. Workers' demands included:

1. An increase in salaries in general

2. Payment of gratuities on the basis of half a month's pay for every complete year spent in the service of the company, provided that the workers had served for a continuous period of no less than five years

3. Medical treatment in hospitals in accordance with privileges enjoyed by other government employees

4. Payment of compensation to those injured while on duty in accordance with the Workmen's Compensation Ordinance

5. Every vacancy in the company should be filled by competent Sudanese staff who should have preference over foreigners in this respect.[92]

The strike took the government by surprise, and created a crisis in the Three Towns since the tram was the main means of transportation for government employees. The municipal authorities took emergency steps: tolls for taxis on the White Nile Bridge were removed, lorries were allowed to carry passengers, government cars and trucks were used, and a barge service in the capital was organized. The strike lasted four days and was called off after the mediation of the two sectarian leaders, 'Abd al-Rahman al-Mahdi and 'Ali al-Mirghani, and other notables.

Despite its failure, the action of the tramway workers forced the government to reexamine the conditions of permanent workers. Even before the end of the strike, the secretary of the Labour Committee wrote to the governor of Khartoum expressing his fears that the strike might "stimulate native discontent with current wages for casual and semi-skilled laborers."[93] The secretary admitted that the cost of living for urban workers was too high. He stressed the need to investigate the circumstances which had led to the strike and the necessity to raise wages for workers in both government service and private firms to rates "more compatible with present post-retrenchment standards of living."[94] However, when the issue was presented to the financial secretary, his response was not sympathetic. The workers' demand of a gratuity at the end of five years' service was considered "unreasonable."[95] On the subject of compensation, it was admitted that the government rules on this subject were unsatisfactory and should be amended along the lines of the workmen's compensation scheme, which would relate the compensation more directly to the extent of disability.[96]

Strikes increased during the war years. In 1941 and 1942 different groups of workers struck no less than fourteen times in different parts of the country.[97] The government did not pay attention to the conditions of permanent workers until after World War II when labor protests grew.

Khartoum workers were active participants in postwar labor protests. These protests involved both wage and nonwage workers. Following the legalization of trade unions, bakery workers, carpenters, builders, and tailors formed unions and became affiliated with the Sudan Workers' Trade Union Federation. Even unemployed workers formed their own union.[98] Strikes increased during the following years. In response to an increase in the Traders' License fee, taxi drivers struck for four days in January and for two days in May 1949. Bakery workers struck for five days in March 1950 and were followed by the employees of the Sudan Light and Power Company. Similar actions were taken by medical dressers in April 1950.[99] During the same year the SWTUF moved its headquarters from Atbara to Khartoum. The Workers' Club in Khartoum became a meeting place for urban workers and trade unions, and the capital was transformed into a center of agitation and political unrest.

The widespread labor unrest in the postwar years threatened the social and political order and forced the government to deal with the labor question which had been ignored for several decades. Indeed, these labor protests took place in different parts of Africa and prompted the colonial governments to adopt new labor and social policies. According to Frederick Cooper, the new strategies aimed at the creation of a stable and productive working class, a task that involved provision of stable housing and family life and other social services. This goal would also require the separation of the working class from the urban "riffraffs" and the eradication of casual labor.[100] Cooper's argument may not apply to those African cities such as Atbara, which had a relatively stable work force. However, it is certainly relevant to Khartoum where casual labor was predominant. In the postwar years colonial officials in the Sudan engaged in lengthy debate on casual labor and urban migration. They also launched a massive campaign of clearing slums and rehousing urban workers in Khartoum.

THE DEBATE ON URBAN MIGRATION AND CASUAL LABOR

During the early period of colonial rule the presence of ex-slaves and other dislocated people in Khartoum was tolerated because it provided cheap labor. However, the continuing migration and presence of a floating population and "unproductive" elements in the cities were considered potentially threatening to urban order and to the economic well-being of the country. As one colonial official put it:

> The only class of persons who were excessive and therefore undesirable were casual laborers: the other type of persons, such as artisans, educated persons, etc. seeking to live in Khartoum were not undesirable.[101]

From the mid-1940s, administrators engaged in lengthy deliberations on how to curb the rural-urban migration and on how to purge the city of "unproductive" people. Indeed, the "drift to towns" became a common cliché in the colonial literature across Africa.

In June 1944, the civil secretary wrote to the governors of Khartoum, Kassala, Kordofan, and the northern provinces inquiring about the state of rural-urban migration in their provinces, particularly the immigration and settlement of the Fallata, and what measures they had taken to prevent it.[102] A committee was set up in Khartoum, comprising senior municipal staff, to study the drift to towns and to recommend measures to check it. The governor of Khartoum Province instructed his district commissioners to compile data on the rate and the nature of population growth in Khartoum

North, Omdurman, and Khartoum. With no expertise in social survey or statistical method, municipal officials began to compile information on population growth, birth and mortality rates, rural-urban migration, geographical origin of immigrants in the capital, etc. Massive data was produced and files on the subject became thicker. But the findings were marred by inaccuracies and discrepancies, usually based on figures that were mere guesses.

The greatest attention was given to Omdurman where the majority of urban residents lived and engaged in nonwage activities. J. Longe, the district commissioner in the early 1940s, had this to say about Omdurman:

> Omdurman is obviously far too big for so poor a country as the Sudan. No where else in the world is there so large a community which is so unproductive. It has not even one secondary industry in which a single firm employs as much as 20 people regularly. It is a parasitic wen on the body politic of the country, owing its origin largely to the stupidity of the Khalifa and its subsequent spread to our reluctance to face the problem he left us. It can have no future as a town unless it begins to be productive. At present it is only what the London papers recently called: "The Largest Village in the World," a village that grows no crops and pastures no herds.[103]

The district commissioner went on to suggest several measures to discourage settlement in the city. These included the refusal to issue ration cards except to: (1) children whose parents were established residents in Omdurman; (2) government officials who were transferred from outside districts; (3) employed persons who carried certificates from their employers; (4) women who came to join their husbands; and (5) persons whose original home was Omdurman and who came for permanent residence in it. The most important measures, however, were: abolition of the freehold land system; control of housing loans, which was given to government officials; the establishment of zoning and the enforcement of strict building specifications in certain areas; and control of traders licenses.[104] The substitution of leasehold for freehold was adopted by the Omdurman Municipal Council in March 1946.[105]

The antipathy of colonial officials was not limited to casual labor but to urbanization itself.[106] It emanated from their resistance to social change and their fear of its consequences. Moreover, in their view urbanization was an anachronism:

The Sudan is essentially an agricultural country and there is no reason to suppose that it will ever be anything else, and as such every effort must be made to prevent its becoming an importer of food and all our energy should be directed to make it if possible, an exporter or at least self sustaining in the basic agricultural commodities.[107]

Hence, every possible attempt was made to encourage people to remain in the countryside and to prevent them from coming to the cities. But the conditions that impelled people to leave their home areas remained unmeasured by colonial administrators.

At its meeting in January 1946, the municipal council recommended that the best strategy to curb immigration from the north was to improve the social and economic conditions in that part of the country. As for the West Africans and Nuba immigrants, the council suggested that they should be repatriated.[108] The solution proposed by the governor of Khartoum Province to the civil secretary was to establish a labor bureau to control employment and to restrict rations. Furthermore, the "Native Lodging Area" should be classified as a "fourth-class" residential neighborhood, which meant that it would not be entitled to government services such as water and electricity. The governor also felt that it might be necessary to introduce legislation prohibiting overcrowding by making it an offense for anyone to provide lodging for more than a specified number of people in one house. In order to cut out petty traders and middlemen, the governor proposed setting up cooperative groceries and shops in various neighborhoods.[109]

It was realized that these measures would have no effect unless the problem was tackled at its roots: living conditions in rural areas. Thus the drift to towns had finally awakened colonial officials to the neglect of remote parts of the country. In their view, rural-urban migration could be checked by "making life in the rural areas more attractive" and at the same time making it "less attractive in the urban centers." With regard to the first, ideas were debated about the development of water supplies, introduction of mechanized farming, the supply of consumer goods, etc. Yet ideas about rural development were phrased as wishes and hopes, while the task of making urban life less desirable for immigrants was pursued with great vigor and enthusiasm. In June 1948 the civil secretary wrote to the provincial governors proposing several measures to be taken in order to make life in the urban centers "less attractive" for immigrants.[110] They included strict prosecution of vagabonds, fighting the black market, keeping the price of grain high, making town water more expensive, increasing the price of traders licenses, and spending less money on capital works in towns.[111] The governor of Khartoum Province showed little enthusiasm for these proposals and voiced objections to most of them. It had become clear that the whole question of rural-urban migration was blown out of proportion as a result of unreliable data. He argued that

> it would be highly dangerous to take any *drastic* measures to interfere with the growth and development of any of the Three Towns *unless such measures were preceded by an expert social survey which showed beyond doubt that they were both necessary and socially sound.*[112]

Instead, in line with the postwar strategy toward migrant labor, and in its attempt to create a decent, efficient, and modernized working class, the government launched a "slum clearance" campaign and began to take steps to demolish the Daims and relocate their residents farther south.

REHOUSING URBAN WORKERS

A central element in the postwar approach was housing. Housing was closely linked to the stability and the reproduction of the labor force. During the early decades, colonial governments tolerated the huts and hovels that accommodated casual workers. But the creation of a more stable and productive work force required decent and healthy housing.

As mentioned previously, the Daims were classified by the government as a "Native Lodging Area," which was meant to provide "temporary" lodging for urban workers.[113] By World War II there were eighteen Daims comprising 5,777 houses and accommodating approximately 30,000 people. The quality of housing in the Daims remained unchanged from the turn of the century. Inhabitants continued to live in mud houses with an average area of 30 to 60 square meters. There were no toilets or pit latrines; the population used the open spaces adjoining the Daims.[114]

The removal of the Daims, on health and sanitary grounds, had been on the agenda of municipal authorities since the 1930s. In 1937 it was decided that 200 square meters was the minimum area adequate for a single house and a layout was drawn up accordingly, which enabled a pit latrine to be dug for each house. But owing to lack of funds, no systematic action was taken and authorities continued to tolerate existing residential patterns in the Daims. Conditions wrought by postwar immigration generated an enormous demand for housing, especially in the first- and second-class areas in which European expatriate and senior Sudanese civil servants lived. These conditions also increased overcrowding in the Daims. Since Khartoum was surrounded by rivers on the north, east and west, the only direction for further expansion was to the south, where the Daims were located. Hence, the Daims were an obstacle to any future development. Municipal authorities had two alternatives: either remove them or leave them where they were and plan a new residential area to the south of them. The first alternative was the more attractive, owing to the fact that land classified as a "Native Lodging Area" was owned by the government and the government had the right to evict residents at any time on one month's notice.[115] A new plan was devised in 1946–1947 according to which 550 people from the old Daims were allotted plots in the New Daims to the southeast of the old ones. They were required to sign a contract that they would demolish their houses in the old Daims as soon as they had built new houses. In practice the allottees moved to the "New Daims," leaving their houses in the old Daims intact, and started renting them out to tenants. Such rents became a major source of income for the landlords, who vehemently opposed resettlement when it was undertaken later on. By 1948 the demand for land in Khartoum had become acute; the gap between the old Daims and the town had been completely filled and there was no room for expansion farther south. The allottees therefore profited considerably at the expense of newcomers to the area.

In March 1949, the government appointed a retired Sudanese district commissioner as Daims Resettlement Officer and instructed him to carry out a "social survey" to determine the ownership of the plots and the length of residence.[116] A Workers' Housing Committee under the chairmanship of the commissioner of labor was established in 1952. With the help of Khartoum University College, a survey of 8,000 workers' homes was conducted.[117] In 1949 the Daims residents were classified into three main groups:

Group A. Comprised "absentee allottees" who had been allotted new plots and had completed and moved into houses on them but had continued to retain possession of their original plots in the old Daims.

Group B. Comprised "occupying allottees." This category included persons who either by original allotment or by purchase or inheritance from an allottee had acquired a house in the old Daims and were living in it.

Group C. Comprised the tenants of the absentee allottees of Group A.

The municipal authorities then decided to allot free 200-square-meter plots in the New Daims, subject to the payment to the municipality of a sum of fifteen piastres per month as ground rent and property tax, to all occupying allottees in Group B and all tenants in Group C who had resided in the old Daims for at least ten years, had their families living with them, and had permanent employment in Khartoum. At the same time, notice was given to all occupying allottees in Group B and tenants in Group C who had been given plots in the New Daims in 1946–1947 and had completed their houses there, informing them that they must move into their new houses within three months, after which their old houses in the old Daims would be demolished. Considerable opposition came from the landlords, who did not want to lose the income from rent. Despite the opposition, the authorities decided in June 1949 to move ahead and issued warnings to the effect that if occupants did not move to their new plots by the end of the year, they would lose them.[118] It was anticipated that most of these people could use the material from their old houses to build the new ones. Those who could not afford to build would either be left in their old houses and would receive an ex gratia payment by way of compensation for vacating them, or, if destitute, would be accommodated in the Alms House.

The demolition of the old Daims commenced in 1949, and by April, Daim Fallata had been completely destroyed. The absentee landlords from Daim Salman and al-Gashasha raised storms of protest, but their opposition was suppressed when the government repossessed 103 plots in the New Daims from those residents who had been allotted plots in 1946–1947. After long negotiations the plots were restored to their original allottees on the condition that they complete their new houses and demolish the old ones by the end of the year.[119] By the end of 1949, 1,036 houses had been demolished in Daim Salman, al-Gashasha, and Telegraph. At the beginning, the demolition was done by prison gangs, but as demand increased, paid labor was used. The steady pace of demolition continued and 1,009 houses were demolished in 1950, 1,884 in 1951, and 1,848 in 1952. By January 1953, the seventy remaining ruined houses and eight shops had been demolished and all that remained in the old Daims were two mosques, three bakeries, and one flour mill. Thus within three years, 5,855 houses and shops had been demolished. The construction of houses in the New Daims was carried out simultaneously with the demolition of the old Daims. By 1953 about 8,000 plots had been allotted in the New Daims. However, about 100 persons who lived in the old Daims and were qualified for plots, did not wish to receive them as they could not afford to develop them, and therefore each was given LE 10 as compensation. An additional eighty people who did not qualify for plots were also compensated, while twenty-five destitute West Africans were accommodated in the Alms House in the New Daims.[120]

Allottees were required to build their houses according to standard building plans prepared by the municipal engineer. Each plan provided for a family room, guest room, veranda, kitchen, bathroom, and pit latrine. Houses were arranged in blocks, each block containing approximately fifty plots.[121] At the same time, a plan provided open spaces in the middle of every fifty plots. One shop was also provided for every two blocks. Realizing the importance of marisa for urban workers, the authorities allotted twenty-two plots to marisa makers in 1950 in the southwestern area of the New Daims.[122] At the beginning, all the plots in the New Daims were allocated on Native Lodging Area terms, which meant that no written leases were prepared. The lease term for the standard third-class area was twenty years, renewable for two periods of ten years.[123]

Large-scale relocation did not fragment the old neighborhood. This was due to the manner in which the resettlement was carried out. The residents of each Daim were moved together and settled within one or two blocks. Even today the blocks continue to advertise their ethnic heritage in such names as Daim Banda and Daim Zubayriya. However, with the continuing flow of immigrants, neighborhoods became more diverse.

Meanwhile migration to the Three Towns continued unabated. As the Daims and other "native lodging areas" became saturated, the new immigrants settled in shantytowns and squatters' slums on the outskirts of the Three Towns. One of the earliest of such settlements was 'Ishash Fallata on the southern edge of Khartoum. As the name indicates it was inhabited mainly by West African immigrants as well as other western Sudanese. The 1951 Khartoum annual report described it as the "worst and most overcrowded slum in Khartoum."[124]

The influx of rural poor continued to increase, especially from the south as a result of the civil war. In the late 1960s, squatters in the Three Towns were estimated at 40,000, of whom 17,000 were in Khartoum North. Approximately 84.6 percent of the latter worked in the textile factory there. About 58.2 percent of the squatters were from Kordofan and 35.1 percent were from Dar Fur.[125] In 1969 the government appointed a committee to deal with the "problem." After a great deal of deliberation, the committee recommended that the existing "carton" villages should be removed, and that families of Sudanese origin should be given plots of 200 square meters in an area that would be classified as a fourth-class residential area. Municipal authorities were urged to provide water, electricity, and health facilities in these neighborhoods. It was further decided that foreign nationals as well as unemployed Sudanese migrants should be removed. By the early 1970s a large number of the Khartoum North squatters had been moved to the new residential area of al-Haj Yusuf.

Postindependence Sudanese governments maintained colonial urban policies. Houses were divided into first-class, second-class, and third-class categories. In the 1950s, a first-class house had a minimum of 400 square meters, a second-class house had 300 square meters, and a third-class house had 200 square meters. These figures were adjusted later to 750 square meters, 500 square meters, and 300 square meters, respectively.[126] The first-class areas had a building density of three to four houses per acre. They were inhabited by high-income groups including senior government officials, merchants, and businessmen. Their design followed a European style. The same applied to the second-class houses. In terms of inhabitants, the first-class area was almost exclusively dominated by the more prosperous and more educated riverain northerners and expatriates.[127] However, in the third-class areas, the building density was between ten and fifteen houses to one acre, while in the Fallata village it was between thirty-three and thirty-five houses to the acre.[128] The contrast was not limited to density of houses only but also included building materials, physical appearance, and the type of social services each area received. While houses in the first- and second-class areas were built from red brick, the Daims' houses (known locally as *jaloos*) were built from mud and were easily damaged by heavy rains. However, the worst housing conditions prevailed in the shantytowns such as the Fallata and *Kartoon* (carton) villages, in which there were no facilities, and even drinking water was drawn from shallow wells dug by the inhabitants.[129] Once again, the convergence of class and ethnicity was manifested in the pattern of urban residences in the Three Towns. While the first- and the second-class residential neighborhoods were dominated by riverain northern Sudanese, the vast majority of immigrants from the southern and western Sudan and West Africans lived either in the Daims or in the shantytowns and squatters' settlements.

Like its predecessor, the postcolonial state exhibited a great deal of hostility toward the squatter settlements, which were periodically bulldozed and their residents rounded up and expelled from the capital. Since independence, several plans have been drawn up to remove the Fallata village but for political reasons they have never been carried out. Another major squatter settlement was the Kartoon village (carton village), which was established in Khartoum North in the 1960s by immigrants from Dar Fur and Kordofan who worked in the industrial area there. Several attempts by the municipal authorities to remove them were blocked by the central government at the time for political reasons. The vast majority of these immigrants were ardent supporters of the Umma Party whose leaders made every effort to keep them in Khartoum for electoral purposes. In the 1970s the *kasha* (rounding up) became a daily routine for the municipal police. The hostility toward squatters has become more intense in recent years, with the influx of refugees fleeing the famine and the civil wars in the south and the west. Harassment of squatters and other migrants from remote parts of the Sudan underlines the political and cultural hegemony of the dominant classes and reveals their views about Sudanese identity.[130] By preventing migrants from the remote parts of the country from residing in the capital, the central government has tried to emphasize the marginality of these regions and perpetuate the political and economic inequalities in the country.

War, drought, and famine have continued to drive thousands of people from the south and the west to Khartoum, with far-reaching demographic and political consequences. In the 1986 parliamentary elections, Philip 'Abbas Ghabosh of the Sudanese National Party won in al-Haj Yusuf District of Khartoum North. A Nuba from Kordofan, Ghabosh has been a champion of the Nuba and other non-Arab groups in the country. His victory in Khartoum is a clear illustration of how ethnic composition of the northern Sudanese population in general, and in the capital in particular, has changed.

CONCLUSION

By the second decade of colonial rule, the vast majority of Khartoum slaves were able to redeem themselves and were joined by streams of immigrants from the rural areas. Ex-slaves became part of a diverse group of people. Urban residents took advantage of their proximity to the Gezira and moved back and forth between the city and the countryside. In this way the Three Towns continued to function as a labor reservoir. This pattern persisted until World War II. However, after the war, the demand for casual labor in the capital decreased and unemployment became rampant. Nevertheless, rural-urban migration increased in the postwar era. Ex-slaves, workers, and immigrants in Khartoum built viable communities and created a dynamic popular culture.

The majority of Khartoum residents clustered in nonwage activities. Yet this urban mass engaged in various forms of labor protests and were active participants in the postwar labor movement. The growing labor and urban unrest prompted the colonial government to initiate new policies toward casual labor and urban planning. Nonetheless, labor protests increased, rural immigration continued, and the "floating population" remained an integral part of life in Anglo-Egyptian Khartoum.

CONCLUSION

⌁

The central subjects of this study have been the process of slave emancipation and the fate of liberated slaves in the city of Khartoum during a period of extraordinary transformation. Perhaps the most important points this study has tried to stress are that the questions of Sudanese ethnicity, class, ideology, and the unfolding events in contemporary Sudan cannot be fully understood without reference to slavery and the manner in which it was abolished.

The conditions that prevailed in the Sudan at the beginning of the twentieth century were created by historical developments that began several centuries earlier. Although institutionalized servitude existed in the Sudan since antiquity, the widespread use of slaves did not occur until the end of the eighteenth and the beginning of the nineteenth century when Turco-Egyptian encroachment was set in motion. These changes included increased commercial contacts with the outside world, the rise of a middle class, and the development of a new ideology that justified domination and enslavement. Hence, the Turco-Egyptian conquest in 1821 consolidated trends that were already underway and created new ones through its policies of taxation, military recruitment, and land tenure. Turkish rule expanded the slave-raiding frontiers and increased the use of slaves, a situation that persisted during the Mahdiyya.

The policies of the Anglo-Egyptian regime toward slavery and labor were shaped by the baggage the British officials brought with them. The toleration of slavery during the first three decades of colonial rule stemmed from the fear of an economic collapse and from administrators' anxieties about the social consequences of manumission and large-scale proletarianization. The colonial economy itself guaranteed the persistence of slavery and other forms of precolonial labor and consolidated the position of the slaveholders.

The period of emancipation excited a struggle that involved the colonial regime, the slaveholders, and the slaves. To the slaveholders, slavery was a divinely ordained institution that should be preserved. They vehemently resisted colonial antislavery legislation. When they began to lose their male slaves through desertion and manumission, the slaveholders made every possible effort to keep their female slaves through Islamic courts, thereby delaying their manumission.

British officials, on the other hand, were convinced that slavery had always been an integral part of Sudanese life and saw no reason to abolish it. They adopted the slaveholders' view that Sudanese slavery was basically benign and that slaves were members of their owners' households. Furthermore, colonial officials understood freedom in economic terms and stressed the link between emancipation and free labor. From their perspective, the main problem was how to transform slaves into hardworking, disciplined low-wage workers.

For the most part, the slaves' responses to emancipation were determined by their material and social conditions. Rather than facing economic uncertainties, some slaves chose to remain with their owners or to redefine their relationships, while others moved away and broke all ties with their former owners. In general, ex-slaves had their own version of freedom. When colonial officials insisted on work, thrift, and discipline, ex-slaves insisted on autonomy. They occupied vacant land, joined the communities of ex-slaves and discharged soldiers, or migrated to the cities.

Despite the efforts of the colonial regime to maintain the status quo, the colonial economy generated a great demand for wage labor. But in the Sudan, as elsewhere in Africa, the British had great difficulty in attracting a sufficient number of workers. The majority of the Sudanese population either evinced little interest in wage employment or did not work steadily. Hence, labor recruitment required constant intervention by the colonial state.

Throughout this book I have argued that there was a strong link between slave emancipation, ethnicity, and labor. From the beginning, colonial British officials conceived of labor in ethnic terms and held subtle convictions about the working capacity of each group. Accordingly, the Arabic-speaking northern Sudanese were considered indolent and averse to manual labor, while the slaves were regarded as energetic but in need of discipline, and were, therefore, targets for labor recruitment. However, the task of converting ex-slaves into wage earners remained a difficult problem.

With the expansion of cash crop production in the mid-1920s, the demand for labor became more acute and the colonial authorities had no alternative but to turn to non-Arab groups such as West African residents and immigrants, as well as western Sudanese. These groups became the backbone of the seasonal agricultural labor force in the Gezira and in other agricultural schemes, and were reduced to a quasi-proletarian status. Although socioeconomic transformation in the rural areas in the late colonial era prompted other Sudanese groups to seek wage employment, the labor force remained segmented along ethnic lines. By the beginning of World War II a Sudanese working class began to emerge. This class was heterogeneous in composition, mode of employment, and ethnic and regional origins. Yet it gave birth to a powerful labor movement that played a vital role in Sudanese society and politics.

Additionally, this study addresses the question of what the urban alternative meant for liberated slaves. Indeed, the city offered ex-slaves numerous economic and social opportunities. It allowed them to rebuild their lives, make a living, rejoin kin, and create new ethnic and cultural identities. Yet while city life yielded opportunities for self-determination, it also created new forms of coercion that threatened the mobility and economic independence of ex-slaves. They became targets of the colonial vagrancy laws, a registration system, and labor recruitment. However, ex-slaves were not just pawns whose fates were determined by the actions of the colonial officials. They had their own goals and strategies. They sought alternatives or sold their labor at times of their own choosing.

Finally, this study focuses on the role of the Three Towns in the colonial labor market. This urban complex functioned as a labor reservoir for the growing demands of the colonial economy. Following the establishment of colonial rule, the Three Towns became the political and economic hub of the country and attracted a large number of ex-slaves and other dislocated people. Although the presence of this floating population was deplored by administrators, these "undesirables" were considered a source of cheap labor that could be deployed to the countryside. Yet the recruitment of these people into the labor force required a great deal of coercion. Ex-slaves and other urban residents had their own motives and strategies. They established their own neighborhoods in the city and were joined by a steady stream of immigrants. They sought wage employment when they needed cash and moved between the city and the countryside in search of favorable conditions.

By the time of World War II, an urban working class with deep roots in the city began to emerge. Khartoum workers established their own institutions and engaged in various forms of protest. They created viable communities in the Daims and developed a dynamic working-class culture. Indeed, ex-slaves played a major role in the growth of that culture.

While official abolition brought redemption and economic independence to many former slaves, ex-slaves and their descendants are still considered socially and culturally inferior in Sudanese society. Former slave owners have not relinquished their perceptions of ex-slaves and continue to reproduce ideologies that justify domination and subordination. Politically and culturally, ex-slaves have an ambiguous status; they have not been fully integrated into the society that enslaved them. At the same time they are not considered members of the communities from which they were taken.

Despite this continued disfranchisement, former slaves and their descendants have developed new identities and a particular form of consciousness that reflects their position in Sudanese society. They have formed ethnically based organizations that have taken the lead in defending the interests of the non-Arab groups in the country. Rather than vagrants, ex-slaves could arguably be called pioneers. They have changed the ethnic composition and influenced the cultural tradition of northern Sudanese society. Ex-slaves and non-Arabs formed the backbone of the colonial wage labor force and played a leading role in the development of a dynamic urban popular culture in Khartoum and other Sudanese towns. These issues are particularly relevant to the current debate on Sudanese identity, cultural pluralism, and the persistent inequalities in the country.

PETITION BY SIXTY-EIGHT NOTABLES FROM OMDURMAN TO KITCHENER, SIRDAR OF THE EGYPTIAN ARMY.[1]

∽

PETITION BY SIXTY-EIGHT NOTABLES OF OMDURMAN TO KITCHENER

∽

His Excellency, The Sirdar,
The Egyptian Army

We respectfully want to state to your Excellency that the best help the government could give to the natives to ameliorate their present state and save them from danger, want, and hunger is to allow them to keep their slaves. At present, they are all confused as a result of the intrusion of some government soldiers and their allies from the Dervishes' slaves who enter the natives' homes and the womens' quarters under the pretext that they are searching for male slaves for enlistment in the army. In the process, they take away female slaves as well as dark-skinned freeborn men. This is happening despite the fact that the majority of those taken are not suitable for military service, but were merely enticed by the soldiers and their allies, who are driven by personal greed and have no regard for the interest of the government. In the past the government stopped the slave trade but did not interfere with slaves who were living with their masters except in cases when the slaves had grievances against their masters. Your Excellency is aware that the natives are really suffering as a result of the Dervishes' intransigence, and are anxious for government help. All the residents of Omdurman are loyal to the government and are looking forward to its help. Those who fought against the government have perished during the wars and their remnants have escaped with the Khalifa to the West. The restoration of the saqiyas and agriculture, which are essential for the reconstruction of the country, cannot be achieved without the slave labor. Without that, there will be no prosperity for any native and there will be no progress in the Sudan to be able to catch up with the rest of the world. In order to remove our suffering and improve our conditions, we present this petition to you on behalf of all the people, hoping that it will have a favorable consideration. If the government needs soldiers, they can be provided from different parts of the country once peace and security are established.

Signed by Sixty-eight Omdurman Notables
2 October 1898

❧

SUDAN PENAL CODES REGARDING KIDNAPPING, ABDUCTION AND FORCED LABOR[2]

❧

302 Kidnapping

Whoever takes or entices any minor under 14 years of age if a male, or under 16 of age if a female, or any person of unsound mind, out of the keeping of the lawful guardian of such minor or person of unsound mind, without the consent of such guardian, or conveys any such minor or any person of unsound mind beyond the limits of the Sudan without the consent of some person legally authorized to consent to such removal, is said to kidnap such minor or person of unsound mind.

Explanation: The words "lawful guardian" in this section include any person lawfully entrusted with the care or custody of such minor or other person and authorized to consent to the taking.

303 Abduction

Whoever by force compels, or by any deceitful means induces, any person to go from any place, is said to abduct that person.

304 Punishment for Kidnapping.

Whoever kidnaps any person shall be punished with imprisonment for a term which may extend to seven years, and shall also be liable to fine.

305 Kidnapping or Abducting in order to Murder.

Whoever kidnaps or abducts any person in order that such person may be murdered or may be so disposed of as to be put in danger of being murdered, shall be punished with imprisonment for a term which may extend to fourteen years, and shall also be liable to fine.

306 Kidnapping or Abducting with Intent Secretly and Wrongfully to Confine Person.

Whoever kidnaps or abducts any person with intent to cause that person to be secretly and wrongfully confined, shall be punished with imprisonment for a term which may extend to seven years, and shall also be liable to fine.

307 Kidnapping or Abducting a Woman to Compel her to Marriage, Etc.

Whoever kidnaps or abducts any woman with intent that she may be compelled, or knowing it to be likely that she will be compelled, to marry any person against her will, or in order that she may be forced or seduced to illicit intercourse, or knowing it to be likely that she will be forced or seduced to illicit intercourse, shall be punished with imprisonment for a term which may extend to ten years, and shall also be liable to fine.

308 Kidnapping or Abducting in order to Subject Person to Grievous Hurt, Etc.

Whoever kidnaps or abducts any person in order that such person may be subjected, or may be so disposed of as to be put in danger of being subjected, to grievous hurt, or to the unnatural lust of any person, or knowing it to be likely that such person will be so subjected or disposed of, shall be punished with imprisonment for a term which may extend to ten years, and shall also be liable to fine.

309 Wrongfully Concealing or Keeping in Confinement Kidnapped or Abducted Person

Whoever, knowing that any person has been kidnapped or has been abducted, wrongfully conceals or confines such person, shall be punished in the same manner as if he had kidnapped or abducted such person with the same intention or knowledge or for the same purpose as that with or for which he conceals or detains such person in confinement.

310 Buying or Selling Minor for Purpose of Prostitution, Etc.

Whoever buys, sells, hires, lets to hire, or otherwise obtains possession or disposes of any minor under the age of 16 years, with intent that such minor shall be employed or used for the purpose of prostitution or for any unlawful or immoral purpose, or knowing it to be likely that such minor will be employed or used for any such purpose, shall be punished with imprisonment for a term which may extend to ten years and shall also be liable to fine.

311 Unlawful Compulsory Labor

Whoever unlawfully compels any person to labor against the will of that person, shall be punished with imprisonment for a term which may extend to one year or with fine or with both.

312 Kidnapping or Abducting in order to Subject to Unlawful Compulsory Labor

Whoever kidnaps or abducts any person with intent that such person may be unlawfully compelled to labor against his will, shall be punished with imprisonment for a term which may extend to seven years and shall also be liable to fine.

& Transferring Control of Person with Intent to Subject to Unlawful Confinement or Unlawful Compulsory Labor

Whoever, for money or money's worth, transfers or purports to transfer the control of the person of any man or woman to another person with intent to enable such other person to unlawfully confine such man or woman, or to unlawfully compel him or her to labor against his or her will, shall be punished with imprisonment for a term which may extend to seven years, and shall also be liable to fine.

313 Whoever, for money or money's worth, transfers or purports to transfer the possession or control of any person to another with intent to enable such other person to confine such person unlawfully or to compel him unlawfully against his will, shall be punished with imprisonment for a term which may extend to seven years and shall be liable to fine.

314 Possession or Control of Person Obtained outside the Sudan by Acts Constituting Offence if Done within the Sudan

Whoever is in possession or control of any person within the Sudan having obtained such possession or control outside the Sudan by acts which would have constituted an offence if done within the Sudan, shall be punished in the same manner as if such acts had been done within the Sudan.

315 Transferring outside the Sudan Possession of Person Obtained within the Sudan

Whoever, being in possession or control of any person within the Sudan, conveys such person outside the Sudan and there transfers or purports to transfer the possession or control of such person in any manner which could constitute an offence if such transference or purported transference took place within the Sudan, shall be punished in the same manner as if such transference or purported transference had taken place within the Sudan.

∽

SUDAN GOVERNMENT "CONFIDENTIAL" CIRCULAR MEMORANDUM NO. 22[3]

∽

REGULATIONS AS TO SUDANESE WHO LEAVE THEIR MASTERS

Sudan Government "Confidential" Circular Memorandum No. 10 of the 28th January 1902, is hereby canceled, and the following substituted:

(1.) Regulations as to Escaped Slaves

1. Any Sudanese, who is still in slavery, has the right to leave his master if he or she wishes.

2. Of the Sudanese who leave their masters and come into the towns in expectation of obtaining an easy living, many are reduced to want. Others being unwilling or unable to obtain regular employment take, the men to thieving and the women to prostitution. The following regulations aim at preventing the growth of this class.

3. Sudanese who have no means of honestly earning their living can be treated as idle persons under the "Vagabonds Ordinance, 1905," and under Section 6 may be required to find a surety for good behavior for one year, in default of which they may be imprisoned until the period for which they have been ordered to find a surety expires, or until they find a surety.

Before, however, requiring surety under this section, the magistrate must be careful to satisfy himself that the Sudanese has no honest means of livelihood.

4. If a Sudanese, who is still in slavery, applies for his freedom, or a master complains that a Sudanese has recently run away from him, an enquiry should be held. The Sudanese, and his or her master, should be questioned on the following points:

(a.) How long the Sudanese has been in the service of his or her master, and how he or she came into the possession of his or her master.

(b.) Whether the Sudanese has been treated well by his or her master or the reverse.

(c.) What is the reason for the Sudanese leaving his or her master.

(d.) From what part of the country the Sudanese originally came and whether he or she has any friends or relations willing to assist him or her.

(e.) How he or she proposes to live.

5. If the magistrate finds that the Sudanese has an honest means of livelihood he will not interfere with him or her.

If, on the other hand, the magistrate finds that the Sudanese is an idle person as defined in the Vagabonds Ordinance, he can deal with him or her under that ordinance, as explained in Section 3 of these regulations. But, as an alternative, if the Sudanese has been with his or her master since before the reconquest and the magistrate is satisfied that he or she has been well-treated and that he or she has no honest means of subsistence, the magistrate may recommend such Sudanese to return to his or her master, upon such terms as may seem fair, and if the Sudanese accepts, the magistrate will not deal with him or her under the Vagabonds Ordinance.

6. Idle persons and vagabonds who conduct themselves well in imprisonment should, wherever possible, be assisted by the Governors in earning their livelihood.

(2.) Sudanese Soldiers Enticing Girls from the People of the Country

1. No soldier will be allowed on his own initiative to take away a girl from anyone upon the grounds that she is his sister or relative, or for any other reason. If a soldier finds a sister or relative of his living with a man, and wishes to complain, he must make his

complaint to his commanding officer, who will forward the case to the Governor. Any soldier who takes away a Sudanese girl from anyone contrary to this regulation on whatever pretence will be punished by his commanding officer.

2. All cases in which it is alleged that a soldier has taken away a girl from any person, or in which a soldier complains that his sister or relative is the slave of someone, will be sent by the commanding officer in his battalion to the Governor. The Governor, or an inspector appointed by him, will hear the case personally. The case itself will not be referred to the Kadi, but if the question of the validity or non-validity of a marriage arises in the case, that question should be referred to the Kadi, and his decision as to the marriage, subject to the rights of appeal to the Grand Kadi, will be accepted as final.

3. If the girl is married to the person, the Governor will carry out the orders of the Mahkama Shari'a as to the girl's returning to her husband.

4. If the Governor comes to the conclusion that the girl is not the sister of the soldier or related to him within the prohibited degrees of marriage, and if she has no honest means of subsistence and refuses to return to her master or other person with whom she was living, he will treat her as an idle person under the Vagabonds Ordinance.

5. If the Governor finds that the girl is the soldier's sister or related to him within the prohibited degrees of marriage he will, if the soldier has applied in accordance with these regulations and the commanding officer agrees to her living in the Harimat lines, hand her over to the soldier, upon his undertaking to clothe and feed her suitably and to produce her if demanded, and in the event of her marrying to be responsible that the marriage is a suitable one.

If the commanding officer does not consent, the Governor must not hand her over to the soldier, but will hand her over to some trustworthy person, taking proper guarantees, or will confine her in the ward for vagabonds, as the case may demand.

(3.) Registration of Sudanese

In provinces where this registration has not been completed, the Governor-General desires that Governors should complete the same, as far as, and as soon as, possible. The registration is to be made in the books provided for the purpose by the Slavery Repression Department. The truth of the particulars entered in the registers should be substantiated by omdas, shaykhs or other responsible persons.

By order of the Governor-General,
P. R. Phipps, Miralai,
Civil Secretary.
Khartoum, 4 January 1907

∽

CONFIDENTIAL CIRCULAR MEMORANDUM NO. 33[4]

∽

REGULATIONS AS TO SUDANESE SERVANTS

1. Confidential Circular Memorandum No. 22 of the 4th January 1907 is cancelled and this Circular substituted.

2. In this Circular unless the context otherwise requires the words "Sudanese Servants" mean persons who were in a state of slavery or considered as such by natives and apply to both sexes, and the word "Master" includes "Mistress."

3. Every Sudanese servant not under contract has the right to leave his master if he wishes and may not be compelled or persuaded to return against his will.

4. It is not desirable in the interests of the community that Sudanese should through leaving the homes in which they have been brought up and finding themselves without work take to thieving or prostitution and the following regulations aim at preventing this but they must be very carefully applied. They are not intended to enable masters to retain Sudanese in slavery but for the protection of Sudanese themselves and in the interests of the whole community.

5. Sudanese who are not honestly earning their livelihood and come within the definition of the idle persons or vagabonds as set out in Section 2 of the Vagabonds Ordinance 1905 may be treated under Section 6 of that ordinance and required to find surety for good

behavior and imprisoned in default. But before a surety can be required under this section proceedings must be taken in the form laid down by the Criminal Procedure Code and the Sudanese must be convicted of being an idle person or a vagabond on proper and sufficient evidence. It is an abuse of the powers of the ordinance to order a Sudanese to find a surety merely to apply pressure on him to go back to his former master.

6. If a Sudanese who is still living with his master applies for his freedom or a master complains that a Sudanese has recently run away from him an enquiry should be held by the Inspector of the District where the Sudanese actually is and they should both be questioned on the following points:

(a) How the Sudanese originally came into the service of the master

(b) How long the Sudanese has been in the master's service

(c) Whether the Sudanese has been treated well or ill by the master

(d) What is the reason for the Sudanese wishing to leave

(e) From what part of the country the Sudanese originally came and whether he or she has any friends or relatives willing to assist him

(f) How the Sudanese proposes to support himself.

Complaints by a master must be heard by the Inspector in whose District the Sudanese is actually living and a Sudanese is not to be sent to another district for enquiry except at his or her own request or under warrant on a criminal charge.

Complaints made by a master of theft by a runaway Sudanese servant should be viewed with grave suspicion as they are often made without any foundation.

If the Inspector finds that the Sudanese has an honest means of livelihood he will not interfere with him and will if requested give him a freedom paper.

8. If on the other hand the Inspector finds that the Sudanese is an idle person or vagabond as above he can sit as a Magistrate and try him under the Vagabonds Ordinance. But as an alternative if the

Sudanese has been with his master's or his mistress' family since before the reconquest of the Sudan and the Inspector is satisfied that he has been well-treated the Inspector may recommend such Sudanese to return to his master upon any terms on which master and servant agree provided they seem to the Inspector to be fair and the Inspector will not then cause the Sudanese to be tried under the Vagabonds Ordinance.

9. As not infrequently it happens that Sudanese servants who have lived many years with their masters are really happier and better off if they still remain part of their masters' families and that when complaints are made it is due to some temporary cause of disagreement and the Inspector may try and reconcile the parties but such reconciliation must be quite voluntary and pressure is not to be put in any way on Sudanese to accept terms.

10. Sudanese imprisoned as idle persons and vagabonds who conduct themselves well in prison should as far as possible be assisted by Governors in earning their own livelihood when released.

11. In the case of children underage the regulations laid down for dealing with adults are not always applicable.

The right to their custody is to be given first to their parents or other natural guardians but in the event of their being without such they are not to be taken out of the custody of their de facto guardians except for the same reasons that natural guardians would be deprived of their custody, viz., that the children are ill-treated or the guardians are unfitted for their post.

12. As regards women difficult questions sometimes arise by reason of Moslem Law. The Mohammedan Law Courts will follow the Egyptian practice and administer the law of marriage and guardianship on the footing that the status of slavery does not exist and if there is necessity will apply to the administrative authority for the issue of freedom papers in order to render their decision formally correct.

As in some parts of the country it appears to be a practice to make marriage with Sudanese women a pretext for their enslavement such cases should be carefully watched but the decision as to whether any particular marriage is valid or not is for the religious court to say and in any case it may be remembered that if a woman is a wife she must under Moslem Law be a free woman.

13. As the Government does not recognize the status of slavery it follows that any claim by a master to the property of a servant who has left him must be based on contract or agreement such as agency partnership or trusteeship as it would be between master and servant in other countries and not on rules of Moslem Law applicable only to the status of slavery.

14. The registration of Sudanese is as far as possible to be kept up to date but it must be remembered that the register is for the protection of Sudanese.

15. The Governor-General holds Governors and Inspectors responsible for the carrying out of this Circular in the spirit and the letter.

(Signed) R. M. Feilden
Lewa,
Civil Secretary
Khartoum,
1 May 1919

෴

SUDAN GOVERNMENT CIRCULAR MEMORANDUM NO. C.S./60-A-1[5]

෴

SLAVERY

1. The fixed policy of the Sudan Government has always been that all slavery in the Sudan should in due course come to a natural end. Its aim therefore has been to do nothing that will delay the natural ending of slavery, but it was not desirable and would not have been fair to other classes of the people of the Sudan to take active steps to produce that result in too short a time.

2. This natural end will be brought about by the decision of the Government that no person born after the reoccupation of the country in 1898 is otherwise than free and by the recognition of the principle that no master has the right to retain Sudanese servants against their will.

3. In view of the time that has lapsed since the reoccupation of the country, the time has come for the Government to restate its policy in clearer terms.

4. Where servants who have been brought up by particular masters in a status equivalent to the status of slavery under Mohammedan law wish to break that relation and for that purpose apply to the Government, no obstacle is to be placed in their way, but it is not necessary for Government officials to take the initiative except on application of the servant. The District Commissioner dealing

with the case may, however, attempt a reconciliation if he considers it to be in the interests of both parties, but in so doing he shall not only bear in mind himself that the servant has an absolute right to freedom but make it quite clear to the servant that he has this right and abstain from putting any pressure on the servant. He will not, however, attempt reconciliation in the following cases.

(a) Where the master has hired out the Sudanese servant to another which is an offence under Sec. 311 of the Penal Code

(b) When the Sudanese servant was born since 1898

(c) Where the master has ill-treated or neglected to support the servant.

5. A Sudanese servant is never to be sent (with or without an escort) to another district for inquiry except at his or her own request or under warrant on a criminal charge. Complaints made by a master of theft by a runaway Sudanese servant should be viewed with grave suspicion, as they are often made without foundation to secure the return of the servant to his old district.

6. In cases where reconciliation has been effected District Commissioners will when subsequently visiting the place where the Sudanese servant resides see the servant and ascertain whether promises made at the time of reconciliation have been carried out.

7. District Commissioners will take steps to make sure that Sudanese servants have an opportunity of complaining to them if they wish to, and if they have reason to believe that servants are being badly treated they will make inquiries and take steps to put an end to such treatment.

8. District Commissioners shall keep a record of all cases of complaints and of the manner in which they are dealt with and furnish annual returns to the Governor for inclusion in the statistics furnished with the Province Annual Report.

9. Duties arising under this circular shall not be carried out by any official of lower rank than an Assistant District Commissioner, but it is the duty of every official to assist any Sudanese servant to obtain access to the District Commissioner and to report cases of hardship and cruelty that come under his notice.

10. The Governor-General holds Governors and District Commissioners responsible for the carrying out of this circular in the spirit of the letter.

11. All former circulars on this subject are cancelled.

(Signed) C. E. Lyall
Civil Secretary
Khartoum, 6 May 1925

∽

LETTER FROM SAYYID 'ALI AL-MIRGHANI, SHARIF YUSUF AL-HINDI, AND 'ABD AL-RAHMAN AL-MAHDI TO THE DIRECTOR OF INTELLIGENCE DEPARTMENT[6]

∽

6th March, 1925

The Director of Intelligence,
Khartoum

We find it our duty to point out to you our opinion on the subject of slavery in the Sudan with the hope of drawing the attention of the government to it.

We have followed the policy of the government toward this class since the reoccupation; naturally we cannot criticize a matter which the whole civilized world has combined to stop and is one of the most important matters under the consideration of international law. However, what interests us in the matter is the fact that slavery in the Sudan is not what it is supposed to be generally. The Sudanese who work on agricultural land are really partners to the landowners and have many privileges and rights which would really make them a class by themselves, and cannot be termed slaves in the ordinary sense. People of the Sudan who still have Sudanese at the present time do really treat them more as members of their families, owing to their great need for their work. If there is any party to complain it would now be the masters who are at the mercy of their servants.

As you are well aware, labor at present is the most important question in the Sudan, which should be considered with greatest interest. The

Government, the companies and the individuals who are interested in agriculture are in need of every single hand that can be obtained and which would contribute to the success of these schemes.

Further, the government and its officials must have remarked during the past few years that the majority of freed Sudanese have become useless for any work. The women folk among them generally turned to prostitution, and men are addicted to drinking and laziness.

For these reasons we urge the Government to consider very carefully the wisdom of indiscriminately issuing freedom papers to persons who look upon these papers as granting them freedom from any liability to work or to carry out the obligation under which they stand.

Since these Sudanese are not really slaves in the sense understood by International Law, there is no more need to give freedom papers to them than to the landowners for whom they work. But it is in the best interest of all those concerned, that the Sudanese should remain on the land and work, and if the policy of encouraging them to leave the land to loaf in the towns is maintained, nothing but ill can ensue.

We hope that the Government would take this matter into earnest consideration and will issue its orders to all officials not to issue any freedom certificates unless the Sudanese can prove ill-treatment.

(Signed) 'Ali al-Mirghani
Sharif Yusuf al-Hindi
'Abd al-Rahman al-Mahdi
6 March 1925

಄

PETITION BY AMNA BINT AHMAD TO THE ASSISTANT CIVIL SECRETARY FOR NATIVE AFFAIRS[7]

಄

مقدمت هذا آمنة بنت أحمد برقاوية الجنس ومن أهالي مديرية دارفور والآن بديم التعايشة شياخة وعمودية عمر كويس ويرشد عنِّي حسين محمد يونس البرقاوي بديم التعايشة.

المدعى عليه عبدالله آدم من قبيلة المجانين مقيم بحلة الضليل شياخة نضل الله عمودية نصرالله أمبدة نظارة جمعة سهل تبع مديرية كردفان.

حضرة صاحب السعادة مدير الشؤون الأهلية بالخرطوم

بكل أدب وأحترام رفعت هذا لسعادتكم عن الآتي :

أنندم بما أني برقاوية الجنس ومن أهالي مديرية دارفور في سنة ١٩١٦ الحكومة فتحت مديرية دارفور وفي أيام الفتوح إختطفوني الكبابيش وباعوني إلى المدعى عليه وأخيه [إبراهيم] المتوفى وأصبحت بطرف المدعى عليه جارية وكان المدعى عليه يخدِّمني الخدمات الشاقة وهي نشل المياه لسقاية الجمال وكنت متجولة بالخلا مع الجمال وفي أثناء تجولي إجتمعت برجل سوداني ورزقت منه بولد وبنتين دون عقد شرعي الولد اسمه سعيد والبنت الاولى اسمها سعيدة والثانية ام سعدين. الولد عمره ٦ سنوات تقريبا واحد البنات عمرها ٥ سنة والثانية ثلاثة سنوات ونصف. ومن تاريخ مباعي للمدعى عليه لغايت سنة ١٩٢٢ أنا في أشد تعب ومعاملتي كانت كمعاملة المسجون القاتل وما كنت أعرف الطريق الذي يوصلني إلى الحكومة لأشكي عن حالتي واخيراً أخذت أولادي وهربت ووصلت بالأبيض وأفهمت العمدة صالح عمدة النلاتة والبرقو عن ما حصل وأصبحت مقيمة بمنزل العمدة صالح بالأبيض والمدعى عليه لما علم بوجودي بالأبيض حضر بمنزل العمدة وطلب مني أن أرجع معه. رفضت واخيراً المدعى عليه إتفق مع العمدة صالح والعمدة صالح سلم إبني ولما رأيت ذلك قدمت لجناب مفتش الأبيض ووضحت لجنابه كل

ما حصل وجناب طلب الدعى عليه يحضر ولدي ويسلمني إياه ونعلاً إستلمت
منه الولد وجناب المفتش منعه مني ومن أولادي وعاد المدعى عليه إتفق مع
العمدة صالح ورفع ضدي قضية شرعية إدعى أولادي أولاده والحقيقة بخلاف
ذلك. أنا جارية مملوكة وأولادي رقيق وما يثبت ذلك أسماءهم توري أنهم
رقيق. بخلاف ذلك ما بيني وبين المدعى عليه عقد باطل والمحكمة قبلت منه
القضية وأخذت بناتي والولد وسلمتهم إليه وبما أني إمرأة مسكينة وغريبة
وكنت مخطوفة من أهلي زمن عديد والآن بناتي وولدي أخذوا مني دون
وجه حق ولفراقهم أصبحت مريضة والآن حضرت بالخرطوم وبادرت برفع هذا
لسعادتكم ألتمس من عدلكم المساعدة وإحضار أولادي أمام سعادتكم
وتسليمي إياهم وإعطائي أمر حرية بيدي وأمر حرية بناتي والولد بعد
إستلامي إياهم والامر مفوض لاهل العدل   أنندم

١٩٢٤/٢/١٢   مقدمته أمنه بنت أحمد

∽

PETITION BY AMNA BINT AHMAD TO THE ASSISTANT CIVIL SECRETARY FOR NATIVE AFFAIRS[7]

∽

Submitted by Amna bint Ahmad, a Bergo from Dar Fur Province, now residing at Daim Ta'isha, under omda 'Umar Kuwayyis, represented by Hussayn Muhammad Yunis al-Bergawai, Daim Ta'isha; against 'Abdalla Adam of the Majanin Tribe, now residing at al-Dilayl village, under shaykh Fadlalla, and omda Nasralla Umbada, and nazir Jum'a Sahal, Kordofan Province.

His Excellency Assistant Civil Secretary for Native Affairs:
   With respect, I present this to your Excellency. I am a Bergo from Dar Fur Province. In 1916 when the government occupied Dar Fur, I was kidnapped by the Kababish who sold me to 'Abdalla Adam and his late brother Ibrahim Adam. I remained with them as a slave, and they used to force me to carry out very hard work such as bringing water for the camels. While I was shepherding camels in the desert, I had an illegal sexual relationship with a Sudanese [slave] from whom I got a son named Sa'id and two daughters, named Sa'ida and Um Sa'adayn. The boy is now six years old, and my daughters are now five and three and a half years old, respectively. Since the time I was sold to the defendant until 1932 I was suffering and I was treated like a criminal prisoner. I did not know how to reach the government to submit my complaint. At last I ran away with my children to al-Ubayyid where I explained my case to Omda Salih of the Fallata and Bergo, and remained with him. When the defendant learnt that I was in al-Ubayyid, he came to Omda Salih's house and asked me to go back with him, but I refused. Finally the defendant arranged with the Omda to take my son with him. When I discovered that, I went to see the District Commissioner of al-Ubayyid and presented my case to him. He then

summoned the defendant and ordered him to bring back my son, which he did. But, with the help of Omda Salih, the defendant raised a Shari'a suit against me and alleged that I was his wife and my children were his. The truth is that we are all slaves and my children's names prove that. Moreover, there is no marriage contract between him and myself. Despite all of this the court accepted his pledge and gave him my children.

I am a poor foreign woman who was kidnapped from her family a long time ago. Now my children were unjustly taken away. As a result of their separation I fell sick. Now I came to Khartoum to present my case to you and I beg for your help to get my children back and give all of us freedom papers.

Submitted by: Amna bint Ahmad
12 March 1934

◜

SAMPLE LABOR
CONTRACT 1[8]

◜

نحن الموقعين أدناه مقدم وسبعة شغالة قد إتفقنا أن نشتغل مع المستر ج ٥ جرانت من مصلحة الري في وادي المقدم حسب الشروط الآتية :

(أولاً) نتعهد أن نقوم بالأشغال اللازمة للمساحة في وادي المقدم .

(ثانيا) مدة الشغل تكون خمسة عشر يوماً ولكن إذا إقتضت الحال لبقائنا هناك خمسة عشر يوما أخرى نكون ملزومين بالبقاء بدون إبداء أدنى معارضة .

(ثالثا) ماهية المقدم تكون خمسة قروش صاغ في اليوم والنفر خمسة قروش صاغ في اليوم ايضا ولكن إذا أحداً منا أظهر عدم كفاءت في الشغل أو كان كسلان تخفض أجرته إلى أربعة قروش صاغ يوميا .

(رابعا) يعطى لنا مياه بواقع فنطاس صغير لكل ثمانية أنفار يوميا هذا إذا كان يوجد مياه كفاية وفي عدم وجود مياه كفاية لا يعطى لنا حتى المقدار الموقع أعلاه .

(خامسا) ساعات العمل غير محدودة مطلقا واننا نكون مستعدين للشغل في أي وقت مدة النهار وللزوم في الليل إذا إقتضت ضرورة الشغل لذلك .

(سادسا) يجب أن نأخذ طعامنا معنا وعلى مصاريفنا ولكن يخصص لنا جملين لحمل الطعام وعفشنا .

(سابعا) يعطى لنا خيمة واحدة لأجل إستعمالها .

(ثامنا) رجوعنا إلى الخرطوم يكون على مصاريف الحكومة.

(تاسعا) إذا مرض أحدنا وكان مرضه مسببا عن الشغل يعالج على مصاريف الحكومة ويعطى له ماهية عن الأيام التي يكون مريضا فيها. أما إذا كان مرضه متسببا من نفسه لا يعطى له ماهية ويلزم بدفع معالجته.

(عاشرا) يدفع لنا أجرة أسبوعين مقدما.

عملت هذه على صورتين تحريرا في الخرطوم ٢٢ سبتمبر سنة ١٩١٢

عبد الله حمد   محمد عمر   حسب الكريم إدريس   خير السيد الجاك

سعيد عبد الله   اسماعيل عبد الله   طه اسماعيل   صالح فضل الله

SAMPLE LABOR CONTRACT 1

We the undersigned, one muqqadam and seven laborers, agreed to work for Mr. G. H. Grant of the Irrigation Department, at Wadi al-Muqqadam under the following conditions:

1) We will do the necessary works at Wadi al-Muqqadam.

2) The period of work is fifteen days, but if the situation requires that we stay for another fifteen days, we are obliged to remain there without any objection.

3) The wage for the muqqadam is five piastres per day, and for the laborer is five piastres per day. However, if any of us showed that he is incompetent or lazy, his wage will be reduced to four piastres per day.

4) We will be provided with water, on the basis of a small tank for every eight men, provided that there is a sufficient amount of water. If there is not sufficient water, we will not be provided with the above mentioned amount.

5) The working hours are absolutely unlimited and we will be prepared to work at any time, day and night, if it is required.

6) We must take with us our own food at our own expense; but we will be provided with two camels to carry our food supplies and luggage.

7) We will be provided with one tent.

8) Our return trip to Khartoum will be at the government's expense.

9) If any of us get sick during work, he will be treated at the government's expense and will receive his wage for the days he was out of work. However, if his sickness was due to his own fault, he would lose his wage and will be responsible for his own treatment.

10) We will be given two weeks' wage in advance.

Made in two copies at Khartoum on 22 September 1912.

Signed by: 'Abdalla Hamad, Muhammad 'Umar, Hasab al-Karim Idris, Khayr al-Sayyid al-Jak, Sa'id 'Abdalla, Isma'il 'Abdalla, Taha Isma'il, Salih Fadlalla.

∽

SAMPLE LABOR CONTRACT 2

∽

We the undersigned muqqadams and laborers agree to work with the Sudan Industries Limited on the following conditions:

1) To do whatever work, wherever, and whenever desired by the manager or his representative.

2) To work for a period of two months from the day of arrival at the work site.

3) The wages will be five piastres and two rotls of dura (a rotl is 12 ounces) for the muqqadam and three and a half piastres and two rotls of dura for each laborer per diem, commencing from the date of leaving Khartoum and ceasing on the date of returning to Khartoum.

4) Fifteen days' pay in cash will be paid to us in advance before leaving Khartoum. The rest of our pay for the remaining period will be paid to us on returning to Khartoum, making from it such deduction as may have been paid to our families at Khartoum as per the list left in the Central Labour Bureau. The dura ration will be issued to us every three days in advance. The muqqadams will be responsible for the fifteen days' wages given to laborers in advance.

5) Any laborer who ceases to work on account of sickness will lose cash pay during the time he is out of work but will receive the dura wages. If he is accidently hurt he will receive full cash and dura wages and will be exempt from hospital charges if his case necessitates his admission into hospital.

6) No muqqadam or laborer is allowed to make or use marisa or any other intoxicating drinks. Anyone disobeying will be fined half a piastre for drinking and one piastre for making marisa.

7) Anyone ceasing to work before the termination of this contract will be struck off pay at once and will forfeit his free passage back to Khartoum. He will also be prosecuted in civil courts for breach of contract.

8) Any women taken with muqqadams and laborers for cooking, etc. will be at their own expense. The employers will only be responsible for the transport of such women from Khartoum to the place of work and back to Khartoum.

9) Each of us must have with him one pair of pantaloons and one pair of puttees at our own expense. The employer will only supply us with one blanket and one mosquito curtain each on loan which we shall hand back to the manager or his representative in case of discharge or resignation. In case of any willful damage being done to these we agree to take them and pay their price.

10) We agree to work ten hours every day commencing at an early hour in the morning as the manager or his representative may fix and continue to work in daytime at hours appointed by the said manager or representative provided the hours do not exceed ten in number in the day time. We agree also to do any extra work as may be required from us whether in the day- or nighttime and we will be paid half a piastre for the extra work provided that it does not exceed one hour beyond the twelve hours every day.

Signed at Khartoum on this 17th day of January, 1911.

NOTES

INTRODUCTION

1. 'Ushari Mahmoud and Sulayman Baldo, *El-Di'ayn Massacre* (Khartoum: N.p., 1987).

2. The exception is Heather Sharkey's thesis, "Domestic Slavery in the Nineteenth and Early Twentieth-Centuries in Northern Sudan," Master's thesis, Durham University, 1992.

3. R. S. O'Fahey and J. L. Spaulding, *Kingdoms of the Sudan* (London: Methuen & Co., Ltd., 1974). R. S. O'Fahey, "Slavery and the Slave Trade in Dar Fur," *Journal of African History* XIV, no. 1, (1973): 29–43; and "Slavery and Society in Dar Fur," from John Willis, ed. *Slaves and Slavery in Muslim Africa*, Vol. II (London: Frank Cass, 1985), 83–100. Jay Spaulding, *The Heroic Age in Sinnar* (East Lansing: African Studies Center, Michigan State University, 1985).

4. Lidwien Kapteijns, *Mahdist Faith and Sudanic Tradition. The History of the Masalit Sultanate, 1870–1930* (London and Boston: KPI, 1985); and "The Use of Slaves in Pre-colonial Western Dar Fur: The Case of Dar Masalit, 1870–1905," *Northeast African Studies* 6, nos. 1 and 2, (1984): 105–126. Janet Ewald, *Soldiers, Traders, and Slaves* (Madison: University of Wisconsin Press, 1990).

5. R. S. O'Fahey, "Fur and Fartit: The history of a frontier," *Culture History in the Southern Sudan*, eds. John Mack and Peter Robertshaw (Nairobi: The British Institute in Eastern Africa, 1982), 76–87; Wendy James, "Social Assimilation and Changing Identity in the Southern Funj," *Sudan in Africa*, ed. Yusuf Fadl Hasan (Khartoum: Khartoum University Press, 1971), 197–211; *'Kwanim PA. The Making of the Uduk People* (Oxford: Clarendon Press, 1979); and "Perceptions from an African Slaving Frontier," *Slavery and Other Forms of Unfree Labor*, ed. Leonie J. Archer (London and New York: Routledge, 1988), 130–141.

6. Richard Gray, *A History of the Southern Sudan, 1839–1889* (Oxford: Oxford University Press, 1961); Dennis Cordell, *Dar al-Kuti and the Last Years of the Trans-Saharan Slave Trade* (Madison: University of Wisconsin Press, 1985).

7. Jay Spaulding, "Slavery, Land Tenure, and Social Class in the Northern Turkish Sudan," *International Journal of African Historical Studies* 15, no. 1, (1982): 1–20; Anders Bjorkelo, *Prelude to the Mahdiyya. Peasants and Traders in the Shendi Region, 1821–1885* (Cambridge: Cambridge University Press, 1989).

8. Douglas H. Johnson, "Sudanese Military Slavery From the Eighteenth to the Twentieth Century," *Slavery and Other Forms of Unfree Labor*, ed. Leonie J. Archer (London and New York: Routledge, 1988), 142–156; "The Structure of a Legacy: Military Slavery in Northeast Africa," *Ethnohistory* 36, no. 1 (Winter

1989): 72–88; and "Recruitment and Entrapment in Private Slave Armies: The Structure of the Zaraib in the Southern Sudan," *Slavery & Abolition* 13, no. 1, (April 1992): 162–173.

9. A. I. M. Ali, *The British, the Slave Trade and Slavery in the Sudan, 1820–1881* (Khartoum: Khartoum University Press, 1972); T. M. Hargey, "The Suppression of Slavery in the Sudan, 1898–1939," Ph.D. diss., Oxford University, Oxford, 1981.

10. These include Saad ed Din Fawzi, *The Labor Movement in the Sudan, 1946–1955* (London: Oxford University Press, 1957); Abdel Rahman el Tayib Ali Taha, "The Sudanese Labor Movement: A Study of Labor Unionism in a Developing Society," Ph.D. diss., University of California, Los Angeles, 1970; Jay O'Brien, "Agricultural Labor and Development in Sudan," Ph.D. diss., University of Connecticut, 1980, and "The formation of the agricultural labour force in Sudan," *Review of African Political Economy* 26, (1983): 15–34; El-Wathig Mohamed Kameir, *The Political Economy of Labor Migration in the Sudan. A Comparative Case Study of Migrant Workers in an Urban Situation* (Hamburg: Institut Fur Afrika-Kunde, 1988).

11. Jay Spaulding and Lidwien Kapteijns, "The Orientalist Paradigm in the Historiography of the Late Precolonial Sudan," *Golden Ages, Dark Ages. Imagining the Past in Anthropology and History*, eds. Jay O'Brien and William Rosebury (Berkeley, Los Angeles, and Oxford: University of California Press, 1991), 143.

12. On the debate on slavery, see Suzanne Miers and Igor Kopytoff, eds., *Slavery in Africa. Historical and Anthropological Perspectives* (Madison: University of Wisconsin Press, 1977); Frederick Cooper, *Plantation Slavery on the East Coast of Africa* (New Haven and London: Yale University Press, 1977); Paul Lovejoy, *Transformation in Slavery: A History of Slavery in Africa* (Cambridge: Cambridge University Press, 1983); Paul Lovejoy, ed., *The Ideology of Slavery in Africa* (Beverly Hills: Sage Publications, 1981). On emancipation in Africa, see Frederick Cooper, *From Slaves to Squatters. Plantation Labor and Agriculture in Zanzibar and Coastal Kenya, 1890–1925* (New Haven and London: Yale University Press, 1980); Suzanne Miers and Richard Roberts, eds., *The End of Slavery in Africa* (Madison: University of Wisconsin Press, 1988); and Fred Morton, *Children of Ham, Freed Slaves and Fugitive Slaves on the Kenya Coast, 1873 to 1907* (Boulder and San Francisco: Westview Press, 1990).

13. Cooper, *From Slaves to Squatters*, 46–61.

14. Morton, *Children of Ham*, 77–97.

15. Miers and Roberts, eds., *The End of Slavery in Africa*, 3–24.

16. Frederick Cooper, ed., *Struggle for the City: Migrant Labor, Capital and the State in Urban Africa* (Beverly Hills: Sage Publications, 1983); and *On the African Waterfront: Urban Disorders and the Transformation of Work in Colonial Mombasa* (New Haven: Yale University Press, 1987). Paul Lubeck, *Islam and Urban Labor in Northern Nigeria: The Making of a Muslim Working Class* (Cambridge: Cambridge University Press, 1986); Peter Gutkind, C. W. Cohen, and Jeane Coppan, eds., *African Labor History* (London: Sage Publications, 1978); Bill Freund, *The African Worker* (Cambridge: Cambridge University Press, 1989).

17. Charles Van Onselen, Chibaro: *African Mine Labour in Southern Rhodesia 1900–1922* (London: Pluto Press, 1977); and *New Babylon: Studies in the Social and Economic History of the Witwatersrand 1886–1914* (London: Longman, 1982); Luise S. White, *The Comforts of Home. Prostitution in Colonial Nairobi* (Chicago: University of Chicago Press, 1990); and Jacklyn Cock, *Maids and Madams: A Study in the Politics of Exploitation* (Johannesburg: Raven Press, 1980).

18. Claire C. Robertson, *Sharing the Same Bowl: A Socio-Economic History of Women and Class in Accra* (Bloomington: Indiana University Press, 1984); Margaret Strobel, *Muslim Women in Mombasa, 1890–1975* (New Haven: Yale University Press, 1979).

19. Cooper, *Struggle for the City*, 53.

20. Abner Cohen, *Customs and Politics in Urban Africa: A Study of Hausa Migrants in Yoruba Towns* (London: Routledge and Kegan Paul, 1969).

21. Leroy Vail, ed., *The Creation of Tribalism in Southern Africa* (Berkeley: University of California Press, 1989).

CHAPTER 1

1. C. A. Willis, *Report on Slavery*, 1926, NRO Civsec 60/2/7, 2.

2. For this chapter I have relied on the numerous studies that have appeared during the last two decades. For precolonial Sudanese slavery, see R. S. O'Fahey and J. L. Spaulding, *Kingdoms of the Sudan* (London: Methuen & Co., Ltd., 1974); R. S. O'Fahey, "Slavery and the Slave Trade in Dar Fur," *Journal of African History* XIV, 1, (1973): 29–43; and "Slavery and Society in Dar Fur," *Slaves and Slavery in Muslim Africa*, Vol. II, ed. John Ralph Willis (London: Frank Cass, 1985): 83–100; Jay Spaulding, *The Heroic Age in Sinnar* (East Lansing: African Studies Center, Michigan State University, 1985). Lidwien Kapteijns, *Mahdist Faith and Sudanic Tradition. The History of the Masalit Sultanate, 1870–1930* (London & Boston: KPI, 1985), and "The Use of Slaves in Pre-colonial Western Dar Fur: The Case of Dar Masalit, 1870–1905," *Northeast African Studies* 6, nos. 1 & 2, (1984): 105–126. Janet Ewald, *Soldiers, Traders, and Slaves* (Madison: University of Wisconsin Press, 1990).

3. Jay Spaulding, *The Heroic Age in Sinnar*, 75–77.

4. Ibid., 75–77.

5. Ibid., 86–87.

6. W. Nicholas, "Sakia in Dongola Province," *Sudan Notes and Records* 1, no. 1 (1918): 23–25.

7. Spaulding, *The Heroic Age*, 86.

8. Abd al-Ghaffar Muhammad Ahmad, *Shayks and Followers. Political Struggle in the Rufa'a and al-Hoi Nazirate in the Sudan* (Khartoum: Khartoum University Press, 1974): 35–58.

9. Ibid.

10. Ian Cunnison, *Baqarra Arabs* (Oxford: Clarendon Press, 1966): 59.

11. Ibid., 66–67.

12. Suzanne Miers and Igor Kopytoff, eds., *Slavery in Africa. Historical and Anthropological Perspectives* (Madison: University of Wisconsin Press, 1977): 5–7.

13. Frederick Cooper, "The Problem of Slavery in African Studies," *Journal of African History* 20, no. 1, (1979): 103–125; Paul Lovejoy, *Transformations in Slavery. A History of Slavery in Africa* (Cambridge: Cambridge University Press, 1983); and Claude Meillassoux, *The Anthropology of Slavery. The Womb of Iron and Gold* (Chicago: The University of Chicago Press, 1991): 23–40.

14. A. M. H. Sheriff, "The Slave Mode of Production Along the East African Coast, 1810–1873," *Slaves and Slavery in Muslim Africa*, Vol. 2 (London: Frank Cass, 1985): 161–181.

15. J. O. Hunwick, "Black Africans in the Islamic World: An Understudied Dimension of the Black Diaspora," *Tarikh* 5, no. 4, (1978): 21; and Muhammad 'Abd al-Wahab Fayid, *Al-Riq fil Islam* (Cairo: N.p., n.d.): 21–22.

16. Walid 'Arafat, "The attitude of Islam to slavery," *Islamic Quarterly* 10 (1966): 12–19.

17. Ibid.

18. Fayid, *Al-Riq fil Islam*, 82–90.

19. James Bruce, *Travels to Discover the Source of the Nile, in the Years 1768, 1769, 1770, 1772, and 1774*, Vol. 4 (Edinburgh: J. Ruthven, 1790): 459.

20. O'Fahey and Spaulding, *Kingdoms of the Sudan*, 56–80.

21. Ibid., 117–121.

22. See W. G. Browne, *Travels in Africa, Egypt, and Syria, from the year 1792 to 1798* (London: T. C. Cadell Junior and W. Davies, 1799): 213, 350; Gustav Nachtigal, *Sahara and Sudan*, Vol. 4 (London: C. Hurst & Co., 1971): 197.

23. O'Fahey, "Slavery and the Slave Trade in Dar Fur," 29–43.

24. O'Fahey, "Slavery and Society in Dar Fur," 89.

25. Ibid.

26. Ibid.

27. O'Fahey and Spaulding, *Kingdoms of the Sudan*, 81.

28. Ibid.

29. R. S. O'Fahey, *State and Society in Dar Fur* (London: N. p., 1980): 49–68; R. S. O'Fahey and M. I. Abu Salim, *Land in Dar Fur. Charters and Related Documents From the Dar Fur Sultanate* (Cambridge: Cambridge University Press, 1983): 15–17.

30. Paul E. Lovejoy, ed., *The Ideology of Slavery in Africa* (Beverly Hills and London: Sage Publications, 1981): 1–38.

31. Paulo Fernando de Moraes Farias, "Models of the world and categorical models: the enslaveable Barbarians as a mobile classificatory label," from John Willis, ed. *Slavery and Slaves in Muslim Africa*, vol. 2, (London: Frank Cass, 1985): 27–56.

32. Indeed the use of Nubian slaves in Egypt dates back to the Pharaonic period. See William Y. Adams, *Nubia: Corridor to Africa* (Princeton: Princeton University Press, 1977): 211, 231–232, 437, 451–452.

33. Yusuf Fadl Hasan, "External Islamic Influences and the Progress of Islam-

ization in the Eastern Sudan Between the Fifteenth and the Nineteenth Centuries," from *Sudan in Africa*, ed. Yusuf Fadl Hasan (Khartoum: Khartoum University Press, 1972): 73.

34. R. S. O'Fahey, "Fur and Fartit: The history of a frontier," in John Mack and Peter Robertshaw, eds., *Culture and History in the Southern Sudan* (Nairobi: The British Institute in Eastern Africa, 1982): 76–87; Wendy James, *'Kwanim PA. The Making of the Uduk People* (Oxford: Oxford University Press, 1979), and "Perceptions from an African Slaving Frontier," from *Slavery and Other Forms of Unfree Labor*, ed. Leonie J. Archer (London: Routledge, 1988): 130–141.

35. O'Fahey, "Fur and Fartit," 78.

36. Ibid.

37. Ahmad Alawad Sikainga, *The Western Bahr al-Ghazal Under British Rule: 1898–1956* (Athens: Ohio University, 1991): xiv-xv.

38. James, "Perceptions," 14.

39. Spaulding, *The Heroic Age*, 221.

40. O'Fahey and Spaulding, *Kingdoms of the Sudan*, 58.

41. Spaulding, *The Heroic Age*, 221.

42. Ewald, *Soldiers, Traders, and Slaves*, 15–53.

43. O'Fahey, "Slavery and Society in Dar Fur," 86.

44. Kapteijns, *Madhist Faith*, 50.

45. Terence Walz, *Trade Between Egypt and Bilad al-Sudan, 1700–1820* (Cairo: Institut Francais D'Archeologie Orientale Du Caire, 1978): 39–40.

46. John Lewis Burckhardt, *Travels in Nubia* (London: John Murray, 1822): 299.

47. Ibid.

48. Walz, *Trade*, 33.

49. Burckhardt, *Travels*, 307.

50. Ibid., 297.

51. Ibid., 303.

52. Kapteijns, "The Use of Slaves," 105–126.

53. Ibid.

54. Ibid., 113.

55. Ibid., 121.

56. Hasan Ahmad Ibrahim, *Muhammad 'Ali Pasha fi al-Sudan* (Khartoum: Khartoum University Press, 1991): 25.

57. Spaulding, *The Heroic Age*, 276–277.

58. Hasan Ahmad Ibrahim, *Muhammad 'Ali Pasha*, 5, 58.

59. Ewald, *Soldiers, Traders, and Slaves*, 57–58.

60. These efforts included the building of boats to transport captives by river and the provision of medical facilities.

61. Ibrahim, *Muhammad 'Ali Pasha*, 81.

62. For more detail on the expansion of the slave raiding frontier, see Richard Gray, *A History of the Southern Sudan, 1839–1889* (Oxford: Oxford University Press, 1961); and Dennis Cordell, *Dar al-Kuti and the Last Years of the Trans-Saharan Slave Trade* (Madison: University of Wisconsin Press, 1989).

63. For these changes see Jay Spaulding, "Slavery, Land Tenure, and Social Class in the Northern Turkish Sudan," *International Journal of African Historical Studies* 15, no. 1, (1982): 1–20; and Anders Bjorkelo, *Prelude to the Mahdiyya. Peasants and Traders in the Shendi Region, 1821–1885* (Cambridge: Cambridge University Press, 1989).

64. Spaulding, *The Heroic Age*, 282–288; James, '*Kwanim PA*, 38.

65. Ibid., 58–69.

66. Abbas Ibrahim Muhammad Ali, *The British, The Slave Trade, and Slavery in the Sudan, 1821–1881* (Khartoum: Khartoum University Press, 1972): 107.

67. Spaulding, *The Heroic Age*, 291.

68. A. I. M. Ali, *The British, The Slave Trade*, 6.

69. Ewald, *Soldiers, Traders, and Slaves*, 173.

70. Hill, *A Biographical Dictionary of the Sudan*, 2nd ed. (London: Frank Cass Co. Ltd., 1967): 180.

71. W. K. R. Hallam, *The Life and Times of Rabih Fadl Allah* (Devon: Arthur H. Stockwell Ltd., 1977).

72. Cordell, *Dar al-Kuti*, 105–108, 129–130.

73. Dennis Cordell, "Warlords and Enslavement: A Sample of Slave Raiders from Eastern Ubangi-Shari, 1870–1920," *Africans in Bondage, Studies in Slavery and Slave Trade*, ed. Paul Lovejoy (Madison: University of Wisconsin Press, 1986): 335–336.

74. For military slavery in Islam, see Daniel Pipes, *Slave Soldiers and Islam: The Genesis of a Military System* (New Haven and London: Yale University Press, 1981); Patricia Crone, *Slaves on Horses: The Evolution of the Islamic Polity* (Cambridge: Cambridge University Press, 1980). On the Sudan, see Douglas H. Johnson, "Sudanese Military Slavery From the Eighteenth to the Twentieth Century," *Slavery and Other Forms of Unfree Labor*, ed. Leonie J. Archer (London: Routledge, 1988): 142–156; "The Structure of a Legacy: Military Slavery in Northeast Africa," *Ethnohistory*, Vol. 36, no. 1, (Winter 1989): 72–88; and "Recruitment and Entrapment in Private Slave Armies: The Structure of the Zaraib in the Southern Sudan," *Slavery & Abolition*, Vol. 13, no. 1, (April 1992): 162–173.

75. See Johnson, "Sudanese Military Slavery," 142–156; "The Structure of a Legacy," 72–88; and "Recruitment and Entrapment," 162–173.

76. Richard Hill, *Egypt in the Sudan 1820–1881* (London: Oxford University Press, 1959): 25.

77. Ibid., 25.

78. Ibid., 25–26.

79. Gerard Prunier, "Military Slavery in the Sudan During the Turkiyya, 1820–1885," *Slavery & Abolition*, Vol. 13, no. 1, (April 1992): 132.

80. Muhammad Mahmoud al-Suruji, *al-Jaysh al-Misri fi al-Qarn al-Tasi'ashr* (Cairo: Dar Al-Ma'arif, 1967): 75.

81. Muhammad Mahmoud al-Suruji, *Al-Jaysh al-Misri fi al-Qarn al-Tasi'ashr* (Cairo: Dar Al-Ma'arif, 1967): 75.

82. G. R. F. Bredin, "The Life of Yuzbashi 'Abdullahi Adlan," *Sudan Notes and Records* 42, (1961): 37.

83. Hill, *Egypt in the Sudan*, 104. Among the officers honored were Muhammad Bey al-Maz and Muhammad Bey Sulayman. Hill, *A Biographical Dictionary*, 251 and 274.

84. Prunier, "Military Slavery," 132.

85. Ibrahim, *Muhammad 'Ali Pasha*, 92–94.

86. Al-Suruji, *al-Jaysh al-Misri*, 432.

87. Hill, *Egypt in the Sudan*, 138.

88. Johnson, "Sudanese Military Slavery," 142–156.

89. Ibid.

90. Georg Schweinfurth, *The Heart of Africa*, Vol. 2 (New York: Harper & Brothers Publication, 1874): 322, 427.

91. Johnson, "Recruitment and Entrapment," 166–167.

92. Hill, *A Biographical Dictionary*, 147–148.

93. Ibrahim, *Muhammad 'Ali Pasha*, 135.

94. Spaulding, "Slavery, Land Tenure," 4–8.

95. Ibid., 16.

96. Ewald, *Soldiers, Traders, and Slaves*, 172–173.

97. Ibid., 173.

98. Ibid., 54–55.

99. Ibid., 172.

100. Yusuf Mikhail, *Mudhakirat Yusuf Mikhail* (London: N.p., n.d.): 10.

101. Ibid., 168.

102. Spaulding, *The Heroic Age*, 295.

103. Claire C. Robertson and Martin A. Klein, eds., *Women and Slavery in Africa* (Madison: University of Wisconsin Press, 1983): 3–25.

104. Ibid.

105. Margaret Strobel, "Slavery and Reproductive Labor in Mombasa," in Robertson and Klein, eds., *Women and Slavery*, 67.

106. Robertson and Klein, *Women and Slavery*, 119.

107. Willis Report, NRO Civsec 60/2/7, 68.

108. Paul E. Lovejoy and Jan S. Hogendorn, *Slow Death for Slavery. The Course of Abolition in Northern Nigeria, 1897–1936* (Cambridge: Cambridge University Press, 1993): 234–260.

109. Paul E. Lovejoy, "Concubinage and the Status of Women in Early Colonial Northern Nigeria," *Journal of African History* 29, no. 2, (1988): 245–266; and "Concubinage in the Sokoto Caliphate (1804–1903)," *Slavery and Abolition* 11, no. 2, (1990): 159–189.

110. Fayid, *Al-Riq fi-Al-Islam*, 82.

111. Burckhardt, *Travels in Nubia*, 299.

112. Ibid.

113. During the Mahdiyya a young female slave was sold for 110 to 160 dollars, while a male was sold for 50 to 80 dollars; Rudolf Slatin, *Fire and Sword in the Sudan* (London: Edward Arnold, 1896): 558.

114. O'Fahey, "Slavery and Society in Dar Fur," 89.

115. Kapteijns, *Mahdist Faith*, 169.

116. Spaulding, *The Heroic Age*, 194.

117. Willis Report, NRO Civsec 60/2/7, 10–11.

118. Claude Meillassoux has rejected this notion and argued that slavery in West Africa was sustained by continued acquisition of new slaves by purchase or by capture and not by natural reproduction; Claude Meillassoux, "Female Slavery," in Robertson and Klein, eds., *Women and Slavery*, 51.

119. Heather Jane Sharkey, "Domestic Slavery in the Nineteenth and Early Twentieth-Century Northern Sudan," Master's thesis, Durham, 1992, 37–38.

120. Willis, *Report on Slavery*, 1926, NRO Civsec 60/2/7, 31.

121. Paul Santi and Richard Hill, eds., *The Europeans in the Sudan 1834–1878* (Oxford: Oxford University Press, 1980): 1–34.

122. Kapteijns, *Mahdist Faith*, 168.

123. Acting Governor General to British High Commissioner in Egypt, 29 September 1929, NRO Civsec 60/6/19.

124. Lidwien Kapteijns, "Islamic Rationales for the Changing Social Roles of Women in the Western Sudan," *Modernization in the Sudan*, ed. M. W. Daly (New York: Lilian Barber Press, 1985): 63.

125. Eilas Toniolo and Richard Hill, *The Opening of the Nile Basin*, 33.

126. Santi and Hill, *The Europeans in the Sudan*, 218.

127. R. C. Stevenson, "Khartoum during the Turco-Egyptian occupation," *Urbanization and urban life in the Sudan*, ed. Valdo Pons (Hull: Development Studies Center, Hull University, 1980): 115.

128. Ibid.

129. Santi and Hill, *The Europeans in the Sudan*, 217.

130. Muhammad Ibrahim Abu Salim, *Tarikh al-Khartoum* (Beirut: Dar Al-Jeil, 1991): 39.

131. Ibid., 129.

132. Hill, *Egypt in the Sudan*, 161–162.

133. Lidwien Kapteijns and Jay Spaulding, *Een Kennismaking met de Afrikaanse Geschiedenis* (Muiderberg: Coutinho, 1985): 122–123.

134. Ibid. I am grateful to Jay Spaulding for translating this letter.

135. Hill, *Egypt in the Sudan*, 78.

136. Stevenson, "Khartoum during the Turco-Egyptian Occupation," 116.

137. Dorothea McEwan, *A Catholic Sudan. Dream, Mission, Reality* (Rome: N.p., 1987): 20.

138. Ibid., 116.

139. Leonzio Bano, *Mezzo Secolo Di Storia Sudanese 1842–1898* (Verona, N.p., 1976). The vast majority of the converts were baptized in Khartoum; others were baptized at the mission's station in Gondokoro.

140. McEwan, *A Catholic Sudan*, 72.

141. According to Licurgo Santoni a slave woman could be purchased for about 100 dollars. Santi and Hill, *The Europeans in the Sudan*, 218.

142. Ibid.

143. Ibid., 22.

144. Ibid.

145. Ibid., 24.

146. Ibid.

147. Ibid., 218.

148. Ibid., 25.

149. McEwan, *A Catholic Sudan*, 88.

150. Bano, *Mezzo Secolo Di Storia*, 13.

151. Ibid., 11.

152. Ibid., 279.

153. Ibid., 10–11.

154. Ewald, *Soldiers, Traders, and Slaves*, 174–176.

155. Mikhail, *Mudhakirat*, 28.

156. Willis Report, NRO Civsec 60/2/7, 3.

157. Robert O. Collins, *The Southern Sudan 1883–1898: a Struggle for Control* (New Haven: Yale University Press, 1964): 142.

158. Ibid.

159. Rudolf C. Slatin, *Fire and Sword in the Sudan* (London and New York: Edward Arnold, 1896): 556.

160. Ibid., 565.

161. Ibid.

162. Mikhail, *Midhakirat Yusuf Mikhail* (London: N.p., N.d.): 46.

163. Ibid.

164. Muhammad Sa'id al-Gaddal, *Al-Siyasa al-Iqtisadiyya lil Dawla al-Mahdiyya* (Khartoum: Khartoum University Press, 1986): 58.

165. Ibid., 69.

166. Ibid., 64.

167. For instance, Isa wad al-Zayn, the Mahdist emir in al-Ubayyid, had one male and six female slaves. J. A. Reid, "Story of a Mahdist Amir," *Sudan Notes and Records* 9, no. 2, 1926: 79–82.

168. Robert S. Kramer, "Holy City On the Nile: Omdurman, 1885–1898," Ph.D. diss., Northwestern University, 1991, 226–227.

169. Ibid., 225.

170. Hill, *A Biographical Dictionary*, 297.

171. Mahdist followers.

172. P. M. Hot, *The Mahdist State in the Sudan 1881–1898*, 2nd ed. (Oxford: Oxford University Press, 1970): 159–161.

173. Ibid., 253.

174. F. R. Wingate, *Ten years' captivity in the Mahdist camp 1882–1892. From the original manuscripts of Father Joseph Ohrwalder* (New York: Charles Scribner's Sons, 1892): 383.

175. Ibid.

176. Slatin, *Fire and Sword*, 558.

177. Interview with 'Abbas Qadah Ad-Dam, 22 October 1989.

178. Ibid.

179. Ibid.

180. Wingate, *Ten Years' Captivity*, 163.
181. Ibid.
182. Ibid., 387.
183. Mikhail, *Mudhakirat Yusuf Mikhail*, 61–62.
184. Ibid., 354.
185. Slatin, *Fire and Sword*, 472.
186. Ibid., 385.
187. Interview with Sayyid Daw al-Bayt, 29 October 1989.

CHAPTER 2

1. H. C. Jackson, *Behind the Modern Sudan* (London: MacMillan & Co., Ltd., 1955): 94–95.
2. Willis to Civil Secretary, 2 July 1918, NRO Civsec 60/1/1.
3. Paul E. Lovejoy and Jan S. Hogendorn, eds., *Slow death for slavery. The course of abolition in Northern Nigeria, 1879–1936* (Cambridge: Cambridge University Press, 1993): 6.
4. C. A. Willis, *Report on Slavery*, 1926, NRO Civsec 60/2/7, 18.
5. Richard Hill, *Slatin Pasha* (London: Oxford University Press, 1965): 104.
6. Jackson, *Behind the Modern Sudan*, 94.
7. Willis Report, NRO Civsec 60/2/7, 10.
8. M. W. Daly, *Empire on the Nile* (London & New York: Cambridge University Press, 1986): 212.
9. Ibid., 212–213.
10. Ibid., 215–216.
11. Civil Secretary to Director, Egyptian Railway Administration, 6 December 1900, NRO CAIRINT 10/6/26.
12. Willis Report, 75.
13. Ibid.
14. Ibid., 69.
15. Ibid., 66.
16. Susan Lee Grabler, "From Concessionaire to Shaykh: The Shaping of Colonial Economic Policy in Sudan, 1898–1930," Ph.D. diss., University of Wisconsin, Madison, 1986, 18–67.
17. Daly, *Empire on the Nile*, 221–222.
18. Grabler, "From Concessionaire to Shaykh", 52.
19. Ibid., 54.
20. Ibid., 75.
21. Ibid.
22. Ibid., 195.
23. Daly, *Empire on the Nile*, 223.
24. Ibid., 217.
25. Yusuf Mikhail, *Mudhakirat Yusuf Mikhail*, 3.
26. Ibid., 43.

27. Ibid., 83.

28. Sudan Report, 1902, 260.

29. Jay Spaulding, "The business of slavery in Central Anglo-Egyptian Sudan, 1910–1930," *African Economic History* 17, (1988): 29.

30. Willis Report, NRO Civsec 60/2/7, 78.

31. Note on Sitt Amna, by Intelligence Department. Willis Report, 19 May 1922, NRO B.N.P. 1/61/424, 72.

32. Willis Report, NRO Civsec 60/2/7, 57.

33. 'Abbas Ahmed Mohammed, *White Nile Arabs* (London: N.p., 1980): 25.

34. Willis Report, NRO Civsec 60/2/7, 89.

35. Sudan Intelligence Reports, No. 14, 1913, Appendix 1, 26.

36. Quoted in Taj Mohammed Hargey, "The Suppression of Slavery in the Sudan, 1898–1939," Ph.D. diss., Oxford University, 1981, 75.

37. Yacoub Pasha Artin, *England in the Sudan* (London: MacMillan and Co., Ltd., 1911): 141.

38. Ibid.

39. H. MacMichael, *The Sudan* (London: N.p., 1954): 72.

40. Hargey, "The Suppression of Slavery," 209.

41. Ibid.

42. Ibid., 73–104.

43. Gabriel Warburg, "Slavery and Labor in the Anglo-Egyptian Sudan," *Asian and African Studies* 12, (1978): 225–226.

44. Hill, *Slatin Pasha*, 107.

45. Ibid.

46. Warburg, "Slavery and Labor," 231.

47. Jackson, *Behind the Modern Sudan*, 94.

48. Hargey, "The Suppression of Slavery," 85.

49. Scarcity of Labor in Khartoum, 1910, NRO Civsec 60/1/1.

50. G. S. Symes, *Tour of Duty* (London: Collins, 1946): 145.

51. Sudan Reports, 1906, 7.

52. Symes, *Tour of Duty*, 143.

53. Circular Memorandum No. 22, 1907, NRO Civsec 60/1/1.

54. Memorandum by the Governor of the Red Sea Province, 26 January 1915, NRO Civsec 60/1/1.

55. Ibid.

56. Ibid.

57. Ibid.

58. W. P. D. Clarke to the Governor, Blue Nile Province, 24 August 1918, NRO Civsec 60/1/1.

59. Ibid.

60. Ibid.

61. Policy With Regard to Sudanese by the Governor of the Blue Nile Province, 3 July 1918, NRO Civsec 60/1/1.

62. Willis to Civil Secretary, 23 July 1918, NRO Civsec 60/1/1.

63. C. Kerr to Assistant Director of Intelligence, 6 March 1911, NRO Intel. 4/5/39.

64. G. S. Symes to Director of the Railways, 11 March 1911, NRO Intel. 4/5/39.

65. Traffic Manager to Director of the Sudan Railways, 18 March 1911, NRO Intel. 4/5/39.

66. Willis Report, NRO Civsec 60/2/7, 20.

67. Enclosed in the Acting Governor-General, Sudan, to Secretary-General, League of Nations, 29 August 1925, PRO FO 371/10901.

68. Ibid.

69. Hargey, "The Suppression of Slavery," 103.

70. Richard Roberts and M. A. Klein, "the Banamba Slave Exodus of 1905 and the Decline of Slavery in the Western Sudan," *Journal of African History* 21, (1980): 375–394. Lovejoy and Hogendorn stated that several hundred thousands or 10 percent of the slave population in northern Nigeria had deserted immediately after the conquest; see Lovejoy and Hogendorn, 31–32.

71. Fred Morton, *Children of Ham. Freed Slaves and Fugitive Slaves on the Kenya Coast, 1873–1907* (Boulder: Westview Press, 1990): 1–19.

72. Frederick Cooper, *From Slaves to Squatters* (New Haven and London: Yale University Press, 1980): 46–61.

73. C. A. Willis, *Report on Slavery*, 1926, NRO Civsec 60/2/7, 113.

74. Ibid.

75. Ibid., 4.

76. Ibid.

77. C. Terysson to Wingate, 16 June 1902, SAD 272/4.

78. Willis Report, NRO Civsec 60/2/7, 78.

79. The term Malakiyya literally means civilian. However, it usually refers to neighborhoods that are inhabited by discharged soldiers of the Black battalions of the Egyptian Army, most of whom were former slaves. These quarters are found in many Sudanese towns, bearing the same name.

80. Ian Cunnison, *Baqqara Arabs* (Oxford: Clarendon Press, 1966): 80–85.

81. Willis Report, NRO Civsec 60/2/7, 85.

82. Ibid., 89.

83. Ibid., 97.

84. Southern Policy was introduced by the British administration in the Sudan in the 1920s to check the spread of Islam and the Arabic language in the South.

85. Willis Report, NRO Civsec 60/2/7, 97.

86. Ibid., 13.

87. Spaulding, "The business," 29.

88. Lovejoy and Hogendorn, eds., *Slow Death for Slavery*, 99.

89. Willis Report, NRO Civsec 60/2/7, 32.

90. Claire C. Robertson, "Post-Proclamation Slavery in Accra: A Female Affair?" in Robertson and Klein, *Women and Slavery in Africa*, 223–224.

91. Slatin to Wingate, 27 January 1900, SAD 270/1.

92. Reminiscence in Kordofan in 1906, SAD 294/18.

93. *Sudan Reports*, 1902, 288–290, 312, 334

94. Natale O. Akolawin, "Islamic and Customary Law in the Sudan: Problems of Today and Tomorrow," *Sudan in Africa*, ed. Yusuf Fadl Hasan (Khartoum: Khartoum University Press, 1971): 279.

95. J. N. D. Anderson, *Islamic Law in Africa* (London: Frank Cass, 1978): 301.

96. Ibid., 311.

97. Akolawin, "Islamic and Customary Law in the Sudan," 287.

98. Such practices were also common in other Muslim parts of Africa such as Murtaina; see E. Ann McDougall, "A Topsy-Turvy World: Slaves and Freed Slaves in the Mauritanian Adrar, 1910–1950," *The End of Slavery in Africa*, ed. Suzanne Miers and Richard Roberts (Madison: University of Wisconsin Press, 1988): 376.

99. *Sudan Law Journal and Reports*, 1972, 1–3.

100. Circular No. 2 by the Grand Qadi, September 1902, NRO Civsec 60/1/10.

101. Ibid.

102. R. H. Dun, Legal Secretary to Civil Secretary, 21 June 1924, NRO Civsec 60/1/2.

103. Hargey, "The Suppression of Slavery," 431.

104. Willis Report, NRO Civsec 60/2/7, 13.

105. Bennet Burleigh, *Khartoum Campaign 1898* (London: Chapman & Hall, Limited, 1899): 2.

106. Andrew Haggard, *Under Crescent And Star* (Edinburgh and London: William Black and Sons): 74.

107. F. R. Wingate, *Mahdism and the Egyptian Sudan* (London: Frank Cass & Co., Ltd., 1968): 221.

108. Richard Hill, *A Biographical Dictionary of the Sudan*, 2nd ed., (London: Frank Cass & Co., Ltd., 1967): 47.

109. Ibid., 324–325.

110. Wingate, *Mahdism*, 222.

111. G. R. F. Bredin, "The Story of Yuzbashi 'Abdallah 'Adlan," *Sudan Notes and Records* 42, (1961): 44–45.

112. Wingate, *Mahdism*, 225.

113. *Handbook of the Egyptian Army*, 1912, SAD 203/12, 12.

114. Bredin, "The Story," 51.

115. *Handbook of the Egyptian Army*, 46–47.

116. Daly, *Empire on the Nile*, 113.

117. Memorandum on the Bahr al-Ghazal, 7 April 1895, SAD 261/1.

118. Burleigh, *Khartoum Campaign*, 3.

119. Douglas H. Johnson, "Sudanese Military Slavery from the Eighteenth to the Twentieth Century," *Slavery and Other Forms of Unfree Labor*, ed. Leonie J. Archer (London and New York: Routledge, 1988): 150.

120. Slatin to Wingate, 27 January 1900, SAD 270/1.

121. Daly, *Empire on the Nile*, 115.

122. Hargey, "The Suppression of Slavery," 249.

123. Ibid., 251.

124. Interview with Muhammad Faraj 'Allam, Omdurman, 28 September 1978.

125. Interview with Zahir Sirur al-Sadati, Omdurman, 11 December 1978.

126. Historical Records, Nuba Territorial Company, SAD 106/5/2.

127. Kaid Am to Civil Secretary, 1 December 1936, NRO Dakhlia 1/1/4.

128. Ahmad Alawad Muhammad, *Sudan Defence Force: Origin and Role 1925–1955* (Khartoum: Institute of African and Asian Studies, n.d.): 7–11.

129. Asser to Wingate, 6 August 1913, SAD 187/2.

130. Allen Isaacman and Anton Rosenthal, "Slaves, Soldiers, and Police: Power and Dependency Among the Chikunda of Mozambique, ca. 1825–1920," *The End of Slavery in Africa*, ed. Suzanne Miers and Richard Roberts (Madison: University of Wisconsin Press, 1988): 220–243.

131. Bredin, "The Story," 51.

132. Note on the mutiny of Omdurman, December 1899–January 1900, SAD 270/1.

133. Daly, *Empire on the Nile*, 36.

134. Ibid.

135. Wingate to Crost, 1 March 1911, SAD 300/3.

136. Historical Records, Nuba Territorial company, n.d., SAD 106/5.

137. Hargey, "The Suppression of Slavery," 253.

138. Ibid.

139. Hill, *A Biographical Dictionary of the Sudan*, 324–325.

140. Wingate to Garcia, 14 October 1914, SAD 157/10.

141. Jay O'Brien, "Culture Concepts, Cultural Dynamics, and Class Formation in Sudan." Paper presented at the Sudan Studies Association Annual Conference, Boston, April 1994; and Jay Spaulding and Lidwien Kapteijns, "The Orientalist Paradigm in the Historiography of the Late Precolonial Sudan," *Golden Ages, Dark Ages*, eds. Jay O'Brien and William Roseberry (Berkeley: University of California Press, 1991): 139–151.

142. Leroy Vail, ed., *The Creation of Tribalism in Southern Africa* (Berkeley and London: University of California Press, 1989): 11.

143. In South Africa, for instance, the notion of the "lazy Kafir" was popular among white settlers; see Keletso E. Atkins, *The Moon Is Dead! Give Us Our Money! The Cultural Origins of an African Work Ethic, Natal, South Africa, 1843–1900* (Portsmouth: Heinemann, 1993): 2–7.

144. Labor Bureau Report, 1909, NRO Intel. 4/3/15.

145. Labor Bureau Annual Report, 1909, NRO Intel. 4/3/15.

146. Quoted in Cooper, *From Slaves to Squatters*, 15.

147. Mark R. Duffield, "The Fallata: Ideology and the National Economy in Sudan," *Economy and Class in Sudan*, eds. Norman O'Neill and Jay O'Brien (Aldershot and Brookfield, USA: Avebury, 1988): 122–136.

148. Mark Duffield, *Maiurno: Capitalism and Rural Life in Sudan* (London: Ithaca Press, 1981): 16.

149. *Sudan Reports*, 1908, 558.

150. Ibid.

151. Ibid., 40.

152. See Keletso E. Atkins, *The Moon Is Dead*, 2–7.

153. *Sudan Reports*, 1903, 6.

154. *Sudan Reports*, 1904, 14.

155. Circular Memorandum, 12 February 1901, SAD 542/21.

156. *Sudan Reports*, 1905, 160.

157. *Sudan Reports*, 1903, 5.

158. *Sudan Reports*, 1908, 71.

159. Scarcity of Labor in Khartoum, 1910, NRO Civsec 60/1/1.

160. Labor Bureau Report, 1909, NRO Intel. 4/3/15.

161. Ibid.

162. Sudan Government Orders No. 610, 1 February 1909, NRO Intel. 4/3/15.

163. G. S. Symes to the Governor, Khartoum Province, 17 December 1910, NRO Intel. 4/1/6.

164. G. S. Symes to the Directors of Departments, 11 August 1909, NRO Intel. 4/1/6.

165. Ibid.

166. These methods of registration involved checking the background of a prospective laborer such as his name, address, age, tribe, and a photo identification.

167. Jackson to Civil Secretary, 12 July 1914, SAD 452/276.

168. Ibid.

169. Warburg, *Sudan Under Wingate*, 165.

170. Willis to Civil Secretary, 12 February 1918, NRO Intel. 4/1/1.

171. Feilden to Governors of Dongola, Berber, and Red Sea provinces, 16 May 1918, NRO Intel. 4/2/8.

CHAPTER 3

1. El-Sayed El-Bushra Mohammed, "The Khartoum Conurbation: An Economic and Social Analysis," Ph.D. diss., London University, 1970, 95.

2. M. W. Daly, *Empire on the Nile. The Anglo-Egyptian Sudan, 1898–1934* (London: Cambridge University Press, 1986): 2; Philip Ziegler, *Omdurman* (London: Collins, 1973): 216.

3. Babikr Bedri, *The Memoirs of Babikr Bedri*, vol. 1, (London: N.p., 1969): 213, 241.

4. Ziegler, *Omdurman*, 213.

5. Petition by Omdurman Notables, 2 October 1898, SAD 430/6/4. See Appendix.

6. Ziegler, *Omdurman*, 213.

7. C. A. Willis, *Report on Slavery*, 1926, NRO Civsec 60/2/7, 4.

8. Bedri, *The Memoirs of Babikr Bedri*, Vol. 2 (London: Ithaca Press, 1980): 81.

9. Under these circumstances, some former slaves resold themselves into slavery. It was reported that a woman under the influence of alcohol sold herself to three Arabs while her sixteen-year-old son was trying to stop her. See Jackson, *Pastor on the Nile* (London: S.P.C.K., 1960): 29.

10. Wingate to McMurdo, 16 December 1906, SAD 279/6/80.

11. Sudan Government Orders, No. 1255, 16 November 1904, NRO CAIRINT 10/6/27.

12. Jackson, *Pastor on the Nile*, 22.

13. Willis, *Report on Slavery*, 1926, NRO Civsec 60/2/7, 80.

14. Willis report, NRO Civsec 60/2/7, 80. Population estimates for the early period of the Condominium are based on sheer guess. The population of the Three Towns at the turn of the century was estimated at 80,000.

15. *Sudan Reports*, 1913, 453.

16. Wingate to Cromer, 11 December 1903, PRO FO 141/318.

17. *Sudan Reports*, 1910, 122.

18. *Sudan Reports*, 556.

19. Memorandum on the Riverain Estate Labor Supply, 23 March 1911, NRO Intel. 4/5/42.

20. Governor, Khartoum Province to Civil Secretary, 22 December 1918, NRO Civsec 60/1/1.

21. W. H. McLean, The Planning of Khartoum and Omdurman, Town Planning Conference, London, 10–15 October 1910, SAD 235/1.

22. On this perspective, see Kenneth J. Perkins, *Port Sudan: The Evolution of a Colonial City* (Boulder: Westview Press, 1993).

23. Gabriel Warburg, *Sudan Under Wingate, Administration in the Anglo-Egyptian Sudan, 1899–1916* (London: Frank Cass & Co., Ltd., 1971): 162.

24. *Sudan Reports*, 1902, 312.

25. Interview with Ibrahim Osman, Ahmad Muhammad Ali, Shaykh Idris 'Abd al-Qadir, and Yusuf Abu Bakr, 17 December 1989.

26. *Blue Nile Handbook, 1922–1926*, NRO Civsec 57/33/122.

27. E. G. Sarsfield-Hall, *Handbook of Khartoum Province* (Typescript, N. d.): 17.

28. *Sudan Reports*, 1912, 144.

29. S. R. Simpson, "Town Planning and Development during the Condominium: Two Extracts from a Memoir," *Modernization in the Sudan*, ed. M. W. Daly (New York: Lilian Barber Press, Inc., 1985): 73.

30. El-Sayed El-Bushra Mohammed, "The Evolution of the Three Towns," *African Urban Notes* 6, no. 2, (1971): 18.

31. Warburg, *Sudan Under Wingate*, 162.

32. Abner Cohen, *Customs and Politics in Urban Africa: A Study of Hausa Migrants in Yoruba Towns* (London: Routledge and Kegan Paul, 1969); Enid Schildkrout, *The People of the Zongo. The Transformation of Ethnic Identity in Ghana*, eds. Abner Cohen and Leroy Vail (Cambridge: Cambridge University Press, 1978).

33. Leroy Vail, ed., *The Creation of Tribalism in Southern Africa* (Berkeley: University of California Press, 1989): 14.

34. Igor Kopytoff, "The Cultural Context of African Abolition," *The End of Slavery in Africa*, eds. Suzanne Miers and Richard Roberts (Madison: University of Wisconsin Press, 1988): 495–507. Thomas J. Herlehy and Rodger F. Morton, "A Coastal Ex-Slave Community in the Regional Colonial Economy of Kenya: The

WaMisheni of Rabai, 1880–1963," in Suzanne Miers and Richard Roberts, eds., *The End of Slavery in Africa* (Madison: University of Wisconsin Press, 1988): 308–331.

35. Interview with Ibrahim Osman, Shaykh Idris 'Abd al-Qadir, Ahmad Muhammad 'Ali, and Yusuf Abu Bakr, 17 December 1989.

36. *Blue Nile Handbook, 1920–1926*, NRO Civsec 57/33/122.

37. *Blue Nile Handbook, 1920–1926*, NRO Civsec 57/33/122. I am grateful to Dr. Jay Spaulding who provided me with this document, which was misfiled under the Blue Nile Province.

38. This information is based on a series of interviews with Ibrahim Osman, Shaykh Idris 'Abd al-Qadir, Ahmad Muhammad 'Ali, and Yusuf Abu Bakr, 17 December 1989; Jaragandi 'Abdullah, 5 November 1989; and Ibrahim Mahjub, 23 October 1989. See also Sarsfield-Hall, *Handbook of Khartoum Province*, (Typescript, n.d.): 17.

39. W. H. McLean, The Planning of Khartoum and Omdurman, Town Planning Conference, London, 10–15 October 1910, SAD 235/1.

40. El-Sayed E-Bushra Mohammed, "The Khartoum Conurbation: An Economic and Social Analysis," 201.

41. Bennet Burleigh, *Khartoum Campaign 1898* (London: Chapman & Hall Limited, 1899): 229–230.

42. Bedri, *Memoirs of Babikr Bedri*, Vol. 2, 81.

43. E. G. W. Sandes, *The Royal Engineers in Egypt and the Sudan* (Chatham: the Institution of Royal Engineers, 1937): 473–474.

44. Ibid.

45. Ibid., 420.

46. Memoir of Scott Hill, SAD 466/4/2.

47. *Sudan Reports*, 1902, 305.

48. Jackson, *Pastor on the Nile*, 48.

49. Taj Hargey, "The Suppression of Slavery in the Sudan 1898–1939," Ph.D. diss., Oxford University, 1981, 201.

50. It was reported that freeborn parents were reluctant to send their children to these workshops because they associated these jobs with slavery. Memorandum on Agricultural Labor in the Anglo-Egyptian Sudan, 1908, NRO Intel. 4/3/15.

51. Memorandum on Agricultural Labor in the Anglo-Egyptian Sudan, by Director of Intelligence, 13 March 1910, NRO Intel. 4/3/15.

52. John Lewis Burckhardt, *Travels in Nubia* (London: John Murray, 1822): 198.

53. Luise White, *The Comforts of Home. Prostitution in Colonial Nairobi* (Chicago: University of Chicago Press, 1990): 1–28.

54. *Sudan Reports*, 1903, 69.

55. Edward Fothergill, *Five Years in the Sudan* (New York: D. Appleton And Company, 1911): 286.

56. H. C. Jackson, *Sudan Days and Ways* (London: MacMillan & Co., Ltd., 1954): 81–82.

57. *Sudan Reports*, 1906, 662.

58. Daly, *Empire on the Nile*, 211.

59. *Sudan Reports*, 1908, 558.

60. George Frederickson, *White Supremacy. A Comparative Study in American and South African History* (Oxford, New York, Toronto: Oxford University Press, 1982): 60–61.

61. Vagabonds Ordinance, 1905, NRO Intel. 4/4/29.

62. Ibid.

63. *Sudan Reports*, 1907, 460.

64. Central Labor Bureau Annual Report, 1909, NRO Intel. 4/3/15.

65. Ibid.

66. *Sudan Reports*, 1905, 111.

67. The information on the card included name, age, tribe, and an identification mark to show if he had a master. Labor Bureau Annual Report, 1909, NRO Intel. 4/3/15.

68. G. S. Symes to Governor, Khartoum Province, 17 December 1910, NRO Intel. 4/1/6.

69. Laborers for the Central Experimental Farm, 1912, NRO Intel. 4/1/2.

70. Contract, n.d., NRO Intel. 4/1/3.

71. Report on the Labor Bureau, 1911, NRO Intel. 4/1/15.

72. Report on the Central Labor Bureau, 1911, NRO Intel. 4/1/15.

73. Susan Lee Grabler, "From Concessionaire to Shaykh: The Shaping of Colonial Economic Policy in Sudan, 1898–1930," Ph.D. diss., University of Wisconsin, Madison, 1986, 129.

74. *Sudan Reports*, 1908, 556.

75. Governor of Khartoum Province to Assistant Director of Intelligence, 24 March 1912, NRO Intel. 4/5/57.

76. *Sudan Reports*, 1907, 293.

77. Interview with Ibrahim Osman, Shaykh Idris 'Abd al-Qadir, Ahmad Muhammad 'Ali, and Yusuf Abu Bakr, 17 December 1989; and Ibrahim Mahjub, 23 October 1989.

78. Sudan Government Order No. 610, 1 February 1909, NRO Intel. 4/3/15.

79. Riverain Estates Labor Supply, by the Assistant Director of Intelligence, 30 April 1911, NRO Intel. 4/5/42.

80. Riverain Estates Labor Supply, 30 April 1911, NRO Intel. 4/5/42.

81. Ibrahim M. Fagiri and Muqqadams to Assistant Director of Intelligence, 28 October 1913, NRO Intel. 4/6/46.

82. P. F. M. McLoughin, "Labor Market Conditions, and Wages In the Three Towns, 1900–1950," *Sudan Notes and Records* 51, (1970): 110.

83. Ibid., 116.

84. *Sudan Reports*, 1905, 160.

85. Ibid.

86. Ibid., 161.

87. Governor of the Red Sea Province to Assistant Director of Intelligence, 22 February 1915, NRO Intel. 4/6/46.

88. Assistant Director of Intelligence to Muqqadams, 2 November 1913, NRO Intel. 4/6/46.

89. Memoir of Scott Hill, SAD 466/4/2.

90. Robin Cohen, "Resistance and hidden forms of consciousness among African workers," *Review of African Political Economy* 19, (1980): 8–22.

91. Interview with Ibrahim Osman, Shaykh Idris 'Abd al-Qadir, Ahmad Muhammad 'Ali, and Yusuf Abu Bakr, 17 December 1989.

92. *Sudan Reports*, 1907, 114.

93. Assistant Director of Intelligence to Chief Engineer, Experimental Farm, 30 March 1910, NRO Intel. 4/1/2.

94. District Commissioner, Wad Medani to Adjutant General, 28 May 1911, NRO Intel. 4/1/4.

95. The Legal Secretary to Assistant Director of Intelligence, 3 August 1910, NRO Intel. 4/1/3.

96. Advocate General to Assistant Director of Intelligence, 15 June 1911, NRO Intel. 4/5/45.

97. Contract between the Director of Public Works and Laborers, 15 June 1911, NRO Intel. 4/1/3.

98. Contract, 1 September 1910, NRO Intel. 4/1/3.

99. Contract, 17 January 1911, NRO Intel. 4/1/3.

100. *Sudan Reports*, 1902, 312.

101. Assistant Director of Intelligence to Governor of Khartoum Province, 14 February 1917, NRO Intel. 4/1/1.

102. *Blue Nile Handbook*, 1922–1926, NRO Civsec 57/33/122.

103. Assistant Director of Intelligence to Governor, Khartoum Province, 14 February 1917, NRO Intel. 4/1/1.

CHAPTER 4

1. M. W. Daly, *Empire on the Nile, the Anglo-Egyptian Sudan, 1898–1934* (Cambridge: Cambridge University Press, 1986): 423–425.

2. Arthur Gaitskell, *Gezira, a story of development in the Sudan* (London: N.p., 1959); Tony Barnett, *Gezira: An Illusion of Development* (London: Frank Cass, 1977); and Daly, *Empire on the Nile*, 420–433.

3. Ibid., 425.

4. Isam Ahmad Hassoun, "Western Migration and Settlement in the Gezira," *Sudan Notes and Records* 33, part 1, (1952): 79.

5. Susan Lee Grabler, "From Concessionaires to Shaykh: The Shaping of Colonial Economic Policy in Sudan, 1898–1930," Ph.D. diss., University of Wisconsin, Madison, 1986, 227–255.

6. M. W. Daly, *Imperial Sudan. The Anglo-Egyptian Condominium, 1934–1956* (Cambridge: Cambridge University Press, 1991): 96.

7. Assistant Director of Intelligence, 7 February 1921, NRO Intel. 4/1/7.

8. Daly, *Empire on the Nile*, 392–394.

9. District Commissioner, Khartoum, to Governor, Khartoum Province, 22 November 1939, NRO 2 Kh.P. 21/1/1

10. K. M. Barbour, *The Republic of the Sudan. A Regional Geography* (London: University of London Press, 1961): 161.

11. Ali Taisier and Jay O'Brien, "Labor, Community, and Protest in Sudanese Agriculture," *The Politics of Agriculture in Tropical Africa*, ed. Jonathan Barker (Beverly Hills: Sage Publications, 1984): 205–238.

12. Tim Niblock, *Class & Power in Sudan. The Dynamics of Sudanese Politics, 1898–1985* (Albany: State University of New York, 1987): 86.

13. Taisier and O'Brien, "Labor, Community and Protest in Sudanese Agriculture," 224–225.

14. Ibid.

15. Daly, *Empire on the Nile*, 429–430.

16. Daly, *Imperial Sudan*, 98.

17. Ibid., 172–174.

18. Abdel Basit Saeed, "Merchant Capital, the State and Peasant Farmers in Southern Kordofan," *Economy and Class in Sudan*, eds. Norman O'Neill and Jay O'Brien (Aldershot: Avebury, 1988): 190.

19. Daly, *Imperial Sudan*, 302–304.

20. Grabler, "From Concessionaires to Shaykh," 322.

21. John Tait, "Capitalist Penetration and the Genealogy of the Capitalist Mode of Production in the Gezira Scheme," *Economy and Class in Sudan*, eds. Norman O'Neill and Jay O'Brien (Aldershot: Avebury, 1988): 92; Grabler, "From Concessionaires to Shaykh," 255–269.

22. Jay Spaulding, "The Business of Slavery in the Central Anglo-Egyptian Sudan, 1910–1930," *African Economic History* 17, (1988).

23. L. Stack to British Consul General in Addis Ababa, 2 June 1920, NRO Intel. 2/23/186; and Willis Report, NRO Civsec 60/2/7, 98.

24. P. G. W. Diggle to Governor General, 11 February 1924, NRO Civsec 60/1/2.

25. Ibid.

26. Ibid.

27. Ibid.

28. Taj Mohammed Hargey, "The Suppression of Slavery in the Sudan 1898–1939," Ph.D. diss., Oxford University, Oxford, 1981, 275.

29. Sayyid Ali al-Mirghani, al-Sharif Yusuf al-Hindi, and Sayyid 'Abd al-Rahman al-Mahdi to the Director of Intelligence, 6 March 1925, NRO Civsec 60/1/3.

30. Ibid.

31. Circular Memorandum, 6 May 1925, NRO Civsec 60/1/3.

32. Hargey, "The Suppression of Slavery," 283.

33. Note by the Governor General, 30 November 1925, NRO Kh.P. 1/9/206.

34. Willis Report, NRO Civsec 60/2/7, 6.

35. Acting Governor General to British High Commissioner in Egypt, 29 September 1929, NRO Civsec 60/6/19.

36. A. J. Arkell to Governor, White Nile Province, 28 May 1928, NRO Civsec 60/6/18.

37. Daly, *Empire on the Nile*, 405.

38. For more details on Southern Policy see Robert O. Collins, *Shadows in the Grass: Britain in the Southern Sudan, 1918–1956* (New Haven: Yale University Press, 1983).

39. Ahmad Alawad Sikainga, *The Western Bahr Al-Ghazal Under British Rule: 1898–1956* (Athens: Ohio University, 1991).

40. P.R.O. F.O. 37/1/27, 494, Governor-General, Sudan, to Secretary-General, League of Nations, 18 April 1941.

41. W. P. Clarke to Hewin, 24 February 1921, NRO Intel. 4/2/8.

42. Willis Report, NRO Civsec 60/2/7, 57.

43. P. Murro to Civil Secretary, 11 May 1920, NRO Civsec 5/6/33.

44. C. A. Willis to Governor, Blue Nile Province, 11 and 29 March 1926, NRO B.N.P. 1/28/211.

45. Willis Report, NRO Civsec 60/2/7.

46. Ibid., 75.

47. Dongola Province Annual Report, 1923, NRO Civsec 60/1/1.

48. Ibid.

49. Ibid.

50. Ian Cunnison, *Baqqara Arabs. Power and the Lineage in a Sudanese Nomadic Tribe* (Oxford: Oxford University Press, 1966): 83.

51. Ibid.

52. Willis Report, NRO Civsec 60/2/7, 86.

53. Assistant District Commissioner, Southern Jabals to Governor, Kordofan Province, 12 May 1929, NRO K.P.N. 1/19/90.

54. Willis Report, NRO Civsec 60/2/7, 85.

55. Ibid.

56. Ibid., 86.

57. Saeed, "Merchant Capital, The State and Peasant Farmers in Southern Kordofan," 192.

58. From the Proceedings of the Governors' Meeting, 24 February 1920, NRO Civsec 5/6/33.

59. Ibid.

60. Civil Secretary to Governors, 3 April 1920, NRO Civsec 5/6/33.

61. Civil Secretary Department, January 1923, NRO Civsec 5/6/33.

62. See Ibid., and Mohammed Omer Beshir, *Revolution and Nationalism in the Sudan* (London: Rex Collings, 1974).

63. The White Flag League was founded by Ali 'Abd al-Latif, the son of slave parents, in 1923; it began to call for the "Unity of the Nile Valley" or political union with Egypt. The organization had several branches in different Sudanese towns and attracted many officers from the Sudanese units in the Egyptian Army. See Beshir, *Revolution and Nationalism*, 73–80.

64. Daly, *Empire on the Nile*, 309.

65. Hasan Abdin, *Early Sudanese Nationalism, 1919–1924* (Khartoum: Khartoum University Press, 1986): 86.

66. Douglas Johnson, "Sudanese Military Slavery from the Eighteenth to the

Twentieth Century," in Leonie J. Archer, ed., *Slavery and Other Forms of Unfree Labor* (London and New York: Routledge, 1988): 146.

67. Admad Alawad Muhammad, *Sudan Defence Force: Origin and Role, 1925–1955* (Khartoum: Institute of African and Asian Studies, 1983): 35–36.

68. Ibid.

69. Huddleston to Civil Secretary, 23 September 1926, NRO Civsec 37/1/3.

70. Ibid., 39.

71. Interview with 'Abbas Qadah al-Dam, Omdurman, 8 October 1989.

72. Kaid Am to Civil Secretary, 1 December 1936, NRO Dakhlia 1/1/4.

73. Niblock, *Class and Power in Sudan*, 112.

74. There are two brands of zar, *Burei* and *Tombura*. Although the former has been common in the northern Sudan for many centuries, the latter was introduced by ex-slave soldiers and is popular in their communities. See Susan M. Kenyon, *Five Women of Sennar* (Oxford: Clarendon Press, 1991): 189.

75. Juma'a Jabir, *al-Musiqa al-Sudaniya. Tarikh, turath, hawiya, naqd* (Khartoum: al-Farabi, 1986): 33.

76. Historical Records of Bands and Schools of Music, n.d., SAD 110/21.

77. Ibid.

78. Ibid.

79. Ibid.

80. Jabir, *al-Musiqa al-Sudaniya*, 242.

81. Nasr al-Din Ibrahim Shulqami, *Kosti, al-Qissa wa al-Tarikh* (Khartoum: Khartoum University Press, n.d.): 43, 169.

82. Hargey, "The Suppression of Slavery," 433.

83. Ibid.

84. J. N. D. Anderson, "Recent Developments in Shari'a Law in the Sudan," *Sudan Notes and Records* 31, (1950): 97; Carolyn Fulehr-Lobban, *Islamic Law and Society in the Sudan* (London: Frank Cass, 1987): 46.

85. Anderson, *Islamic Law in Africa*, (London: Frank Cass, 1970): 308–309.

86. Ibid.

87. Amna bint Ahmad to Assistant Civil Secretary for Native Affairs, 12 March 1934, NRO Civsec 60/7/22.

88. Governor, Kordofan Province to D. Newbold, 14 May 1934, NRO Civsec 60/7/22.

89. Civil Secretary to Halima bint Ahmad, 20 May 1934, NRO Civsec 60/7/22.

90. A. M. Hankin to Governor, Kassala Province, 19 October 1934, NRO Civsec 60/7/25.

91. Anderson, *Islamic Law in Africa*, 318.

92. Ibid.

93. H. B. Arber to Qadi, 1 June 1946, NRO K.P. 2/99/428; Sayed Abdullah to Governor, Kassala Province, 4 June 1955, K.P. 2/72/297.

94. Willis Report, NRO Civsec 60/2/7, 45.

95. Author's own observation in the Meroe District, northern Sudan.

96. This discussion is based on personal observation in the region as well as on Hayder Ibrahim, *The Shaiqiya. The Cultural and Social Change of a North-*

ern Sudanese Riverain People (Weisbaden: Franz Steinger, Verlag GMBH, 1979).

97. Ibid., 73.

98. Ahmed S. al-Shahi, "Proverbs and Social Values in a Northern Sudanese Village," *Essays in Sudan Ethnography*, eds. Ian Cunnison and Wendy James (New York: Humanities Press, 1972): 91–92.

99. It is important to mention that in view of their preoccupation with ancestry, the ahl al-Balad also look down upon the halab (who have light complexions) as well as the Arab nomads, who are considered rustic and ignorant.

100. Janice Boddy, *Wombs and Alien Spirits. Women, men, and the zar cult in Northern Sudan* (Madison: University of Wisconsin Press, 1989): 71–79.

101. See Bernard Lewis, *Race and slavery in the Middle East* (New York and Oxford: Oxford University Press, 1990): 92–98.

102. Ibid., 59–60.

103. Saeed, "Merchant Capital, the State and Peasant Farmers in Southern Kordofan," 192.

104. C. A. Willis to Governor, Kordofan Province, 31 January 1926, NRO Civsec 60/7/24.

105. Ian Cunnison, *Baqqara Arabs: Power and Lineage in a Sudanese Nomad Tribe* (Oxford: Clarendon Press, 1966): 83.

106. Ibid., 80.

107. G. K. C. Hebbert, "The Bandala of the Bahr el-Ghazal," *Sudan Notes and Records* 8, (1925): 187–194.

108. Ahmad Alawad Sikainga, "The Legacy of Slavery and Slave Trade in the Western Bahr Al-Ghazal, 1850–1939," *Northeast African Studies* 11, no. 2, (1989): 75–95.

109. Sikainga, *The Western Bahr Al-Ghazal*, 72–76.

110. C. D. O. Farran, *Matrimonial Laws of the Sudan* (London: Bitterworth, 1963): 146–149.

111. Boddy, *Wombs and Alien Spirits*, 71–79.

112. Ibid.

113. Lobban, *Islamic Law*, 126.

114. *Sudan Law Journal and Reports* (Khartoum: Judiciary, 1974): 8–19. See also Lobban, *Islamic Law*, 127–129.

115. *Sudan Law Journal*, 10–12.

116. Ibid., 129.

117. Author's own observation.

CHAPTER 5

1. Jay O'Brien, "Toward a Reconstruction of Ethnicity: Capitalist Expansion and Cultural Dynamics in Sudan," *Golden Ages, Dark Ages: Imagining the Past in Anthropology and History*, eds. Jay O'Brien and William Roseberry (Berkeley: University of California Press, 1991): 128–129.

2. Ibid., 128.

3. Papers on Public Health in the Sudan, by Murry, n.d., SAD 403/8/64.

4. Ibid.

5. Chief Sanitary Inspector, Khartoum Province to Governor of Khartoum, 7 December 1932, NRO Civsec 35/2/7.

6. Ibid.

7. Governor of Kordofan Province to Civil Secretary, 24 March 1932, NRO Civsec 35/2/7.

8. Ibid.

9. Civil Secretary to Governors of Blue Nile, Berber, Fung, Kassala, Khartoum, and White Nile Province, 2 April 1932, NRO Civsec 35/2/7.

10. Civil Secretary to Governors of Blue Nile, Berber, Fung, Kassala, Khartoum, and White Nile Province, 18 December 1932, NRO Civsec 35/2/7.

11. Governor, Fung Province to Civil Secretary, 8 January 1933, NRO Civsec 35/2/7.

12. Governor of Berber to Civil Secretary, 9 January 1933, NRO Civsec 35/2/7.

13. Governor, Kassala Province to Civil Secretary, 14 February 1933, NRO Civsec 35/2/7.

14. Governor of Khartoum Province to Civil Secretary, 10 December 1932, NRO Civsec 35/2/7.

15. From S. J. A. Gillan to Governor, Khartoum Province, 4 March 1933, NRO Civsec 35/2/7.

16. Report of the Labor Committee, 6 April 1921, NRO Intel. 4/4/19.

17. Ibid.

18. Ibid., 2.

19. Ibid., 5.

20. Governor of Berber to the Secretary of Labor Committee, 22 May 1921, NRO Intel. 4/2/9.

21. Meetings of Sudan Agriculturalists, 12 February 1921, NRO Intel. 4/1/7.

22. Report of the Labor Committee, 6 April 1921, NRO Intel. 4/4/9, 6.

23. Report of the Labor Committee, 6 April 1921, NRO Intel. 4/4/9, 4.

24. Cruzon to Scott Webb, 19 August 1920, PRO FO 371/4993.

25. Report of the Labor Committee, 1921, NRO Intel., Appendix IV. p.18

26. Ibid., 19.

27. L. W. G. Andrew to Willis, 11 March 1921, NRO Intel. 4/2/10.

28. Balfore to Cruzon, 24 July 1920, PRO FO 371/4993.

29. Mark R. Duffield, "The Fallata: Ideology and the National Economy in Sudan," *Economy and Class in Sudan*, eds. Norman O'Neill and Jay O'Brien (Aldershot: Avebury, 1988): 127.

30. M. W. Daly, *Empire on the Nile. The Anglo-Egyptian Sudan, 1898–1934* (London & New York: Cambridge University Press, 1986): 441.

31. I. Hassoun, "Western Migration and Settlement in the Gezira," *Sudan Notes and Records* 33, (1952): 75.

32. Taisier Ali and Jay O'Brien, "Labor, Community, and Protest in Sudanese Agriculture," *The Politics of Agriculture in Tropical Africa*, ed. Jonathan Barker

(Beverly Hills: Sage Publications, 1984): 222.

33. Mark Duffield, *Maiurno: Capitalism and Rural Life in Sudan* (London: Ithaca Press, 1981): 37.

34. Hassoun, "Western Migration," 102.

35. P. F. M. McLoughlin, "Economic Development and the Heritage of Slavery in the Sudan Republic," *Africa* 32, (1962): 351–391. S. Al-Arifi, "Landlordism among small farmers: the case of the Gezira tenants in the Sudan," *Sudan Journal of Economic and Social Studies* 1, no. 2, (1975): 11–12.

36. P. F. M. McLoughlin, "Economic Development and the Heritage of Slavery in the Sudan Republic," *Africa* 32, (1962): 355–391.

37. Abbas Abdelkarim, *Primitive Capital Accumulation in the Sudan* (London: Frank Cass, 1992): 38–46.

38. Duffield, "Fallata," 126.

39. Hassoun, "Western Migration," 87.

40. Duffield, "Fallata," 127.

41. Hassoun, "Western Migration," 87.

42. District Commissioner of Khartoum to Governor, Khartoum Province, 22 November 1939, NRO 2 Kh.P. 21/1/1.

43. Ibid., 191.

44. M. W. Daly, *Imperial Sudan. The Anglo-Egyptian Condominium, 1934–1956* (London and New York: Cambridge University Press, 1991).

45. Ibid., 184.

46. Abdel Basit Saeed, "Merchant Capital, the State and Peasant Farmers in Southern Kordofan," *Economy and Class in Sudan*, eds. Norman O'Neill and Jay O'Brien (Aldershot: Avebury, 1988): 194.

47. Hassoun, "Western Migration," 91.

48. Duffield, "Fallata," 129–131.

49. Minutes of the Labor Board Meeting on 19 April 1943, NRO 2 Kh.P. 21/1/4.

50. Ibid.

51. Minutes of the Labor Board Meeting on 28 April 1943, NRO 2 Kh.P. 21/1/4.

52. Duffield, "Fallata," 129–130.

53. Ibid.

54. See Tony Barnett, *Gezira: An Illusion of Development* (London: Frank Cass, 1977); and John Tait, "Capitalist Penetration and the Genealogy of the Capitalist Mode of Production in the Gezira Scheme," *Economy and Class in Sudan*, eds. O'Neill and O'Brien, 90–121.

55. Tony Barnett and B. Founou-Tchuigoua, "De Facto Wage-Earners in the Gezira Scheme (Sudan)," *Africa Development* 3, no. 1, (1978): 25–50.

56. Tim Niblock, *Class and Power in Sudan* (Albany: State University of New York Press, 1987): 88–89.

57. Jay O'Brien, "The Formation and Transformation of the Agricultural Labor Force in Sudan," in O'Neill and O'Brien, *Economy and Class*, 137–156.

58. C. A. Willis, *Report on Slavery*, 1926, NRO Civsec 60/2/7, 57.

59. Niblock, *Class and Power in Sudan*, 88–89.

60. Abbas Abdelkarim, *Primitive Capital Accumulation*, 53–55.

61. Norman O'Neill, "Imperialism and class struggle in Sudan," *Race & Class* XX, no. 1, (1978): 10–11.

62. Ibid.

63. Niblock, *Class and Power in Sudan*, 124.

64. Richard Hill, *Sudan Transport* (London: Oxford University Press, 1965): 96.

65. Yacoub Pasha Artin, *England in the Sudan* (London: MacMillan And Co., Limited, 1911): 13–14.

66. Richard Hill, *Sudan Transport*, 96.

67. Ibid., 96–97.

68. Willis Report, NRO Civsec 60/2/7, 39.

69. K. D. D. Henderson, *A Survey of the Anglo-Egyptian Sudan, 1898–1944* (London and New York, Toronto: Longmans, Green & Co., 1946): 37.

70. Ibid., 37.

71. Gerard K. Wood, "Training Native Engine Drivers on the Sudan Railways," *The Crown Colonist* 5, (1935): 552.

72. Ibid., 553.

73. Ibid.

74. Ibid., 554.

75. Hill, *Sudan Transport*, 157.

76. Railway Department Annual Report, December 1931, SAD 294/12/49, Appendix No. 36a.

77. Ibid.

78. H. MacMichael, *The Sudan* (London: Ernest Benn Limited, 1954): 121.

79. Daly, *Empire on the Nile*, 437.

80. Hill, *Sudan Transport*, 99.

81. M. O. Beshir, *Revolution and Nationalism in the Sudan* (London: Rex Collings, 1974): 123.

82. Sudan Railways Employees, Report of the Independent Committee of Inquiry, Khartoum, April 1948, PRO FO 371/69236.

83. Ibid.

84. Saad ed Din Fawzi, "The Wage Structure and Wage Policy in the Sudan," *Sudan Notes and Records* 35–36, (1954–1955): 160.

85. Report of the Committee of Inquiry, 1948.

86. Notes on a visit to Sudan from 10 to 20 March 1947, PRO FO 371/63088.

87. Report of the Committee of Inquiry, PRO FO 371/69236.

88. Ibid.

89. *Al-Fajr*, 1, no. 7, (September 1934): 366.

90. M. O. Beshir, *Revolution and Nationalism*, 192.

91. See Saad ed Din Fawzi, *The Labor Movement in the Sudan, 1946–1955* (London: Oxford University Press, 1957); and Abdel-Rahman el-Tayib Ali Taha, "Sudanese Labor Movement: A Study of Labor Unionism in a Developing Society," Ph.D. diss., University of California, Los Angeles, 1970.

92. Al-Tayyib Hasan al-Tayyib, *Mudhakirat 'an al-Haraka al'Umaliyya* (Khartoum: Khartoum University Press, 1989).

93. Ibid., 3–4.

94. Henderson, *A Survey of the Anglo-Egyptian Sudan*, 38.

95. Al-Tayyib Hasan al-Tayyib, *Mudhakirat*, 9.

96. Peter Wiler, "Forming Responsible Trade Unions: The Colonial Office, Colonial Labor and the Trade Unions Congress," *Radical History Review* 28, no. 30, 1984, 372.

97. Ibid.

98. Robertson to Speghait, 4 June 1946, PRO FO 371/53254.

99. Fawzi, *The Labor Movement*, 26.

100. Al-Tayyib Hasan al-Tayyib, *Mudhakirat*, 28–29.

101. Ibid., 33.

102. The Egyptian Railway Workers Union donated LE 3,000 in 1948; see Al-Tayyib Hasan al-Tayyib, *Mudhakirat*, 87.

103. Taha, "Sudanese Labor Movement," 68.

104. Report of the Independent Committee of Inquiry, PRO FO 371/69236.

105. Daly, *Imperial Sudan*, 312–313.

106. Ibid., 321.

107. Ibid., 322–323.

108. M. O. Beshir, *Revolution and Nationalism*, 186.

109. Taha, "Sudanese Labor Movement," 75.

110. Niblock, *Class and Power in Sudan*, 122.

111. Taha, "Sudanese Labor Movement," 70.

112. Ibid., 68.

113. K. J. Hird to A. Greenhough, 10 November 1956, PRO FO 371/119703.

CHAPTER 6

1. C. A. Willis, *Report on Slavery*, 1926, NRO Civsec 60/2/7, 80.

2. Ibid.

3. District Commissioner, Khartoum North, to the Governor, Khartoum Province, 14 March 1926, NRO KH.P. 1/9/206.

4. Willis, *Report on Slavery*, 80.

5. Governor of Khartoum Province to Secretary, Labor Committee, 27 August 1921, NRO Intel. 4/2/9.

6. Governor-General Report, 1930, PRO FO 371/15427, 88.

7. K. D. D. Henderson, *A Survey of the Anglo-Egyptian Sudan, 1898–1944* (London, New York, and Toronto: Longman, Green & Co., 1946): 53.

8. *Al-Fajr*, vol. 1, no. 7, (September 1934): 303.

9. *Sudan Reports*, (1932): 129. The community itself became involved in the charity activities and a private shelter called Piaster Shelter was established to cater to orphans and the destitute.

10. P. F. M. McLoughlin, "The Sudan's Three Towns: A Demographic and Economic Profile of an African Urban Complex," *Economic Development and Cultural Change* XII, no. 1, (October 1963): 115.

11. Director of Department of Economics and Trade to Governor, Khartoum Province, 20 October 1940, NRO Civsec 37/2/6.

12. Ibid.

13. Ibid.

14. Information concerning casual labor, by the Secretary, Labor Board, 21 October 1940, NRO Civsec 37/2/6.

15. Note by the Secretary of the Labor Board, 6 February 1941, NRO Civsec 37/2/6.

16. Note by the Civil Secretary, 18 March 1942, NRO Civsec 37/2/7.

17. Minutes of the 5th Meeting of the Labor Board, 1 December 1942, NRO 2 Kh.P. 21/1/4.

18. Ibid.

19. Minutes of the Labor Board Meeting on 2 April 1943, NRO 2 Kh.P. 21/1/4.

20. Ibid.

21. Daly, *Imperial Sudan. The Anglo-Egyptian Condominium, 1934–1956* (London and New York: Cambridge University Press, 1991): 191.

22. Ibid.

23. Ibid.

24. Minutes of the Labor Board Meeting on 14 March 1944, NRO 2 Kh.P. 21/1/4.

25. B. J. Chatterton to Civil Secretary, 16 November 1943, NRO 2 Kh.P. 21/1/4.

26. *Khartoum Province Annual Report, 1945,* 10.

27. Governor, Khartoum Province to Civil Secretary, 28 February 1945, NRO 2 Kh.P. 32/1/1.

28. Daly, *Imperial Sudan,* 312–313.

29. N.R.O. 2 Kh.P. 32/1/1, Governor, Khartoum Province to Civil Secretary, 28 February 1945.

30. This was confirmed by the 1955–1956 population census.

31. District Commissioner, Omdurman, to Governor, Khartoum Province, 6 February 1945, NRO 2 Kh.P. 32/1/1.

32. G. L. Elliot-Smith to Governor, Khartoum Province, 20 January 1945, NRO 2 Kh.P. 32/1/1.

33. District Commissioner, Khartoum, to Governor, Khartoum Province, 16 January 1945, NRO 2 Kh.P. 32/1/1.

34. G. L. Elliot-Smith to Governor, Khartoum Province, 20 January 1945, NRO 2 Kh.P. 32/1/1.

35. *Khartoum Province Annual Report, 1950–1951.*

36. Ibid.

37. McLoughlin, "The Sudan's Three Towns," 78.

38. Ibid., 73.

39. Ibid., 286.

40. El-Sayed el-Bushra Mohammed, "The Khartoum Conurbation: An Economic Analysis," Ph.D. diss., London University, London, 1970, 185–187.

41. Ibid., 181–182.

42. Richard Sandbrook, *The Labouring Poor and Urban Class Formation. The*

Case of Greater Accra (Montreal: McGill University, 1977); and Sara Berry, *Fathers Work for Their Sons: Accumulation, Mobility and Class Formation in an Extended Yoruba Community* (Berkeley: University of California Press, 1985); and Frederick Cooper, *A Struggle for the City* (Beverly Hills: Sage Publications, 1983).

43. District Commissioner, Khartoum, to Governor, Khartoum Province, 14 April 1945, NRO 2 Kh.P. 32/1/1.

44. For a full description of these markets, see El-Sayed el-Bushra Mohammed, "The Khartoum Conurbation," 231–250.

45. Ibid.

46. Ibid., 290.

47. Interview with Ibrahim Osman, Shaykh Idris 'Abd al-Qadir, Ahmad Muhammad 'Ali, and Yusuf Abu Bakr, 17 December 1989.

48. Ibid.

49. Charles Van Onselen, *New Babylon. Studies in the Social and Economic History of the Witwatersrand, 1886–1914*, Vol. 2 (New York: Longman, 1982): 52.

50. Gabriel Warburg, *The Sudan Under Wingate* (London: Frank Cass, 1971): 141.

51. Ibid.

52. *Al-Fajr*, vol. 1, no. 7, (September 1934).

54. Civil Secretary to Governors and Heads of Departments, 11 December 1930, NRO Kh.P. 1/7/167.

55. E. A. Hargreaves to District Commissioners, Khartoum, Khartoum North, and Omdurman, 31 December 1930, NRO Kh.P. 1/7/167.

56. District Commissioner, Omdurman, to Governor, Khartoum Province, 9 March 1931, NRO Kh.P. 1/7/167.

57. Governor of Khartoum Province to District Commissioners, Khartoum, Khartoum North, and Omdurman, 26 May 1934, NRO Kh.P. 1/7/163.

58. District Commissioner, Khartoum North, to Governor, Khartoum Province, NRO Kh.P. 1/7/163.

59. El-Wathig Mohamed Kameir, *The Political Economy of Labor Migration in the Sudan: A Comparative Case Study of Migrant Workers in an Urban Situation* (Hamburg: Institut fur Afrika-Kunde, 1988), 28–31.

60. It is worth mentioning that the institution of amana was practiced since the mid-nineteenth century when a large number of people from the northern regions went to the western and southern Sudan as traders and slave raiders. See Anders Bjorkelo, *Prelude to the Mahdiyya. Peasants and Traders in the Shendi Region, 1821–1885* (London: Cambridge University Press, 1989): 4.

61. Fatima Babikr, *'Amal Saad ed Din Fawzi* (Khartoum: Economic and Social Research Council, 1984), 48.

62. F. Rehfisch, "A rotating credit association in the Three Towns," *Essays in Sudan Ethnography*, eds. Ian Cunnison and Wendy James (New York: Humanities Press, 1972): 189–200.

63. See Christopher Alan Waterman, *Juju. A Social History and Ethnography of an African Popular Music* (Chicago and London: University of Chicago Press, 1990).

64. Interviews with Sayyid Daw al-Bayt and Jaragandi Abdullah, 9 October 1989.

65. Interviews with Ibrahim Osman and others, 17 December 1989.

66. It is interesting to note that the ex-soldiers of Dinka origin who lived in Tanta in Egypt had played a significant role in the spread of the Ahmadiyya in the Daims. Group interview, 17 December 1989.

67. Because of the sensitivity of the subject of slavery in the Sudan, the names of the people who became religious figures cannot be revealed.

68. Jum'a Jabir, *al-Musiqa al-Sudaniya: tarikh, turath, hawiyah, naqd* (Khartoum: Sharikat al-Farabi, 1986): 33.

69. Ibid., 115.

70. Ibid., 29.

71. Ibid., 89.

72. Note on Dr. Mohammed Adam Adham and the Black Block, by J. Robertson, 15 December 1948, PRO FO 371/69209.

73. Note on Dr. Mohammed Adam Adham and the Black Block, by J. Robertson, 15 December 1948, PRO FO 371/69209.

74. Ibid.

75. Note on the Black Block and sister organizations, by Deed Effendi, 4 February 1948, NRO 2 Kh.P. -A.

76. Ibid.

77. Note on the Black Block and sister organizations, by Deed Effendi, 4 February 1949, NRO 2 Kh.P. -A, 9/3/21.

78. Ibid.

79. Ibid.

80. Ibid.

81. Philip 'Abas, "Growth of Black Political Consciousness in Northern Sudan," *Africa Today* 20, no. 3, 1973, 3.

82. N.R.O. 2 Kh.P.—A 9/3/21, Note on the Black Block.

83. Suzanne Miers and Igor Kopytoff, eds., *Slavery in Africa. Historical and Anthropological Perspectives* (Madison: University of Wisconsin Press, 1977), 17.

84. Frederick Cooper, *From Slaves to Squatters. Plantation Labor and Agriculture in Zanzibar and Coastal Kenya*, 1890–1925 (New Haven: Yale University Press, 1980), 165.

85. D. M. H. Evans, to Governor, Khartoum Province, 12 January 1953, NRO 2 Kh.P. 9/3/21.

86. Governor, Khartoum Province, to District Commissioner, Omdurman, 14 April 1953, NRO 2 Kh.P. 9/3/21.

87. Ibid.

88. For a critique of this approach, see Sherry Vatter, "Militant Journeymen in Nineteenth-Century Damascus: Implications for the Middle Eastern Labor History," *Workers and Working Classes in the Middle East. Struggles, Histories, Historiographies*, ed. Zachary Lockman (Albany, State University of New York Press, 1994): 1–20.

89. *Al-Fajr*, vol. 1, no. 7, (September 1934): 366.

90. Hill, *Sudan Transport*, 164.

91. Ibid.

92. Petition by Hussain Muhammad Ahmad, Babikr el-Shafei, Al-Amin Abd al-Rahman, Ahmad Abdullah, Ahmad Hassan, Abd al-Mun'im, Muhammad Ahmad al-Birayr, Sayyid Ahmad Siwar al-Dahab, and Hussain Ibrahim Tarbal, n.d.

93. G. S. Symes to Armstrong, 22 December 1936, NRO Civsec 37/2/6.

94. Ibid.

95. Financial Secretary to Civil Secretary, 9 March 1937, NRO Civsec 37/2/6.

96. Ibid.

97. Mohamed Omer Beshir, *Revolution and Nationalism in the Sudan* (London: Rex Collings, 1974): 192.

98. *Khartoum Province Annual Report, 1949.*

99. Ibid.

100. For a discussion of the new attitudes toward casual labor, see Frederick Cooper, *On the African Waterfront. Urban Disorder and the Transformation of Work in Colonial Mombasa* (New Haven and London: Yale University Press, 1987), 16–21.

101. Minutes of the General Purpose Committee, 20 January 1945, NRO 2 Kh.P. 32/1/1.

102. Civil Secretary to the Governors of Kassala, Khartoum, Kordofan, and Northern provinces, 11 June 1944, NRO 2 Kh.P. 32/1/1.

103. J. Longe to Governor, Khartoum Province, 6 February 1945, NRO 2 Kh.P. 32/1/1.

104. Ibid.

105. District Commissioner, Omdurman, to Governor, Khartoum Province, 13 March 1946, NRO 2 Kh.P.32/1/1.

106. Civil Secretary to Governors of Khartoum, Kassala, Kordofan, Northern, Dar Fur, and Blue Nile provinces, 12 April 1945, NRO 2 Kh.P. 32/1/1.

107. A Note on the Drift to Towns, 1948, NRO 2 Kh.P. 32/1/1.

108. M. M. el-Shaigi, District Commissioner, Khartoum North, to the Governor, Khartoum Province, 2 January 1946, NRO 2 Kh.P. 32/1/1.

109. Governor, Khartoum Province, to Civil Secretary, 28 February 1945, NRO 2 Kh.P. 32/1/1.

110. Civil Secretary's Circular, 8 June 1948, NRO 2 Kh.P. 32/1/1.

111. Ibid.

112. E. J. Wallis to Civil Secretary, 9 September 1948, NRO 2 Kh.P. 32/1/1.

113. Sa'ad ed Din Fawzi, "Social Aspects of Urban Housing in the Northern Sudan," *Sudan Notes and Records* 35 (Part 1), (1954): 92–93.

114. A. J. V. Arthur, Slum Clearance in the Sudan, the removal of the Old Deims in Khartoum, 23 December 1953, SAD 726/7.

115. Arthur, Slum Clearance, 2.

116. Interview with A. J. V. Arthur, 28 January 1992, Chemsford, England.

117. Civil Secretary's Office, Labor Branch Annual Report, 1 July 1952 to 30 June 1953, PRO FO 371/102930.

118. Ibid.

119. Khartoum Province Monthly Diary, April 1949, NRO Civsec 30/6/14.

120. Ibid.

121. Ibid.

122. Ibid.

123. Ibid.

124. Khartoum District Annual Report, January–February 1951, SAD 725/12.

125. Mubarak Uthman Sinadah, Muthakirah Hawl 'ilag Mashakil Manatiq al-Kartoon Bi al-'Asima (Memorandum on the problems of the cardboard areas in the capital), n.d., NRO Departmental Reports 40/1/4.

126. El-Bushra, "Khartoum Conurbation," 253.

127. Mohamed el-Awad Galal el-Din, "Internal Migration in the Sudan Since World War II, With Special Reference to Migration to Greater Khartoum," Ph.D. diss., London University, London, 1973, 199.

128. El-Bushra, "Khartoum Conurbation," 268.

129. Ibid.

130. Frederick Cooper, "Urban Space, Industrial Time, and Wage Labor in Africa," *Struggle for the City: Migrant Labor, Capital, and the State in Urban Africa*, ed. Frederick Cooper (Beverly Hills, London, New Delhi: Sage Publications, 1983), 8.

APPENDICES

1. Petition by Omdurman Notables, 2 October 1898, SAD 430/6/4.

2. N. Henderson to Austen Chamberlain, 5 September 1925, PRO FO 371/10901.

3. Ibid.

4. NRO Kh.P.1 1/9/26.

5. NRO Kh.P. 1/9/206.

6. Sayyid 'Ali al-Mirghani, Al-Sharif Yusuf al-Hindi, and Sayyid 'Abd al-Rahman al-Mahdi to the Director of Intelligence, 6 March 1925, NRO Civsec 60/1/3.

7. Amna bint Ahmad to Assistant Civil Secretary for Native Affairs, 12 March 1934, NRO 60/7/22.

8. NRO Intel. 4/1/3.

GLOSSARY

'abd   slave

'araqi   local liquor

'arabi   nomad

ardeb   a measure, capacity; 1 ardeb = 198 litres

bazingir   slave soldiers

basbuzuq   irregular troops

daim   neighborhood

dura   millet

faki   a holy man or religious teacher

feddan   unit of land measurement; one feddan = 1.038 acres or 0.420 hectares

fidya   money paid by the slave to the owner

fijrawi   morning shift

haddad   blacksmith

halabi   gypsy

jallabi   peddler

jaloos   mud, denoting mud-built houses

jarf   the land between the river's edge and its bank

kantar   a unit of weight; 1 kantar = 100 rotls = 99.05 lbs.

mamur   district administrator

marisa   local beer

nafir   work party

omda   headman of a village or groups of villages

qadi   Muslim judge

saqiya   waterwheel operated by animals or irrigated fields

shayl   credit

Shariʿa   Islamic law
shaykh   tribal or religious chief
ʿushr   one-tenth; a tithe levied on agricultural production
teddan   crop-sharing arrangement; sharecropping
zariba   an enclosure made of thorns

BIBLIOGRAPHY

UNPUBLISHED SOURCES, PUBLIC

A. Oral Sources

A. J. V. Arthur, a former British administrator who was deputy governor and governor, Khartoum Province, 1949–1954, now residing at Chelmsford, England. Interview with author. Chelmsford, 28 January 1992.

Al-Tijani al-Tayyib, a leading figure in the Sudanese Communist Party. Interview with author. Cairo, 17 July 1993.

'Abbas Ahmad Qadah al-Dam, age 70 (in 1989), of Fulani origin and a resident of Mawrada, Omdurman. Interviews with author. Omdurman, 8, 11, and 22 October 1989.

Fadl al-Mula 'Abd al-Khayr, age 75, a tailor residing in Daim Tegali, Khartoum. Interview with author. Khartoum, 8 November 1989.

Group interview with: Shaykh Idris 'Abd al-Qadir, Ibrahim Osman, Ahmad Muhammad 'Ali 'Abd al-Raziq, and Yusuf Abu Bakr Musa, residents of Daim al-Zubayria, Khartoum. Interview with author. Khartoum, 17 December 1989.

Ibrahim Mahjub, age 65, retired railway worker, residing in the Daims. Interview with author. Khartoum, 23 October 1989.

Jaragandi 'Abdulla, age 85, resident of Daim Ta'isha, Khartoum. Interview with author. Khartoum, 5 November 1989.

Muhammad Faraj 'Allam, retired officer who served in the Sudanese battalions of the Egyptian Army; died 1989. Interview with author. Omdurman, 28 September 1978.

Sayid Daw al-Bayt, age 85, of Fur origin, residing at Mawrada, Omdurman. Interview with author. Omdurman, 29 October 1989.

Zahir Sirur al-Sadati, retired officer who served in the Sudanese battalions of the Egyptian Army; died 1989. Interview with author. Omdurman, 11 December 1978.

B. Sudan Government Archives, Khartoum

The archives of the Sudan Government are kept in the National Record Office (previously the Central Records Office), Khartoum. Documents in the NRO are listed by class number, box number, and file number. The following materials have been used:

CAIRINT: This classification deals mainly with intelligence and general administration in the early years of the Anglo-Egyptian rule. 10/2-10/10.

Civsec: Designates files of the civil secretary department. The following materials deal with slavery, labor, Shariʿa courts, and the army: 60/1–7/22, 37/1/1–37/3/10, 42/1, 5/5/19–5/6/36.

Intel.: Contains the archives of the intelligence department, Khartoum; 2/43/363–65 deals with slavery and 4/1–5/6 deals with the Central Labour Bureau.

KHARTOUM PROVINCE, GROUPS I AND 2

Dakhlia: Contains the archives of the ministry of the interior.

Departmental Reports: Contain the files of various government departments.

Security Reports: Contain papers of the public security intelligence branch.

Reports: This is a classification given to official but unpublished miscellaneous reports and drafts.

C. British Government Archives, Public Record Office (PRO), London

FOREIGN OFFICE

FO 371: The following files deal with the question of slavery and labor: 22003, 23318, 23363, 24632, 27494, 4137–80, 53252, 63088, 69170, 69209, 69235–6, 97074, 102930, 113779, and 11378.

FO 141: 3/8, 356, 371, 378, and 493.

UNPUBLISHED SOURCES, PRIVATE

A. University of Durham Library (Sudan Archive)

Below is a list of officials whose papers were used. For specific reference and full citation see notes.

1. A. J. V. Arthur
2. K. D. D. Henderson
3. B. MacKintosh
4. J. W. Robertson
5. W. Scott Hill
6. S. R. Simpson
7. R. S. von Slatin
8. M. E. Wolff and C. L. Wolff
9. F. R. Wingate

10. E. G. Sarsfield-Hall
11. D. M. H. Evans

B. School of Oriental and African Studies, University of London

Papers of the Rev. Dr. A. J. Arkell.

UNPUBLISHED SOURCES, THESES, AND DISSERTATIONS

El-Din, Galal and Mohamed el-Awad. "Internal Migration in the Sudan Since World War II, with Special Reference to Migration to Greater Khartoum." Ph.D. diss., London University, 1973.

Grabler, S. L. "From Concessionaires to Shaykh; The Shaping of Colonial Economic Policy in Sudan, 1898–1930." Ph.D. diss., University of Wisconsin, 1986.

Hargey, T. M. "The Suppression of Slavery in the Sudan, 1898–1939." Ph.D. diss., Oxford University, 1981.

Kramer, R. S. "Holy City on the Nile: Omdurman, 1885–1898." Ph.D. diss., Northwestern University, 1991.

Sayed El-Bushra Mohammed. "The Khartoum Conurbation: An Economic and Social Analysis." Ph.D. diss., London University, 1970.

Sharkey, H. J. "Domestic Slavery in the Nineteenth and Early Twentieth Centuries in Northern Sudan." Master's thesis, Durham University, 1992.

Taha, Abdel Rahman el-Tayib Ali. "The Sudanese Labor Movement: A Study of Labor Unionism in a Developing Society." Ph.D. diss., University of California, Los Angeles, 1970.

PUBLISHED SOURCES, OFFICIAL

A. British Government

1. General Staff, *Handbook of the Egyptian Army, 1912*, London, 1912.
2. Naval Staff Intelligence Division: *Handbook of the Anglo-Egyptian Sudan, 1922*.
3. Reports by His Majesty's agent and consul-general on the finances, administration, and conditions of Egypt and the Sudan, 1899–1919.
4. Reports by His Majesty's high commissioner on the finances, administration, and conditions of Egypt and the Sudan, 1920.
5. Reports on the finance, administration, and conditions of the Sudan, 1921–1945.

B. Sudan Government

1. Anglo-Egyptian Sudan handbook series, *Khartoum Province, 1911*.
2. Civil administration orders
3. Sudan Almanac

4. Sudan Gazette
5. Sudan Intelligence Reports
6. *Sudan Law Journal and Reports*, Judiciary Department, Khartoum.

PUBLISHED SOURCES, SECONDARY

A. Magazines

1. *Al-Fajr*, 1934–1935.

B. Books and Articles

Abbas, P. "Growth of Black Political Consciousness in Northern Sudan." *Africa Today* 20, no.3 (1973): 29–43.

Abdelkarim, A. *Primitive Capital Accumulation in the Sudan*. London: Frank Cass, 1992.

Abdin, H. *Early Sudanese Nationalism, 1919–1925*. Khartoum: Khartoum University Press, 1985.

Abu Salim, M. I. *Tarikh Al-Khartoum*. Beirut: Dar Al-Jeil, 1991.

Adams, W. *Nubia: Corridor to Africa*. Princeton: Princeton University Press, 1977.

Ahmad, Abd al-Ghaffar Muhammad. *Shaykhs and Followers. Political Struggle in the Rufa'a al-Hoi Nazirate in the Sudan*. Khartoum: Khartoum University Press, 1974.

Al-Arifi, S. A. "Landlordism among small farmers: the case of the Gezira Tenants in the Sudan." *Sudan Journal of Economic and Social Studies* 1, no. 2 (1975): 10–12.

Al-Frayh, Siham 'Abd al-Wahab. *al Jawari wa al-shi'r fi al-'asr al-'abasi al-awal*. Cairo: N. p., 1981.

Al-Gaddal, Mohammad Said. *Al-Siyasa Al-Iqtisadiyya lil Dawla Al-Madiyya*. Khartoum: Khartoum University Press, 1986.

Ali, A. I. M. *The British, the Slave Trade and Slavery in the Sudan, 1820–1881*. Khartoum: Khartoum University Press, 1972.

Ali, T., and J. O'Brien. "Labor, Community, and Protest in Sudanese Agriculture." In *The Politics of Agriculture in Tropical Africa*, edited by Johnathan Barker, 205–238. Beverly Hills: Sage Publications, 1984.

Al-Sahid, Muhammad Labib. *mudhakirtan 'an a 'mal al-Jaysh al-Misri fil Sudan wa masat khirujhu minhu*. Alexandria: N.p., n.d.

Al-Shahi, Ahmad, "Proverbs and Social Values in a Northern Sudanese Village." In *Essays in Sudan Ethnography*, edited by Ian Cunnison and Wendy James, 87–104. New York: Humanities Press, 1972.

Al-Suruji, Muhammad Mahmoud. *al-Jayish al-Misri fi al-Qarn al-Tasi'ashr*. Cairo: Dar al-Ma'arif, 1967.

Al-Tayyib, Hassan al-Tayyib. *Mudhakirat 'an Al-Haraka al-'Ummaliyya*. Khartoum: Khartoum University Press, 1989.

Anderson, J. N. D. *Islamic Law in Africa*. London: Frank Cass, 1970.
———. "Recent Development in Shari'a Law in the Sudan." *Sudan Notes and Records* 31 (1958): 83–104.
Arafat, W. "The attitude of Islam to Slavery." *Islamic Quarterly* 10 (1966): 12–18.
Archer, J. L., ed. *Slavery and other Forms of Unfree Labor*. London & New York: Routledge, 1988.
Artin, Y. P. *England in the Sudan*. London: MacMillan and Co., Limited, 1911.
Atkins, K. E. *The Moon Is Dead! Give Us Our Money! The Cultural Origins of an African Work Ethic, Natal, South Africa, 1843–1900*. Portsmouth: Heinemann, 1993.
Baer, G., ed. *Studies in the Social History of Modern Egypt*. Chicago: University of Chicago Press, 1969.
Bano, L. *Mezzo Secolo Di Storia Sudanese 1842–1898*. Verona: N.p., 1976.
Barnett, T. *Gezira: An Illusion of Development*. London: Frank Cass, 1971.
Bedri, B. *The Memoirs of Babikr Bedri*. Vol. 2. London: Ithaca Press, 1980.
Beinin, J., and Z. Lockman. *Workers on the Nile*. Princeton: Princeton University Press, 1987.
Bienefeld, M., "The informal sector and peripheral capitalism." *Bulletin of the Institute of Development Studies* 4 (1975): 53–73.
Berry, S. *Fathers Work for Their Sons: Accumulation, Mobility and Class Formation in an Extended Yoruba Community*. Berkeley: University of California Press, 1985.
Beshir, M. O. *Revolution and Nationalism in the Sudan*. London: Rex Collings, 1974.
Bjorkelo, A. *Prelude to the Mahdiyya. Peasants and Traders in the Shendi Region, 1821–1885*. Cambridge: Cambridge University Press, 1989.
Blassingame, J. *The Slave Community*. New York: Oxford University Press, 1972.
———. *Black New Orleans, 1860–1880*. Chicago: University of Chicago Press, 1973.
Boddy, J. *Wombs and Alien Spirits. Women, Men, and the Zar Cult in Northern Sudan*. Madison: University of Wisconsin Press, 1989.
Bozzoli, B., ed. *Class, Community and Conflict, South African Perspectives*. Johannesburg: Raven Press, 1987.
Bredin, G. R. F. "The Life of Yuzbashi 'Abdullahi 'Adlan." *Sudan Notes and Records* 42 (1961): 37–53.
Browne, W. G. *Travels in Africa, Egypt, and Syria, from the Year 1792 to 1798*. London: T. C. Cadell Junior and W. Davies, 1799.
Bruce, J. *Travels to Discover the Source of the Nile*. Edinburgh and London: N.p., 1805.
Budge, W. E. A. *The Egyptian Sudan. Its History And Monuments*. Vol. 2. London: Kegan Paul, 1907.
Burckhardt, J. L. *Travels in Nubia*. New York: AMS Press, 1978.
Burrleigh, B. *Khartoum Campaign, 1898*. London: Champman and Hall, Limited, 1899.
Cock, J. *Maids and Madams: A Study in the Politics of Exploitation*. Johannesburg: Raven Press, 1980.

Cohen, A. *Customs and Politics in Urban Africa: A Study of Hausa Migrants in Yoruba Towns*. London: Routledge and Kegan Paul, 1969.

Cohen, R. "Resistance and hidden forms of consciousness among African workers." *Review of African Political Economy* 1980:8–22.

Collins, R. O. *The Southern Sudan, 1883–1898: A Struggle for Control*. New Haven: Yale University Press, 1964.

Cooper, F. "Islam and cultural hegemony: the ideology of slaveowners on the East African coast." In *The ideology of slavery in Africa*, edited by P. Lovejoy, 271–300. Beverly Hills and London: Sage Publications, 1981.

———. *Plantation slavery on the East Coast of Africa*. New Haven and London: Yale University Press, 1977.

———. "The Problem of Slavery in African Studies." *Journal of African History* 20, no. 1 (1979): 103–125.

———. *From slaves to squatters. Plantation labor and agriculture in Zanzibar and coastal Kenya, 1890–1925*. New Haven and London: Yale University Press, 1980.

———. ed. *Struggle for the city: Migrant labor, capital, and the state in urban Africa*. Beverly Hills, London, New Delhi: Sage Publications, 1983.

———. *On the African Waterfront: Urban Disorder and the Transformation of Work in Colonial Mombasa*. New Haven and London: Yale University Press, 1987.

Cordell, Dennis. *Dar al-Kuti and the Last Years of the Trans-Saharan Slave Trade*. Madison: University of Wisconsin Press, 1985.

———. "Warlords and Enslavement: A Sample of Slave Raiders From Eastern Ubangi-Shari, 1870–1920." In *Africans in Bondage, Studies in Slavery and Slave Trade*, edited by Paul Lovejoy. Madison: University of Wisconsin Press, 1986.

Crone, P. *Slaves on Horses: The Evolution of the Islamic Polity*. Cambridge: Cambridge University Press, 1980.

Cunnison, I. *Baqqara Arabs. Power and the Lineage in a Sudanese Nomad Tribe*. Oxford: Clarendon Press, 1966.

Daly, M. W. *British Administration and the Northern Sudan, 1917–1924*, Leiden: N.p., 1980.

———. *Empire on the Nile. The Anglo-Egyptian Sudan, 1898–1934*. London, New York, New Rochelle, Melbourne, and Sydney: Cambridge University Press, 1986.

———. *Imperial Sudan*. London, New York, New Rochelle, Melbourne, and Sydney: Cambridge University Press, 1991.

Davis, D. B. *The problem of slavery in the age of revolution. 1770–1823*. Ithaca and London: Cornell University Press, 1975.

———. *Slavery and human progress*, Oxford: Oxford University Press, 1984.

Duffield, M. "The Fallata: Ideology and the National Economy in Sudan." In *Economy and Class in Sudan*, edited by N. O'Neill and J. O'Brien, 122–136. Aldershot: Avebury, 1988.

———. *Maiurno: Capitalism and Rural Life in Sudan*. London: Ithaca Press, 1981.

———. *Review of African Political Economy* 26 (1983): 45–59.

———. "Transformation and Contradictions: Hausa Settlements in the Towns of the Northern Sudan." In *Urbanization and Urban Life in the Sudan*, edited by

V. Pons, 209–246. Hull: Hull University, 1980.

Echenberg, M. *Colonial Conscripts: The Triailleurs Senegalis in French West Africa, 1857–1960.* Portsmouth and London: Heinemann & James Curry, 1991.

Ewald, J. *Soldiers, Traders, and Slaves.* Madison: University of Wisconsin Press, 1990.

Farias, P. F. M. "Models of the world and categorical models: the enslaveable Barbarians as a mobile classificatory label." In *Slavery and Slaves in Muslim Africa*, Vol. 2, edited by J. Willis. London: Frank Cass, 1985.

Farran, C. D. *Matrimonial Laws of the Sudan.* London: Bitterworth, 1963.

Fawzi, Saad ed Din. *The Labor Movement in the Sudan, 1946–1955.* London: Oxford University Press, 1957.

———. "Some aspects of urban housing in Northern Sudan." *Sudan Notes and Records* 35 (1954): 91–110.

———. "The wage structure and wage policy in the Sudan." *Sudan Notes and Records* 36 (1955): 158–180.

Fayid, M. A. *Al-Riq fil Islam.* Cairo: N. p., N. d.

Foner, E. *Nothing But Freedom. Emancipation And Its Legacy.* Baton Rouge and London: Louisiana State University, 1983.

Fothergill, E. *Five Years in the Sudan.* New York: D. Appelton and Company, 1911.

Founou-Tchuigoua, T. "D'Facto Wage-Earners in the Gezira Scheme (Sudan)." *Africa Developement* 3, no.1 (1978): 25–50.

Freund, B. *The African worker.* New York, New Rochelle, Melbourne, and Sydney: Cambridge University Press, 1988.

———. *The Making of Contemporary Africa.* Bloomington: Indiana University Press, 1984.

Fredrickson, G. M. *White Supremacy. A Comparative Study in American & South African History.* Oxford, New York, Toronto, and Melbourne: Oxford University Press, 1982.

Genovese, E. D. *Roll Jordan Roll. The world the slaves made.* New York: Random House, 1976.

———. *The World the Slaveholders Made.* New York: Vintage Books, 1971.

Ghorba, H. "Islam and Slavery." *Islamic Quarterly* II, no. 3 (1955): 153–159.

Gray, R. *A History of the Southern Sudan, 1839–1889.* Oxford: Oxford University Press, 1961.

Gutkind, P., R. Cohen, and J. Copans, eds. *African labor history.* Beverly Hills and London: Sage Publications, 1978.

Haggard, A. *Under Crescent And Star.* Edinburgh & London: William Blackwood And Sons, 1895.

Hallam, W. K. R. *The Life and Times of Rabih Fadl Allah.* Devon: Arthur H. Stockwell Ltd., 1977.

Hasan, Y. F. *The Arabs and the Sudan.* Khartoum: Khartoum University Press, 1973.

———. "External Islamic Influences and the Progress of Islamization in the Eastern Sudan Between the Fifteenth and the Nineteenth Centuries." In *Sudan in Africa*, edited by Y. F. Hasan, 73–86. Khartoum: Khartoum University Press, 1972.

Hassoun, I. "Western Migration and Settlement in the Gezira." *Sudan Notes and Records* 33 (1952): 60–113.

Henderson, K. *Survey of the Anglo-Egyptian Sudan, 1898–1941*. London: The Abbey Press Ltd., 1946.

Hill, R. *A Biographical Dictionary of the Sudan*. London: Frank Cass & Co. Ltd., 1967.

———. *Egypt in the Sudan, 1820–1881*. London, New York, Toronto: Oxford University Press, 1956.

———. *Slatin Pasha*. London: Oxford University Press, 1965.

———. *Sudan Transport: A History of Railway, Marine And River Services in the Republic of the Sudan*. London: Oxford University Press, 1965.

Holt, P. M. *The Mahdist State in the Sudan 1881–1898*. Oxford: Oxford University Press, 1970.

Hunwick, J. O. "Black Africans in the Islamic World. An Understudied Dimension of the Black Diaspora." *TARIKH* 5, no. 4 (1978): 20–40.

———. "Black Slaves in the Mediterranean World: Introduction to a Neglected Aspect of the African Diaspora." *Slavery & Abolition* 13, no. 1 (April 1992): 5–37.

Ibrahim, H. A. *Muhammad Ali Pash fil Sudan*. Khartoum: Khartoum University Press, 1990.

Ibrahim, H. *The Shaiqiyya: The cultural and social change of a northern Sudanese riverain people*. Wiesbaden: Franz Steinger Verlag GMBH, 1979.

Ibrahim, Salah el-Din el-Shazali. "The Emergence and Expansion of the Urban Wage-Labor Market in Colonial Khartoum." In *Sudan: State, Capital, and Transformation*, edited by T. Barnett and A. A. Karim, 181–202. London, New York, Sydney: Croom Helm, 1988.

———. "The Structure and Operation of Urban Wage-Labor Markets and the Trade Unions." In *Economy and Class in Sudan*, edited by N. O'Neill and J. O'Brien, 239–276. Aldershot, Brookfield, Hong Kong, Singapore, Sydney: Avebury, 1988.

Israel, A. "Measuring the War Experience: Ghanian Soldiers in World War II." *Journal of Modern African Studies* 25 (1987): 159–168.

Jabir, Jum'a. *al-Musiqa al-Sudaniya: Tarikh, Turath, Hawiyya, naqd*. Khartoum: al-Farabi, 1986.

Jackson, H. C. *Behind the Modern Sudan*. London and New York: MacMillan and St. Martin's Press, 1955.

———. *Pastor on the Nile*. London: S.P.C.K., 1960.

———. *Sudan Days and Ways*. London and New York: MacMillan and St. Martin's Press, 1954.

James, W. *'Kwanim PA. The Making of the Uduk People*. Oxford: Clarendon Press, 1979.

———. "Perceptions from an African Slaving Frontier." In *Slavery and Other Forms of Unfree Labor*, edited by L. Archer, 130–141. London: Routledge, 1988.

———. "Social Assimilation and Changing Identity in the Southern Funj." In *Sudan in Africa*, edited by Y. F. Hasan, 197–211. Khartoum: Khartoum University Press, 1971.

Johnson, D. H. "Recruitment and Entrapment in Private Slave Armies: The Structure of the Zaraib in the Southern Sudan." *Slavery & Abolition* 13, no. 1 (April 1992): 162–173.

————. "The Structure of a Legacy: Military Slavery in Northeast Africa." *Ethnohistory* 36, no. 1 (1989): 72–88.

————. "Sudanese Military Slavery from the Eighteenth to the Twentieth Century." In *Slavery and Other Forms of Unfree Labor*, edited by L. Archer, 142–156. London and New York: Routledge, 1988.

Kameir, el-Wathiq Mohamed. *The Political Economy of Labor Migration in the Sudan. A Comparative Case Study of Migrant Workers in an Urban Situation.* Hamburg: Institut Fur Afrika-Kunde, 1988.

Kapteijns, L. *Mahdist Faith and Sudanic Tradition. The History of the Masalit Sultanate, 1870–1930.* London: KPI, 1985.

————. "The Use of Slaves in Precolonial Western Dar Fur: The Case of Dar Masalit, 1870–1905." *Northeast African Studies* 6, nos. 1 & 2 (1984): 105–126.

Kapteijns, L., and J. Spaulding. *En Kennismaking met de Afrikaanse Geschiedenis.* Muiderberg: Coutinho, 1985.

Keith, H. "Informal income opportunities and urban employment in Ghana." *Journal of Modern African Studies*, II (1973): 141–69.

Kenyon, S. M. *Five Women of Sennar.* Oxford: Clarendon Press, 1991.

Lewis, B. *Race And Slavery In The Middle East.* New York, Oxford: Oxford University Press, 1990.

Lobban, C. *Islamic Law And Society in the Sudan.* London: Frank Cass, 1987.

Lockman, Z., ed. *Workers and Working Classes in the Middle East. Struggles, Histories, Historiographies.* Albany: State University of New York, 1994.

Lovejoy, P. "Concubinage and the Status of Women in Early Colonial Northern Nigeria." *Journal of African History* 29, no. 2 (1988): 245–66.

————. *The ideology of slavery in Africa.* Beverly Hills and London: Sage Publications, 1981.

————. "Miller's Vision of Meillassoux." *International Journal of African Historical Studies* 24, no. 1 (1991): 133–145.

————. *Transformation In Slavery. A history of slavery in Africa.* Cambridge: Cambridge University Press, 1983.

————, ed. *Africans in bondage. Studies in slavery and the slave trade.* Madison: University of Wisconsin Press, 1986.

Lovejoy, P., and J. S. Hogendorn. *Slow Death For Slavery. The Course of Abolition in Northern Nigeria, 1897–1936.* Cambridge: Cambridge University Press, 1993.

Lubeck, P. M. *Islam and urban labor in Northern Nigeria. The making of a Muslim working class.* London and Cambridge: Cambridge University Press, 1986.

MacMichael, H. A. *The Anglo-Egyptian Sudan.* London: Faber, 1934.

Mahmoud, U., and S. Baldo. *El-Di'ayn Massacre.* Khartoum: N. p., 1987.

Mann, K. *Marrying Well: Marriage, Status, and Social Change Among the Educated Elites in Colonial Lagos.* Cambridge: Cambridge University Press, 1985.

Martin, P. F. *The Sudan in Evolution; a story of the economic, financial and administrative conditions of the Anglo-Egyptian Sudan.* London: Constable and Company Ltd., 1921.

McEwan, D. *A Catholic Sudan: Dream, Mission, Reality.* Rome: N.p., 1987.

McDougall, A. "A Topsy-Turvy World: Slaves and Freed Slaves in the Mauritanian Adrar, 1910–1950." In *The End of Slavery in Africa*, edited by S. Miers and R. Roberts, 362–388. Madison: University of Wisconsin Press, 1988.

McLoughlin, P. "Economic Development and the Heritage of Slavery in the Sudan Republic." *Africa* 32 (1962): 335–391.

———. "Labor Market Conditions and Wages in the Gash and Tokar Deltas, 1900–1955." *Sudan Notes and Records* 47 (1966): 111–127.

———. "Labor Market Conditions and Wages in the Three Towns, 1900–1950." *Sudan Notes and Records* 51 (1970):105–118.

———. "The Sudan's Three Towns: A Demographic And Economic Profile of An African Urban Complex," Part III. In *Economic Development and Cultural Change* 12, no. 1 (October 1963): 286–304.

Meillassoux, C. *The Anthropology of Slavery. The Womb of Iron and Gold.* Chicago: University of Chicago Press, 1986.

———. "Female Slavery." In *Women and Slavery in Africa*, edited by Claire C. Robertson and Martin A. Klein, 49–66. Madison: University of Wisconsin Press, 1983.

Miers, S., and I. Kopytoff, eds. *Slavery in Africa. Historical and Anthropological Perspectives.* Madison: University of Wisconsin Press, 1977.

Miers, Suzanne, and Richard Roberts, eds. *The End of Slavery in Africa.* Madison: University of Wisconsin Press, 1988.

Mikhail, Y. *Mudhakirat Yusuf Mikhail.* London: N.p., n.d.

Miller, J. "The World According To Meillassoux: The Challenging But Limited Vision." *International Journal of African Historical Studies* 22, no. 3 (1989): 473–495.

Mohammed, A. A. *White Nile Arabs: Political Leadership and Economic Change.* London: N.p., 1980.

Mohammed, Sayed El-Bushra. "The Evolution of the Three Towns." *African Urban Notes* 2 (1971): 8–23.

Morrice, H. A. W. "The Development of Sudan Communication," Part 1. *Sudan Notes and Records* 30 (1949): 1–38.

Morton, F. *Children of Ham. Freed slaves and fugitive slaves on the Kenyan coast, 1873 to 1907.* Boulder, San Francisco, and Oxford: Westview Press, 1990.

Niblock, T. *Class & Power in Sudan.* Albany: State University of New York, 1987.

Nichols, W. "The Sakia in Dongola Province." *Sudan Notes and Records* 1 (1918): 21–24.

Oberst, T. "Transport Workers, Strikes and the 'Imperial Response': Africa and the Post-World War II Conjuncture." *The African Studies Review* 31, no. 1 (1988): 117–133.

O'Brien, J. "Formation of the Agricultural Labor Force in the Sudan." *Review of African Political Economy* 26 (1983): 15–34.

———. "The Political Economy of Semi-Proletarianization Under Colonialism: Sudan 1925–50." *Proletarianization in the Third World*, edited by B. Munslow and H. Finch, 121–147. London, Sydney, Dover, New Hampshire: Croom Helm, 1984.

————."Toward a Reconstruction of Ethnicity: Capitalist Expansion and Cultural Dynamics in Sudan." In *Golden Ages, Dark Ages. Imagining the Past in Anthropology and History*, edited by J. O'Brien and W. Rosebury, 126–138. Berkeley, Los Angeles, and Oxford: University of California Press, 1991.

O'Fahey, R. S. "Fur and Fartit: The History of a Frontier." In *Culture and History in the Southern Sudan*, edited by J. Mack and P. Robertshaw, 76–87. Nairobi: The British Institute in Eastern Africa, 1982.

————. *State and Society in Dar Fur*. London: N.p., 1980.

————. "Slavery and the Slave Trade in Dar Fur." *Journal of African History* XIV, no.1 (1973): 29–43.

————. "Slavery and Society in Dar Fur." In *Slaves and Slavery in Muslim Africa*, Vol. 2, edited by J. R. Willis, 83–100. London: Frank Cass, 1985.

O'Fahey, R. S., and M. I. Abu Salim. *Land in Dar Fur*. Cambridge: Cambridge University Press, 1983.

O'Fahey, R., and J. L. Spaulding. *Kingdoms of the Sudan*. London: Methuen & Co. Ltd., 1974.

O'Neill, N., and J. O'Brien, eds. *Economy and Class in Sudan*. Aldershot: Avebury, 1988.

————. "Imperialism and Class Struggle in Sudan." *Race & Class* XX, no. 1 (1978): 1–19.

Pipes, D. *Slave Soldiers and Islam: The Genesis of a Military System*. New Haven: Yale University Press, 1981.

Prunier, G. "Military Slavery in the Sudan during the Turkiyya, 1820–1885." *Slavery & Abolition* 13, no. 1 (April 1992): 129–139.

Rehfisch, F. "Omdurman during the Mahdiyya." *Sudan Notes and Records* 48 (1967): 33–61.

————. "A sketch of the early history of Omdurman." *Sudan Notes and Records* 45 (1964): 35–47.

————. "A Study of Some Southern Migrants in Omdurman." *Sudan Notes and Records* 43 (1962): 50–104.

————. "An unrecorded population count of Omdurman." *Sudan Notes and Records* 46 (1965): 33–91.

Reid, J. A. "Story of a Mahdist Amir." *Sudan Notes and Records* 9, no. 2, 1926: 79–82.

Roberts, R., and M. A. Klein. "The Banamba Slave Exodus of 1905 and the Decline of Slavery in the Western Sudan." *Journal of African History* 21 (1980): 375–394.

Robertson, C. *Sharing the Same Bowl: A Socioeconomic History of Women and Class in Accra*. Bloomington: Indiana University Press, 1984.

Robertson, C., and M. Klein (eds.). *Women and Slavery in Africa*. Madison: University of Wisconsin Press, 1983.

Robertson, J. W. *Transition in Africa: From Direct Rule to Independence*. London: C. Hurst & Company, 1974.

Roboteau, A. J. *Slave Religion. The "Invisible Institution" in the Antebellum South*. Oxford, New York, Toronto, Melbourne: Oxford University Press, 1978.

Said, A. B. "Merchant Capital, the State and Peasant Farmers in Southern Kordofan."

In *Economy and Class in Sudan*, edited by N. O'Neill and J. O'Brien, 186–211. Aldershot: Avebury, 1988.

Sandbrook, R., and J. Arn. *The Labouring Poor and Urban Class Formation: The Case of Greater Accra*. Montreal: McGill University, 1977.

Sandes, E. W. G. *The Royal Engineers in Egypt and the Sudan*. Chatham: The Institution of Royal Engineers, 1937.

Santi, P., and R. Hill, eds. *The Europeans in the Sudan, 1834–1878*. Oxford: Clarendon Press, 1980.

Sarsfield-Hall, E. G. *From Cork to Khartoum: Memoir of Southern Ireland and the Anglo-Egyptian Sudan 1886 to 1936*. Kendal: Carlisle Office Services, 1975.

Schweinfurth, G. *The Heart of Africa*. New York: Harper & Brothers Publication, 1874.

Sheriff, A. M. A. "The Slave Mode of Production Along the East African Coast, 1810–1873." *Slavery in Muslim Africa* 2, edited by J. R. Willis, 161–181. London: Frank Cass, 1985.

Shulqami, N. *Kosti. Al-Qisa wa al-Tarikh*. Khartoum: Khartoum University Press, n.d.

Sikainga, A. A. "The Legacy of Slavery and Slave Trade in the Western Bahr al-Ghazal, 1850–1939." *Northeast African Studies* 11, no. 2 (1989): 75–95.

———. *Sudan Defence Force: Origin and Role, 1925–1955*. Khartoum: Institute of African and Asian Studies, 1983.

———. *The Western Bahr al-Ghazal Under British Rule, 1898–1956*. Athens: Ohio University, 1991.

Shukry, M. F. *The Khedive Ismail and Slavery in the Sudan, 1863–1879*. Cairo: N.p., 1938.

Simpson, S. R. "Town Planning and Development During the Condominium: Two Extracts From a Memoir." *Modernization in the Sudan*, edited by M. W. Daly, 73–84. New York: Lilian Barber, Inc., 1985.

Slatin, R. *Fire and Sword in the Sudan*. London: Edward Arnold, 1896.

Spaulding, J. "The Business of Slavery in the Central Anglo-Egyptian Sudan, 1910–1930." *African Economic History*, 17 (1988): 23–44.

———. *The Heroic Age in Sinnar*. Lansing: Michigan State University, 1985.

———. "Slavery, Land Tenure and Social Class in the Northern Turkish Sudan." *International Journal of African Historical Studies* 15, no. 1 (1982): 1–20.

Spaulding, J., and L. Kapteijns. "The Orientalist Paradigm in the Historiography of the Late Precolonial Sudan." In *Golden Ages, Dark Ages. Imagining the Past in Anthropology and History*, edited by J. O'Brien and W. Roseberry, 139–151. Berkeley, Los Angeles, and Oxford: University of California Press, 1991.

Stevenson, R. C. "Khartoum during the Turco-Egyptian Occupation." In *Urbanization and Urban Life in the Sudan*, edited by V. Pons, 97–131. Hull: University of Hull, 1980.

———. "Three impressions of Khartoum during the Turkiya." *Sudan Notes and Records* 41 (1960): 101–6.

Strobel, M. "Slavery and reproductive labor in Mombasa." In *Women and Slavery in Africa*, edited by C. Robertson and M. Klein, 111–129. Madison: University of Wisconsin Press, 1983.

———. *Muslim Women in Mombasa, 1890–1975.* New Haven: Yale University Press, 1979.

Symes, Sir S. *Tour of Duty.* London: Collins, 1946.

Tait, J. "Capitalist Penetration and the Genealogy of the Capitalist Mode of Production in the Gezira Scheme." In *Economy and Class in Sudan,* edited by N. O'Neill and J. O'Brien, 90–121. Aldershot: Avebury, 1988.

Thompson, E. P. *The making of the English working class.* New York: Vintage, 1963.

Toniolo, E., and R. Hill. *The Opening of the Nile Basin.* London: C. Hurst & Company, 1974.

Tracey, C. B. "Merissa." *Sudan Notes and Records* 8 (1925): 214–215.

Van Onselen, C. *New Babylon: Studies in the Social and Economic History of the Witwatersrand 1886–1914.* London: Longman, 1982.

Vail, L., ed. *The Creation of Tribalism in Southern Africa.* Berkeley: University of California Press, 1989.

Vatter, S. "Militant Journeymen in Nineteenth-Century Damascus: Implications for the Middle Eastern Labor History Agenda." In *Workers and Working Classes in the Middle East. Struggles, Histories, Historiographies,* edited by Z. Lockman, 1–19. Albany: State University of New York, 1994.

Wade, R. C. *Slavery in the Cities. The South 1820–1860.* London, Oxford, and New York: Oxford University Press, 1964.

Walkley, C. E. J. "The Story of Khartoum." *Sudan Notes and Records,* part 2 (1936): 71–92.

Walz, T. *Trade Between Egypt and Bilad As-Sudan, 1700–1820.* Cairo: Institut Français D'Archéologie Orientale Du.CAIRE, 1978.

Warburg, G. "Ideological and Practical Considerations Regarding Slavery in the Mahdist State and the Anglo-Egyptian Sudan: 1881–1918." In *The Ideology of Slavery in Africa,* edited by P. Lovejoy, 145–170. Beverly Hills: Sage Publications, 1981.

———. "Slavery and Labor in the Anglo-Egyptian Sudan." *Asian and African Studies* 12 (1978): 221–45.

———. *The Sudan Under Wingate.* London: Frank Cass & Co. Ltd., 1971.

White, L. *The Comforts of Home. Prostitution in Colonial Nairobi.* Chicago: The University of Chicago Press, 1990.

Wieler, P. "Forming Responsible Trade Unions; The Colonial Office, Colonial Labor, and the Trade Unions Congress." *Radical History Review* 28, no. 30 (1984): 367–392.

Willis, J. R., ed. *Slaves And Slavery in Muslim Africa,* 2 Vols. London: Frank Cass, 1985.

Wingate, F. R. *Mahdism and the Anglo-Egyptian Sudan.* London: Frank Cass & Co., Ltd., 1968.

———. *Ten Years' Captivity in the Mahdi's Camp, 1882–1892.* New York: Charles Scriber's Sons, 1893.

Wood, G. K. "Training Native Engine Drivers on the Sudan Railways." *Crown Colonist* 5, (1935): 550–55.

INDEX